'LIFE THAT IS EXILE'

DANIEL CORKERY AND THE SEARCH FOR IRISH IRELAND

By

Patrick Maume

The Institute of Irish Studies
The Queen's University of Belfast

Published 1993
The Institute of Irish Studies
The Queen's University of Belfast

British Library Cataloguing-in-Publication Data. A catalogue record for
this book is available from the British Library.

ISBN: 085389 492 2 hardback

Printed by W & G Baird Ltd, Antrim
Cover design by Rodney Miller Associates

'LIFE THAT IS EXILE'

DANIEL CORKERY AND THE SEARCH FOR IRISH IRELAND

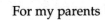

For my parents

TABLE OF CONTENTS

ACKNOWLEDGEMENTS

I would like to express my thanks to those who gave me interviews and other material about their association with Daniel Corkery: Bill and Mary Corkery, Dan O'Donovan, Des Brennan, T.J. McElligott, the late Professor James Barry, the late Professor Aloys Fleischmann, the late James N. Healy, Clara Ni hAnnrachain, Mairead Ni Mhurchu, Seamus de Roiste, Professor Sean O Tuama, Professor John Cronin, Professor Cornelius O'Leary, Dr. Liam O Riain, Helen, Margaret, John and the late Joan Cronin, Professor John A. Murphy, Professor David O'Mahony, the late Dr. Leon O Broin: to Virginia Teehan, UCC Archivist, for allowing me to consult the file on Corkery's appointment to the Chair of English; to Helen Davis and the staff of the UCC archives, Aodh O Tuama and the staff at Cork Municipal Museum, the staff of the Cork Archives Institute, the staff of UCD Archives, the staff of UCD Special Collections, the staff of the National Library of Ireland, Noel Shiels and the staff of RTE Sound Archives; Dr. Niall Buttimer for telling me of the two boxes of Corkery material in the Torna Papers, Traolach O Riordain for references to Corkery in the VEC Minutes and the Cork Examiner, Professor Sean O Coilean for a list of references to Corkery in the Sean O Riordain diaries, Dr. David Doyle for telling me of Arthur Fedel's thesis on Corkery, Gearoid O Cruadhlaoich, Diarmuid O Gilleain and the staff of Roinn Bealoideas UCC for allowing me to use their reader/printer, Fr. J.A. Gaughan and Dr. Brian Girvin for discussing Alfred O'Rahilly and the history of UCC Their help has been invaluable in writing this book; any errors of fact or interpretation are my responsibility alone. Thanks are due to Joan Maguire for proof reading the manuscript.

Above all I am grateful to my Aunt Pat and my Uncle Gerald and Aunt Mary for allowing me to stay with them in Dublin during research, Brian S. Murphy for help, advice and references to the Liam de Roiste diaries, Dr. Tom Dunne for advice and supervision of the original thesis and my parents for their love and support.

I am grateful to Bill and Mary Corkery for their permission to quote material written by their uncle, and to Gill and Macmillan for permission to quote from *The Hidden Ireland*.

The research for this book was undertaken with the assistance of an O'Connor Scholarship, endowed by Mr. Denis J. Doherty of Lynnfield, Massachusetts in memory of his mother Catherine E. Doherty (nee O'Connor) and his sister Kathleen L. Doherty.

Patrick Maume
July 13th, 1992

PREFACE

Most recent studies of twentieth-century Irish history depict Daniel Corkery as the most prominent spokesman for the narrow Gaelic nationalism of post-independence Ireland, a cultural commissar whose rejection of all that was not Catholic and Gaelic betrayed the original inclusive vision of the Gaelic League.[1]

This portrait of Corkery is largely derived from some of the views expressed in his book *Synge and Anglo-Irish Literature* (1931). It is a simplified portrait, reflecting one aspect of a complex man. Other aspects are known: *The Hidden Ireland,* (1924) his book on the poetry of eighteenth-century Gaelic Munster, whose evocation of a lost culture retains strong emotional power despite the multitudinous flaws revealed by social historians; his short stories, which are still anthologised; his relationship with his protégés Sean O Faolain and Frank O'Connor, who immortalised him in their memoirs as a sensitive provincial intellectual who became an embittered doctrinaire.

This book tries to assimilate these aspects into an overall picture. It argues that the key to his attitudes is to be found before his contact with O'Connor and O Faolain, before his first book, in his encounter with the loose network of groups and magazines, trying to preserve what they saw as an endangered national identity, which made up the Irish Ireland movement of the first decade of the twentieth century. He was a hard-worked, gifted, lame apprentice teacher from a well-read artisan family when his discovery of the Irish language and the Gaelic League gave him a new perspective on his discontents with turn-of-the-century Cork and the confidence to articulate them in the pages of the Irish-Ireland weekly *The Leader*. He believed the rediscovery of the Gaelic past could inspire Cork to create for itself a finer and juster civic culture. He established himself as a figure to be reckoned with in Cork literary and intellectual circles, founding the Cork Little Theatre tradition with the Cork Dramatic Society (1908–13); he wrote sensitively about the failings of the educational system, and put some of his ideas into practice in the overcrowded slum classrooms where he taught.

His first books, *A Munster Twilight* (1916) and *The Threshold of Quiet* (1917) established his literary reputation even as he moved from moral force nationalism to physical force Republicanism in the aftermath of the Easter Rising. As the country was transformed, as his old friend Terence MacSwiney rose from being an obscure separatist clerk to become Lord Mayor of Cork and thence to heroic death in a drama witnessed by the whole world, anything seemed possible; Corkery saw this revolution as the product of the Gaelic revival and hoped with his protégés to found a school of local writers, which would further express and extend that revival.

Corkery never entirely recovered from the shock of the Civil War and the Republican defeat; his writing grew more elegiac and a new bitterness entered his polemics as he argued with his former protégés about the cultural nationalism which he treasured as the source of his inspiration and they denounced as sterile fantasy. *The Hidden Ireland* and *Synge and Anglo-Irish Literature* are syntheses of earlier work; he produced little of major significance after 1931 (having come to believe all Irish literature in English, including his own work, was a curiosity of no lasting value) but up to his death in 1964 he remained a gifted painter, a prolific critic in newspapers and periodicals, a respected lecturer, a formidable presence among the intellectuals of Cork. Many Irish artists acknowledged his help and influence.

His achievements were remarkable; yet a reading of the sensitive but limited stories, the magnificent though isolated novel, the great mass of criticism with its mixture of insight, misunderstanding, fantasy and bitterness, shows a mind which could have achieved far more with the right intellectual tools.

The reasons for his failure to acquire those tools lie partly in the limitations of his surroundings and partly in the nature of his inspiration. Corkery's view of the Gaelic past was heavily influenced by the Romantic tradition of cultural criticism, which posited an organic society based on timelessly valid human values in the past in order to criticise the shortcomings of contemporary society. Corkery believed the literary tradition of pre-conquest Gaelic Ireland embodied such timeless human values, and its revival would spontaneously create an organic society. Since the tradition was timelessly valid it need not be adapted to take account of changes which had occurred since its destruction; indeed any such adaptation might destroy the essence of the tradition and any such changes must be superficial or actively evil. In the same way, Corkery expanded a legitimate criticism of the Ascendancy perspective adopted by many professional historians of Ireland into a dismissal of the discipline of history as the work of archive-grubbers who spent constricted lifetimes stitching together patchwork quilts of extracts from state papers without ever attaining the intuitive knowledge contained in a single work of art. Corkery thus cut himself off from the sort of analytic and synthetic approach which would have allowed him to extend his original insights, and increasingly isolated himself from current events in pursuit of an ideal of total Gaelic revival which grew more and more demanding as he worked for it. He was not a believer in "cultural autarky" (total self-sufficiency) but a cultural protectionist who believed the Irish tradition needed a period of recuperation before it could regain its native strength and meet the world on equal terms (though like other protectionists he could not see when recuperation would be complete, or how Ireland should be prepared for such a meeting). He was not a commissar handing down an approved ideology, but a man trying to make sense of his original inspiration.

PART ONE

DANIEL CORKERY 1878-1921

CHAPTER ONE

THE CORK LANES 1878–1901

Daniel Corkery was born on February 14th 1878 in a thatched house (since demolished) at the foot of Gardiner's Hill on what was then the northern fringe of Cork City. He was one of five children born to William Corkery, whose family had been carpenters in Cork for five generations, and his wife (nee Mary Barron) daughter of a Waterford sea-captain lost at sea. Daniel was born with a bone deformity which left his left leg shorter than his right; all his life he walked with a stick and wore a surgical boot.

William Corkery died in 1883 at the age of 34. His wife moved to 31 Barrack Street, in the lanes just south of the River Lee, where she kept a shop and brought up her four surviving children (a son, Richard, died in infancy) with the help of a woman called Kitty who had been a maid in the Barron household. Two sons, Edward and William, became carpenters like their father. (Daniel also acquired some carpenters' skills and made some of his own furniture, including a favourite chair mentioned in *The Threshold of Quiet*). Edward, remembered as a brilliant young man, went to work in London but returned seriously ill and died in 1901. William later became a schoolmaster and eventually headmaster in Passage West, where he died in 1943. He had three children. One of his daughters married an Englishman and went to live in Warwickshire; the other, Maureen, became a teacher of domestic science in Passage West. His son Bill became a master carpenter.[1]

Daniel and the only sister, Mary, looked after the old people. (Mrs. Corkery died in 1923 at the age of 80, having remained active to the end; Kitty survived, blind and bed-ridden, into the mid-1920s, when she was over 90). Mary never married and kept house for Daniel until his death.

Daniel had a lonely childhood, since he could not keep up with his friends when they ran off to play football or ramble around the neighbourhood.[2] Loneliness may have caused his stammer, which he eventually cured by self-discipline; it left him with a distinctive gravelly voice and a habit of pronouncing each word carefully and separately.

The boy learned to explore the city:

3

When talking to you of the life of this city as it was when I grew up, I need not tell you that I only saw a small part of it . . . the little things that an ordinary boy, living with his own people in a quiet little house in an ordinary street on the outskirts or the centre of the city would see. In every city, however small, there are many kinds of life going on alongside each other . . . but the boy doesn't understand that; he thinks that there is only one way of life in the city – his own . . . but I believe that I understood Cork well enough when I was young, because my people understood it. They were born in this city, just as I was, and their ancestors, too, were born in the city – and when that sort of thing happens, knowledge is passed down from generation to generation that is not to be found in books.[3]

He wandered the lanes and the quays; in his only novel, *The Threshold of Quiet* Corkery gave the boy Finbarr Bresnan his fascination with ships.[4] Writing in 1906 after moving to 1 Ophelia Place, in a new suburb at the Lough on the southern fringe of the city, he contrasted the gregarious life of the lanes with the dead sameness of suburbia, where neighbours kept to themselves.[5]

From time to time in the lanes, the boy heard two old men dispute the pronunciation of some strange word; "Boru", "Gougane Barra". When he was twelve a shop put a sign in its window – AIRGEAD SIOS in Gaelic script. Corkery, like all the other boys, thought it was Chinese. They knew an Irish language had existed, but had no idea it was still spoken. They associated it with far-off days of barbarism, ignorance and proselytism. Corkery has recorded his shock when as a boy he came across an elderly neighbour reading a Bible in Irish and realised she was a Protestant – converted by one of the Irish-language missionary societies remembered as "soupers".[6]

Not until adolescence did Corkery realise he lived in a stagnant provincial city. In 1800 Cork was a world centre of the provisions trade, which declined after the Napoleonic Wars. In the second half of the nineteenth century improved transportation brought outside competition which destroyed many traditional Cork industries. The population of the city remained static throughout the century, despite migration from the rural hinterland. The Cork slums were notorious.[7]

Cork rejoiced in the title "The Athens of Ireland" coined in the first decades of the nineteenth century when it produced a number of wits and minor painters, most of whom left the city early in their careers. The poet J.J. Callanan, remembered for a few adaptations of Gaelic poetry, deserves special mention. Corkery never paid him much attention, but his identification of the modern *poete maudit* with the persecuted Gaelic bard and his desire to escape from the indifferent city to the Gaelic hills, prefigure Corkery's aesthetic.[8]

When Corkery was young Cork's cultural life had decayed since Maginn and Sheridan Knowles.

> There was no intellectual life to be found in the city . . . What-
> ever fragments of intellectual life existed were foreign . . . the
> administration of this city had been in the hands of the rich for
> a couple of hundred years . . . there was no museum . . . no free
> library, nor any other sort of library worth talking about – there
> was a picture gallery with no pictures – the music in the churches
> was dreadful – and so forth. There were no books being written
> there, no pictures being composed, no plays being written or
> produced . . . We had only one theatre . . . the stuff there was
> just as bad, and just as foreign as the stuff that is there now. I'll
> say no more – except porter was very cheap then and there was
> a lot of it drunk.[9]

The Corkerys had the traditional artisan respect for learning. There were always books in the house – virtually all English books. Irish books and journals of the same standard did not exist (though they read *The Shamrock* for its endless stories about Mick McQuaid). They saw Irish parliamentary politics, dominated by the land question, as irrelevant to their lives.

> We were not of course anti-Irish. Nor were we pro-English. But
> we despised all that spoke of the countryside – people, ways,
> manners. We did not of course despise the English countryside.
> We seldom seem to have heard of Dublin in those days . . . But
> we knew London from Dickens, Thackeray and others as we
> knew of Scotland from Scott. And in a way we knew the history
> of that country; of our own country we knew no history beyond
> belated facts – we had never seen any reason for knowing any
> more. We had no desire to know any more.[10]

Such a background, and a love of reading heightened by loneliness, helped Corkery to do well at school. He won a King's Scholarship. In his late teens he became a monitor (a senior pupil who supervised classes as an apprentice schoolmaster), but scholastic success did not teach him how his studies could make sense of the life around him. The educational system, strictly based on examination results, left teachers little scope to impart understanding. Corkery kept grateful memories of one or two eccentric Brothers who pursued their own trains of thought regardless of the textbooks, teaching their pupils little except the joy of discovery; but most Brothers stuck to the textbooks.[12]

The textbooks were selected by the government-appointed National Education Board, since the Presentation Brothers whose South Monastery school Corkery attended were too small an order to produce their own textbooks as did the Christian Brothers. The Board claimed to provide "non-political, non-sectarian" textbooks, but their presuppositions, conscious or unconscious, exposed their claims to constant criticism.[13]

> We were taught implicitly, and indeed almost explicitly, not to seek a reflection of our own thoughts and feelings in literature ... We were supposed to read English literature with English eyes ... Such English texts as I studied for examinations had nearly all been edited for nice little Protestant English boys by nice old English Protestant rectors or head-masters of English Schools. Knowledge that I had not – of English customs, religion, home-life, etcetera – was taken for granted. Feelings that I had not, prejudices that I had not, were taken for granted. The knowledge, the feelings, the prejudices I had were never mentioned at all; I was, therefore, all the time being instructed that all these were somehow wrong, that they had no right to be there at all, in me or in anyone else – and that I was somehow out of it, not normal, a kind of freak...
>
> Of course we never did, in spite of the assistance of those nice old English professors and rectors, succeed in reading English classics with English eyes. We read them in a doped sort of way, having dropped nearly all the live contents of our minds before we began. We went from the "known" to the "unknown" with a vengeance dropping the "known" by the wayside.

Corkery had poignant memories of comparing himself with the brave, manly, truth-telling English boys in *Boys' Own Paper* stories of school life, finding himself and everyone around him "very much wanting" and deciding he was a freak and Cork was a wash-out.[14]

Corkery first tried to make sense of his world through socialism. His brothers were trade union activists and subscribed to Robert Blatchford's socialist weekly, *The Clarion*. Corkery read Blatchford's best-selling Manifesto *Merrie England* when it was published in 1894.[15]

Merrie England is heavily influenced by the tradition of socio-cultural criticism associated with John Ruskin (admired by Victorian autodidacts as the master of English prose; Corkery says the writings of Ruskin taught him to observe his surroundings, and the mediaevalism of *The Hidden Ireland* derives from Ruskin's belief that mediaeval society integrated function and ornament, art and morality). *Merrie England* stresses the dehumanising effects of urban industrial capitalism and advocates a decentralised co-operative commonwealth where craftsmanship is valued for its own sake.[16]

Corkery retained elements of this social critique after he became a cultural nationalist; but ultimately Blatchford did not satisfy him. Corkery simply says he drifted away from socialism after joining the Gaelic League, but he may also have been repelled by Blatchford's militant atheism and his jingoism during the Boer War. Blatchford's terms of reference were English, like the textbooks.

In 1896 Brother Calascantus, headmaster of the South Mon., showed Corkery a newspaper report of the first Gaelic League meeting in Cork. "We two . . . put our wise heads together and decided that to bring back the language was the last thing in foolishness".[17] A few years later, under the influence of *The Leader*, a new Irish weekly which declared the Irish language the key to Irishness, he began teaching himself Irish from O'Growney's textbooks.[18] At the age of twenty-three:

> without discussing the matter with anyone I walked into a Gaelic League class with considerable trepidation . . . (and) heard a voice out of Ballyferriter saying "Now that is what you'd say if you struck into a house after being out coursing on the sliabh". Coursing was as much a mystery to me as a sliabh . . . Learning Irish in a night class did not mean that I had joined the Gaelic League. In fact, I did not know that the Gaelic League had any corporate existence outside the dismal school-room where on two nights in the week its students assembled . . . (but) to knit up with your roots is to come on some sense of reality, is to have an energy released within you . . . I would either never have written anything only for the Gaelic League . . . (or) if I had written at all . . . such writing must have been of a very different nature, for the English radicalism of the household would have been its inspiration. And out of that, what could have come except unreality? The Gaelic League, then, drew me home, almost without my knowing it.[19]

CHAPTER TWO

A CITY RUSKIN 1901–9

Soon after joining the League, Corkery wrote his first article for *The Leader*. It appeared on September 14th 1901 under the pen-name "Lee" which he used until 1910.[1]

D.P. Moran, founder and editor of the *Leader*, was the son of a Waterford building contractor. He was educated at Castleknock and went to London in 1888 at the age of 16 to work on the innovative evening paper *The Star*. Moran was a fervent Parnellite but withdrew from politics after the death of Parnell as his boyish dreams of a new 1798 Rising evaporated before the size, power and indifference of London. "I went my ways, unable whole-heartedly to interest myself in England, unable to shake off my interest in Ireland; and yet sharing in the the the general pessimistic feeling that the country was doomed". In 1896 Moran found in the London Gaelic League a new foundation for his nationalism. "I was not an Irishman" he realised when he discovered the Irish language. "I knew nothing of Irish Ireland and was but a creature of British provincial civilization".

In 1898 Moran returned to Ireland and was horrified at the spread of British mass culture. He expounded his views in articles denouncing adolescent separatism, parliamentary oratory, the Celtic Twilight, middle-class gentility and religious tolerance as delusions concealing the erosion of Ireland's Gaelic and Catholic identity; he declared pride in Catholicism, the revival of Irish, encouragement of Irish industries and concerted action against imported smut sufficient by themselves to save Ireland. Politics were irrelevant. "Once Ireland had achieved Home Power she could laugh at those who would deny her Home Rule".

Moran allied himself with the Munster faction of the Gaelic League, who were more explicitly nationalist than the League leadership. After an unsuccessful attempt to instal him as editor of the official League newspaper Moran founded *The Leader*, which first appeared on September 1st 1900. The new paper combined some of the techniques of the new journalism with a talent for ridicule reminiscent of *United Ireland* in the 1880s. Its confident assertions appealed to those who believed the new Ireland created by the political and economic demise

9

of the landlords was about to blossom into economic prosperity and
cultural revival on Catholic and Gaelic lines. The most sophisticated
version of this outlook was represented by a group of Catholic University graduates influenced by Fr. T. A. Finlay and his protégé Professor
William Magennis. Arthur Clery ("Chanel") William Dawson ("Avis")
and Louis J. Walsh had argued with their contemporary James Joyce
about Irish national literature in the Literary and Historical Society;
they became the most prominent contributors to *The Leader* apart
from Moran. "The influence of *The Leader* on the undergraduates of
University College at that time cannot be exaggerated" wrote Dawson.

Outside Dublin the paper attracted provincials with intellectual ambitions. (Moran encouraged them to write articles on local *seoininism*).
Its outspoken Catholicism attracted a clerical audience; Walsh claimed
"The Leader made the fighting Gaelic League curate of thirty years ago,
and the fighting Gaelic League curate made the Gaelic League up and
down the country". Fr. Dineen and an t-Athair Peadar O Laoghaire, the
most distinguished representatives of the Munster faction, regularly
wrote the Irish-language column.[2]

The Leader was often shrewd (and sometimes sinister) but its base of
ideas was narrow. (Moran only visited the Gaeltacht once and never
learned to speak Irish). Within a few years the slogans became a substi-
tute for thought and the paper became the organ of a confidently
self-regarding clique, though Moran's business skills and journalistic
flair kept it profitable. Corkery was respected, but stood apart from the
inner circle of contributors; his closest friend among them was "Imaal"
(J.J. O'Toole) an essayist of no great merit but, like Corkery, solitary,
sensitive and widely-read.[3]

Corkery's contributions to *The Leader* are full of vehement socio-
aesthetic criticism of Cork City, its institutions, and its respectable
classes. Ever since the Normans walled off the city from its hinterland,
Corkery complained, it was ruled by huxtering, short-sighted
merchants who made and spent money in dribs and drabs without ever
creating a true civic culture.

> Imagine Ruskin coming to Cork and telling its history by its art-
> works. He could do it. He would write – No history! – or
> perhaps "Death in Life".[4]
>   . . . One reads of a Greek statue or even a fragment of one
> arriving in an Italian town in the wondrous middle ages, and
> straightaway the craftsmen become artists. A shipload arrive in
> Cork (a collection of casts from Greek statues was presented to
> the Crawford School of Art on its foundation early in the nine-
> teenth century) and the craftsmen became artists – no! Could
> they become artists; were they I mean such as could become
> artists? Certainly they were. I will never believe otherwise; my

fathers were all craftsmen. In the old Italian town the moneyed classes as well as the craftsmen saw the difference between the Greek statue and what the town produced ... In Cork the respectabilities, the intellectuals either did not, do not see the difference or seeing it have no faith in our workmen.[5]

Thus the "respectabilities" rule Cork "the Mean and Ugly", ignorant of art and of their own ignorance, congratulating themselves on the "Beautiful City", the intellectual societies debate whether Bacon wrote Shakespeare, stage-Irishmen cavort on the Opera House stage, clergy and nationalists admire oratory and showy statues which provoke emotion without thought, while the city rots.[6]

It is sad enough to walk Cork at any time; the knowledge of decay in your mind, its presence in ruined factories, scarce a thing thriving except Bung (the drink trade) ... the absence of spiritual life; of intellectual activity; of art; of built beauty; of ornaments; of poets; of museums; of picture galleries; of a healthy Free Library; of anything that would even hint at "soul".

Corkery sympathised with those who tried to improve Cork through trade unionism. "We, having lost our industries, begin to institute Labour Day". He praised Jim Larkin for his endeavours to raise the social and cultural condition of his followers. The personality of Larkin attracted him:

a face and head that anyone that ever did any modelling would like to set to work on – power in every line of it, intellect sitting daringly on the brow, character everywhere in the spare surfaces and firm bones. And then that forward, searching look, that habit of looking at vacancy at odd moments, that indescribable eagerness which the faces of all those take on whose ideas become tyrannous until expressed in the form of a message, a gospel ... by dint of reading, it was his custom to quote poetry as freely as I would myself if I had more courage; by brooding and thinking on problems that for his companions must practically have had no existence – he had raised himself so much above his fellows that he deceived himself if he dreamed he could find lieutenants in their ranks. Here is a drama for any Ibsen that cares to write it – the failure of a leader of the democracy to find lieutenants.[8]

When Larkin was imprisoned on a technicality in 1909, Corkery was one of the few intellectuals to appeal for his release.[9]

Corkery praised Larkin primarily as a nationalist trying to persuade the Irish trade union movement to separate itself from its British counterpart.[10] His own social concern was based on the nationalist belief that the regeneration of the nation would bring with it the betterment of all its people; he ascribed the selfishness of the respectable classes to their un-Irish culture and believed it would be cured with their incorporation into a fully-developed Irish national culture.

> If there are patriots in the true sense of the word among our Irish trade unionists, I would say to them; cut adrift from England, and endeavour to make up for any loss of strength thus brought about by spreading your organisation more widely within Ireland. Ireland has a labour world of its own. It is for you to organise it. This Irish world of labour is not legislated for, it is not understood; it is not even discovered. I read your papers . . . and I see no mention of this Irish industrial world, but I see much of a world which is not here, but which *you believe* to be here. And I see you smiting imaginary enemies – one of them a giant called Capitalist. Which would be comic to witness, if the Irish nation was not dying through your neglect, and others such as you.[11]

In reaction against Cork city and even more against Dublin (at times he wondered if Dubliners were Irish)[12], Corkery sometimes idealised the countryside. Reading *Tess of the D'Urbevilles*, he noted "the peasants in their coarseness are very different from our Irish peasants but then our peasants have not got into print – I know nothing of them".[13] Despite this tendency, Corkery was more often intensely critical of "the wet dullness of Irish rural life".[14] He denounced the new peasant proprietors' habit of cutting down trees on their land even where there was no economic necessity to do so as "uncultured, unpatriotic and ignorant".

> I wish some of those fine characteristics of the Celt would find a means of expressing themselves! The air is loud with their fame and their analysis but it is hard to find their tangible results . . . Possibly there is not a more basely, lazily utilitarian creature in the world than the Irish farmer . . . (In his life) religion itself without emotion becomes mere morality; art, mere skill; life in general without it struggles, kills that it may not be killed; and lacking it, if it could survive the loss even in any form, passion is another name for selfishness.[15]

He complained that the farmers were only interested in the land; he accepted the necessity of the Land War, but believed it hindered the development of an Irish national culture by stifling discussion and ignoring the interests of other elements of Irish society such as the urban workingman[16]. He wrote in his diary that while the mind of the farmer was dominated by land, the townsman valued "personal freedom".

> The farmers in Ireland will cease to hold their grip on the political party – then the towns and cities will give their tone to the policy ... Now I hope for this in Ireland. An individual opinion! How the editors would have to skip and the Bishops and priests wake up – the teachers also and the various boards.[17]

Yet Corkery was not prepared to abandon the "almost hopeless" task of "the spread of culture among those who are hitherto to be rooted in the soil". He believed the peasants had once possessed a developed culture informed by spontaneous emotion, but famine, emigration and the necessary discipline of mass political agitation caused "the vanishing of a people's emotion". The revival of the Gaelic tradition would reconcile and fulfil the values of city and countryside.[18]

When Corkery began to study Irish he saw it as an exercise in romantic antiquarianism, like patching up a ruined castle.[19] Slowly he came to believe it could substantiate the civic culture of Cork and his own artistic stirrings.

> The true spirit of art. .... I have found alone in some Gaelic concerts at which I have been present. The singers were think-ing, the audience were thinking, and was merry; that "bored" look was absent. Hence I knew the spirit of art was abroad.[20]

Slowly he realised there were still people who lived their lives through Irish. In July 1902 he met his first native speaker – an old woman brought from Kerry to be exhibited in the Model Labourer's Cottage built by the Department of Agricultural and Technical Instruction at the Cork Exhibition.[21] In February 1903, visiting Dublin for the second time in his life, Corkery saw his first author – Douglas Hyde playing Raifteiri in his own play *An Posadh*. Corkery later recalled this, with some exaggeration, as "My First Glimpse Of the Gaeltacht"[22].

Soon afterwards Corkery discovered old people in the Cork lanes who could tell stories about eighteenth century Gaelic poets and recite their work. In September 1907 he published an article on "The Memory of Our Poets", presenting the eighteenth-century Munster poets as romantic Bohemians ("One can never hate or moralise over the grave of an adventurous vagabond") who differed from their brethren of *fin de siecle* London and Paris in that (despite their failings) they possessed an "unifying ... simple, undoubting and ardent faith", sang for an audience who knew them and judged their work by accepted traditional standards with

> a warmth, a personal feeling ever and always denied to the poet who sings for millions . . .
>   How the old people love to remember the anecdotes about these poets! For many the lives of the poets seem to have taken the place of popular novels. The poets were their "great" men about whom it was right to tell stories good or bad. . . It was a very old woman gave me this anecdote. I knew her to have lived a life of grinding poverty – yet the daily anguish, the squalid life of the lane had not taken away one of all her stories of these old poets whom she loved to speak of, nor, seemingly, robbed her of one of her thousand lines of poetry. The lane knows her no more. All bright and fresh, perhaps she has had a talk with Eoghan Ruadh before this. . . And I remember meeting an old man who had made sufficient in Chicago to support his old age, talking fluently of Tadhg Gaolach . . .
>   How very nearly these old poets with their wild ways had faded from the national consciousness! . . . Not knowing these and such communities as their lives hint at, what is that tract of Irish history but a uniform grey so far as social life is concerned? We should esteem their memories; we should write about them, speak of them, think of them, until they become part and parcel of the national mind . . . They redeem their time and place from a reproach that in Browning's words, may yet be hurled at our age:
>   Could'st not sing one song for grace?
>   Nor make one blossom man's and ours?[23]

Corkery had found the Hidden Ireland in the Cork lanes before he visited the Gaeltacht. He believed the Gaeltacht tradition could become the basis of a shared national culture which would focus people's attention on the life around them and so inspire them to improve it. He praised the teaching of nature study, whose origins he attributed to Ruskin, because it taught children observation.[24]

Corkery was all the more conscious of this because he was part of the education system which he described as "Juggernaut" and Pearse called the "Murder Machine", no longer as a student but as a teacher trying to encourage

> the spirit of natural art – art that is naturally in one until, with artificiality and want of using, it dies; art that naturally inclines to laugh and play with things rather than to pose and sentimentalise on its own behalf; in a word, art that makes for happiness in people.[25]

In October 1905 Corkery became an assistant teacher in St. Francis'
National School, off North Main Street in the city centre:

> set down in a sort of half-hearted clearance of a network of
> lanes and streets. The backs of a lot of overcrowded, half-
> ancient, four-storey houses looked down on two sides of the
> playground; the other two were bounded by a confused crush
> of stables and yards.[26]

The teachers took turns to go round the surrounding slums looking for
absent pupils. Corkery recorded one such visit in a diary he kept for a
few months in 1907:

> Visited Paul St., Marsh, Main St. All very poor tenement houses.
> All had some features in common. The stairs were leaning to one
> side: vacant "common" rooms seemed frequent; whitewash
> everywhere; intense curiosity on the landings as to whom I might
> be; ashamed look on the faces of those who opened the door for
> me; these faces always unwashed, with hair hanging; an effort
> made to draw the clothes over the breasts; half-naked children
> running round. In a house in Harpur's Lane there were in one
> room a middle aged woman with bare feet, a young girl and a
> soldier, her brother, I should say, and several children. While I
> was talking to a woman in Kyrls Street a neighbour came and put
> her head through window: I was speaking over the half-door;
> she was looking through window expecting some sensation
> presumably. All were very quiet. The only woman who took any
> interest in her children was one a cut above the rest socially. It is
> such lanes as these turn out soldiers.[27]

Corkery was a dedicated teacher, despite discouragement. In
September 1906 he went to St. Patrick's College, Drumcondra, for a
year's teacher training. Corkery was placed in the First Division in his
final Teachers' Examination, but was only marked "good" in English
Composition and "fair" in Progress in Teaching. Since his *Leader* essays
show a distinctive style, viewpoint and concern for critical standards,
and such information as is available about his teaching career shows
him as an exceptional teacher, it seems the college authorities did not
like originality.[28] Years later Denis Breen, his friend and contemporary
at the College, cursed and swore as he told Frank O'Connor how
Corkery suffered there.[29]

Corkery successfully organised a school choir at St. Francis's. It sang
at Gaelic League concerts; he was proud of it and reacted angrily when
an opponent mocked it in the *Leader*[30]. Corkery wrote sadly in his diary
of his pupils' attitude towards him.

A teacher's is one of the most melancholy lives. He is for the great part of the day alone with his children. While with them – and most teachers like to be with them, I have often heard of teachers who came as they get older to really dislike vacation – he seems only to have a small portion of his nature at work. He often gives of his sympathy; even of his love; he seems to get return for both so intently gazing up at his eyes are the pupils; but his back turned they make a joke of it all. This is the case with the young teacher. The old teacher works away, hard enough, earnestly enough, and does not expect any return in the way of sympathy.[31]

The Gaelic League gave Corkery, his sister, and a circle of friends (mostly young teachers like Breen, Daniel and Patrick Harrington, and the Higgins brothers) an outlet for social activities. In its first years the South Parish branch was dominated by a pious elderly man who enforced strict discipline; when he retired the young teachers took over the committee. (Corkery spent several years as secretary and branch representative on the Comhairle Ceanntair). They taught evening classes two nights a week without pay, though sometimes knowing little more Irish than their pupils. (In 1907 Corkery taught pupils studying for the first stage of the five-stage Fleming Companionship examination while he was studying for the second stage; reviewing a book in Irish at the same time, he remarked it was the first Irish book he had read through). They organised historical lectures. They held joint outings down the Harbour with the Blackpool branch, whose secretary Tomas MacCurtain became a close friend of Corkery. They had a choir, supervised by Corkery; some South Parish members joined the Blackpool branch orchestra. (Its conductor, the elderly church musician George Brady, encouraged Corkery's literary endeavours. Corkery played the cello; his sister was second violin). Corkery used League outings as sketching trips; he began painting in watercolours after taking night classes at the Crawford School of Art with the local landscape painter Harry Scully.[32]

He began writing stories. Two conventional pieces appeared in *The Irish Rosary* under the pen-name "Daniel Barron"; one of these reappeared in *A Munster Twilight* (1916) after extensive reworking.[33] Two more appeared in *The Leader*[34], as did two evocative prose-poems, "The Joy of Marching" which describes boys marching the country roads at night to the sound of a fife from sheer exhilaration[35], and "Cantillon's Symphony", which describes the atmosphere of a night in a Dublin lodging-house.[36] "The Joy of Marching" was well-received and inspired the first known article on Corkery's writing, in *Q.C.C.* the new student magazine of Queen's College, Cork (part of the college revival under the presidency of Sir Bertram Windle). The anonymous author (probably the editor, D.L. Kelleher, who had denounced the "Athens of Ireland" myth) praised Corkery as "A City Ruskin" and predicted that Corkery, like other prophets, would be honoured by his city – long after his death.[37]

Corkery was distinguished from most other contributors to *The Leader* by his concern for artistic standards. Many were simply ignorant; others, like Moran, despised art unless it served as propaganda and invoked Gaelic culture as a slogan without bothering to explore its content. The most sophisticated, Clery and Dawson, treated the Abbey with respect until the *Playboy* controversy, but their responses were governed by vague and sentimental ideas of folk-drama; after dismissing as flawed several of the plays for which the Abbey is best remembered, they hailed *Kincora* by Lady Gregory as its first undoubted masterpiece.

At this time Corkery knew little more about Gaelic culture than Moran; but he was prepared to learn and judge its contemporary output by the same standards he applied to any work of art. He saw contemporary Irish-language literature suffered from the absence of a critical reading public, and complained that Gaelic writers ignored literature written in languages other than Irish and favoured simple storytelling without regard for style or subtlety.[38] His criticisms of shoddy and sentimental art provoked regular controversies with other contributors.[39] (Moran encouraged controversies; they helped circulation).[40] The most extensive controversy began when Corkery attacked the pageant play *Eoghan Ruadh O Neill* which had toured Ireland attracting large, enthusiastic audiences. He argued that earlier Gaelic plays, though poor as dramas, tried "to deal honestly with the life of the Irish-speaking districts" and appealed to Irish-speakers' fondness for "vigorous, racy, witty dialogue", but *Eoghan Ruadh* was written in blundering language and relied on elaborate scenery and melodramatic heroics to arouse enthusiasm. "Ah! The pity that we in Irish should think of beginning where English drama in its decrepitude is ending up!" He complained that Irish Ireland, ashamed of the "bawneens and bare legs" of everyday peasant life, was unknowingly killing Irish national drama.[41]

This provoked an uproar. One critic, "Eoin", said the play must be good because it was popular and denied Irish Ireland was ashamed of peasant life.[42] "Buadhthain", a Corkman, jeered at Corkery's multifarious artistic activities as "superficial", claiming Corkery wanted to "stick to the old mud cabin with the manure heap and the malodorous duck's pool in front, and pigs and bare-legged urchins running in and out . . . the stage Irishman . . . Presenting them on the stage, and trying to make people believe they are beautiful and soul-refreshing things, will certainly not help us to get rid of them".[43]

Corkery denied his activities were superficial and pointed out that by encouraging stuff like *Eoghan Ruadh O Neill* the League might disprove the contention that Irish life could only find true expression through the Irish language and, by discouraging talented beginners, destroy any chance of creating a significant Irish drama. "Do you think you are helping forward the Irish language if you force real thought about Ireland to express itself in English? . . . Propagandism that arrives at that – is it not a nice and useful sort of propagandism?"[44]

At this point another contributor, "Siobhan", in an article declaring Donnchadh Ruadh MacCon Mara was not a true poet because he fornicated, turned Protestant, and wrote of drunkenness and seasickness, denounced "Lee's view that the proper foundation for a National Drama is mud". "Siobhan" had neither seen nor read *Eoghan Ruadh*, but praised it as exemplifying Corneille's view that since drama must possess epic dignity it should only deal with kings and nobles. The controversy petered out in a series of acrid exchanges, with Corkery asking if "Siobhan" thought Shakespeare was not a true poet because he wrote "Greasy Joan doth keel the pot", while "Siobhan" complained about his references to obscure Russians and Norwegians (Tolstoi and Ibsen) and "contemporary Irish writers on the value of whose literary work the present generation cannot well pass judgement."[45] Forty years later, in a *Bell* article on Gaelic drama, Peter Kavanagh called this controversy the point when propaganda defeated art, without knowing "Lee" was Corkery.[46]

Not all Corkery's opponents were as obtuse as "Siobhan". The art critic Robert Elliott, having defended Corkery against an accusation that his artistic concerns were simply weaving "flowers for the national tomb" by diverting attention from the need for industrial revival, expressed concern that Corkery was more interested in ornament than the underlying structure. Corkery denied this charge – fairly enough, since he saw cultural criticism as a form of social criticism; but his aesthetic vision of Irish history dismissed or downgraded many aspects of Irish life past and present.[47] Ignorant of the economic forces which shaped his society, suspicious of political activity as a distraction from cultural revival, Corkery drew his idea of a "normal" country from contemporary English escapist literature of rural nostalgia. He explained the difference between the image of English society as "a haunt of ancient peace" and timegrown custom and his own experience of Irish rural society by recalling how "we have been in the wars" for centuries. "When the language went, which of course is the medium of a people's customs, how could the customs remain?"[48] Those darker aspects of English rural society he noticed in his reading were ascribed, in Chestertonian style, to the folly of the English in deserting the land of England for the Flag of England when such deep culture as found expression in the Gaelic *dinnsheanchais* (lore of placenames) could only exist where people could assume their lives and the lives of their children would be bound up with the city or countryside where their ancestors lived:

> Nothing ever surprises a student of Irish so much as to discover
> that all those stone-breakers along the road, in this part of the

country they are all Irish-speakers, are treasuries of old local poems, old ranns and riddles. In an Irish-speaking district every field had a name . . . every hamlet had its song . . . thus it was before people learned to think imperially.[49]

The Irish Ireland view of cultural revival as sufficient in itself to re-create the nation became increasingly problematic as the return of a Liberal government in 1906 opened new political possibilities, while the waning of the first wave of enthusiasm showed the League the limitations of voluntary action. In a 1909 article Corkery lamented that many Gaelic League recruits dropped out soon after joining, over-zealous League denunciations of conventional nationalists often turned ignorant goodwill into hostility, and he knew schoolboys who had decided they must be English since they knew no Irish. He attributed these responses to the tepidity of the political atmosphere. Only a vigorous political movement could engender the nationalist enthusiasm needed to revive the League.[50] Political nationalism might put the power of an Irish government behind cultural nationalism. Believing in the primacy of cultural revival, Corkery was relatively unconcerned about forms of government. (He supported the 1907 Irish Council Bill because it gave Irish control of the educational system,[51] and wrote that membership of the Empire would be acceptable if it became a network of self-governing Dominions.[52]) At the same time he feared a vigorous political movement might swamp the League altogether.

> The swamping of the Gaelic League as a mere organisation is not what would trouble me; it is the wrecking of all the Gaelic League stands for with which I should be concerned. It is the wrecking of that spirit which is keeping our weekly papers alive, which is publishing books in two languages, which is feeling towards education, towards literary culture, towards the works of peace. If all this is to be wrecked, it is a high price. Yet who would hesitate to pay it if there be no other way?[53]

Corkery responded to this dilemma by withdrawing from the *Leader* after 1910 to concentrate on a long-held project; the creation of a local theatre to focus the civic culture of Cork.

In September 1903, seven months after seeing Hyde in *An Posadh*, Corkery reviewed a Cork performance of an tAthair Peadar's play about Queen Maeve. He complained that it used such inappropriate scenery the *Cork Examiner* mistook it for a kitchen comedy, and remarked: "Truly, I wish for talents enough to write a drama in English, for cash enough to produce it here in Cork just to see what the *Examiner* would say of its first performance".[54]

In September 1904 he wrote "the natural thing for a city to do is build itself a theatre. . . . If a city had a life, a heart of its own, which life found expression on its local stage, even a small life and uninspired expression" and mused about a citizen of that city thinking how his own life helped to make these plays which he understood as no later generation could understand them.[55] Another article attacks elaborate scenery; the blank stage with a notice indicating the scene, used by the Chinese, would make the audience listen to the words and allow a society of 'prentice playwrights to stage several new plays a year without bankrupting themselves.[56]

In December 1904 members of local separatist debating societies, having formed the Cork National Theatre Society, staged their first production (a historical play and Yeats' *Pot of Broth*, the first Abbey play Corkery saw). Corkery praised the CNTS though he criticised their imitation of the exaggerated gestures of professional actors. He suggested they should approach local writers like Canon Sheehan and the Youghal novelist William Buckley "to try and get some little plays written here in our own city about our own civic life in the past, but more particularly about our own civic life in the present".[57] The CNTS disappeared after two more productions, having staged only one locally-written play.

In December 1905 Yeats gave a lecture in Cork; he struck Corkery as a *poseur*. When a young man criticised the Abbey for staging the plays of Synge, Yeats responded by discussing *The Well of the Saints*. Corkery's comments show no previous knowledge of Synge's work. He disliked the plot, suggesting Synge should have shown "the peasants" drawn together after the initial shock by shared experiences and memories, finally welcoming blindness lest their love be disturbed again. Corkery denounced Yeats' view that Synge was under no obligation to write about typical peasants; Corkery argued that while "the shallow writer of short stories" gave external descriptions of the words and habits of the *average* peasant, the poet should use his imagination to render the inarticulate, universal qualities of the *typical* peasant.[58]

In August 1907 Corkery visited the Abbey for the first time.

> What you felt about the authors, the actors, the orchestra, about everything, was – how very kind of them! One could hardly understand it. The place was kept so nicely, the plays were, well, so different from what you were given elsewhere, they were so beautifully mounted – this was really well done – that on the whole one felt decidedly thankful to all concerned. To say the least. . . . they are an interesting lot, these Abbey people.[59]

On September 15 and 16 1907 the Abbey paid their first visit to Cork. Corkery attended both nights and was particularly moved by *Riders to the Sea.*[60] A week later, he noted in his diary the idea which became his first play, *The Embers.*[61]

A year later, having written the play, Corkery persuaded some members of the South Parish Branch to begin rehearsals. On November 1st 1908 a public meeting was held in An Dun, the old Gaelic League headquarters over a livery stable. Corkery proposed the establishment of an arts club where different artistic interests could co-operate, rather than a purely dramatic society, but he was outvoted.[62] The Cork Dramatic Society was established and issued a manifesto announcing as its aims "the development of a native school of dramatists . . . to do for Cork what similar societies have done for Dublin and Belfast". It would confine itself to original plays and translations by society members.[63]

On May 23rd 1909 the CDS staged its first production, *The Embers*, at the hall in An Dun.

The Embers is a Moranite satire on Irish politics, constitutionalist and physical force. Corkery got the idea from an incident in 1905, when an old man wandered into An Dun and talked about an obscure Gaelic word on a placard outside. "It's many years since I saw that word".[64] He was Jeremiah O'Donovan Rossa, West Corkman, Fenian leader, native speaker of Irish, whose sufferings in prison after 1866 made him a national hero; after a long career amid the factional disputes of Irish-American separatism, Cork County Council had given him the sinecure office of Corresponding Secretary. The old man's mind was beginning to wander; he resigned within a year and returned to America for family reasons.

In *The Embers* Rossa appears as John Whitelaw O'Loughlin, a worn-out old Fenian released after twenty years in prison; with no home of his own he returns to his native Cooladuv to stay with his old friend William Kiely. Kiely has become a hard-faced, prosperous merchant who secures local government contracts by bribery; he despises his son Lawrence, who has been made unfit for any useful occupation by the genteel "education" inflicted on him by his mother's social ambitions. Kiely plans to instal Lawrence as Workhouse Master. The local "bosses" want to gain popularity by appointing O'Loughlin; they promise to make Lawrence M.P. (The incumbent is dying.) Pitying the broken old man and intoxicated by his own newly-discovered oratorical powers, Lawrence proclaims O'Loughlin's appointment. Lawrence is duly offered the seat when it falls vacant, but stuns the nominating convention with a ferocious denunciation of Parliamentarianism – O'Loughlin has converted him to separatism. Kiely throws O'Loughlin and Lawrence out of his house; they go to the workhouse.

Twenty years later Lawrence is a half-crazed vagabond pelted by drunken Party supporters when he tries to lecture the Manchester Martyrs procession on the memory of John Whitelaw O'Loughlin. His words inspire the adolescent members of the local separatist debating society to make themselves "fools for Ireland's sake"; young Daly their leader, son of Lawrence's ex-fiancee and the Party boss who got the seat, goes out to address the procession in confident expectation of making them all separatists. Left alone in the clubroom, Lawrence collapses and dies; young Daly comes back, having been pelted by the crowd, and pledges himself to follow in the footsteps of Lawrence and O'Loughlin.[65]

Lawrence and O'Loughlin are the most sympathetic characters in the play (O'Loughlin converts Lawrence because no-one else, not even his family and his fiancee, has seen him as more than a means of raising their social standing) but they are shown as futile fantasists. Under Corkery's direction, Lawrence was presented as an affected prig, his patriotic speeches made ridiculous by an acquired English accent; the audience showed a good deal of sympathy when his father called him "a young puppy who never earned a penny". The critic who reviewed *The Embers* for *The Leader* was horrified by its scathing irony, but praised its intellectual force.[66] Other critics admired the style of acting, derived from the Abbey. ("There is not overmuch movement, and the voice is given every prominence".)[67] Despite limitations of scale and finance, the Cork Dramatic Society had achieved a critical success with its first production.

CHAPTER THREE

QUIET DESPERATION 1909–16

In 1904 the Gaelic League opened a teacher training college at Ballingeary in West Cork. In 1907 Ballingeary began to offer summer courses. In August 1909 Corkery attended one of these courses, his first visit to the Gaeltacht. He was deeply impressed by this rural society with its living folk tradition, its memories of the retreat of O'Sullivan Beare and the Tithe War Battle of Keimaneigh, and by the enthusiasm of the other students.[1]

Staying at "The Lodge", a farmhouse two miles north of Ballingeary[2], he made friends with another student, a dark intense young man from the North Parish Branch, whom he already knew slightly through the Cork Dramatic Society. Visiting the separatist Celtic Literary Society once out of curiosity, Corkery had heard him say "We are not ripe enough to start a paper, let us wait" and decided there was something unusual about Terence MacSwiney.[3]

MacSwiney was born in Cork in 1879, the fourth of seven surviving children. His father, John MacSwiney, was a former Fenian and member of the Papal Brigade, an ex-schoolmaster turned tobacco dealer, born in West Cork, a native speaker of Irish who did not transmit it to his children. Family tradition claimed descent from the dispossessed MacSweeney lords of Carraig Dermot Oge Castle, near Macroom. The family was intensely nationalist, though Mrs. MacSwiney was an Englishwoman; the children were taught to recite rebel poems for their father.

In 1885 the family business failed. John MacSwiney emigrated to Australia, hoping to bring out his family; but there was an economic depression in Australia and after some years' hardship he died. His widow brought up the family with the help of her eldest child, Mary; at times the children wore broken shoes and went hungry.[4]

Terence went to the Christian Brothers' North Monastery school, traditionally nationalistic (it taught "Celtic"-Irish); he was one of the most separatist boys in the class. Terence was a bright pupil but he had to leave school at fourteen, becoming a clerk in a large wholesale warehouse to help support the family.[5] A few years later he resumed study in his spare time, restricting himself to four hours' sleep. He maintained this regimen for the rest of his life. He learned accountancy and in 1907 acquired a B.A. in "Mental and Moral Science" from the National University of Ireland, but his studies were not exclusively directed towards professional qualification. He wanted to prepare himself for leadership in a future insurrection.

In 1899 MacSwiney joined the separatist Cork Young Ireland Society which broke away when the Wolfe Tone Society (founded 1898) was taken over by socialists. The Young Ireland Society split in 1900; MacSwiney, like most of the younger and more active members, seceded to form the Celtic Literary Society.

P.S. O'Hegarty wrote that MacSwiney was shaped by "his father's nationalism and his mother's religion". MacSwiney, unlike the agnostic O'Hegarty, refused to distinguish between them. He claimed that since patriotism was divinely ordained it could never conflict with religion; therefore the separatist was not merely a better patriot but a better Catholic.[6] Those who opposed separatism, whether priests or laymen, thereby showed themselves corrupt cowards who had succumbed to "materialism" (personified by Britain, "this hellish materialistic Power"). Not even an overwhelming majority of the Irish people could revoke the right of the Irish nation to separation.[7]

MacSwiney was an ascetic revolutionary of a type common in Europe since the French Revolution, demanding absolute fidelity to the ideal with religious fervour and exerting authority beyond his apparent abilities by force of his austere sincerity. At times his colleagues felt he treated them "as if we were small boys" when he refused to join the IRB because he thought secrecy demoralising or opposed the affiliation of the CLS to the new IRB front organisation Sinn Fein because its dual monarchist programme compromised the principle of complete separation; but his willingness to bear greater burdens than anyone else disarmed criticism.[8]

MacSwiney was eventually persuaded to join Sinn Fein but soon resigned, reproaching himself for acquiescing in compromise, to concentrate on writing and Gaelic League activities.[9] He believed art inseparable from nationalism.[10] In 1906 he published a book of verse, *The Music of Freedom*, naively hoping it might earn enough for him to live in the Gaeltacht a year or two while learning Irish well enough to write it.[11] MacSwiney had once thought Irish must take second place to separatism, but decided "on reflection" Ireland could not remain a separate nationality without Irish.[12]

In 1904 his mother died suddenly. MacSwiney noted in his diary that she was the first of the family buried in Cork, away from their traditional burial place.[13] In February 1906 he recorded the death of an aunt, his last link with the older generation, and recalled her tales of ancient family glories.[14] As he lost other links with the past, his love for the Gaeltacht increased; in the summer of 1906 he cycled through Ballingeary and dreamed of the Gael waiting in the mountains to rush down and restore Freedom to her throne.[15] From 1907 he attended the Ballingeary summer courses annually. His roots in the countryside impressed Corkery. "He could point out the fields which his grandparents had tilled".[16]

Corkery and MacSwiney were drawn together by shared resentment at the city which tolerated slums and condemned them to drudge in dead-end white-collar jobs. (The warehouse where MacSwiney worked was only a few hundred yards from the slum school where Corkery taught; MacSwiney often went over at lunchtime for a few minutes' chat).[17] They shared a love of natural beauty and a desire for artistic creation. MacSwiney accompanied Corkery on his sketching trips, though he could not paint; Corkery remembered him looking at his easel "as if my hobby were some sort of sacred rite".[18] They exchanged their writing for criticism; MacSwiney was the only person apart from a member of Corkery's own household (probably his sister) to read *The Threshold of Quiet*, the novel Corkery worked on for years, before it went to a publisher.[19]

There were differences between them. Corkery thought MacSwiney too sheerly idealistic and wanted more of "the colour and shape and weight of things" in his writing.[20] He disagreed with MacSwiney's separatism, while MacSwiney did not share his admiration for Synge; but their friendship was not disrupted. Between 1909 and 1913 they met almost every day on CDS business.[21]

The committee formed when the CDS was established was soon replaced by a group of directors, each informally given particular responsibilities. Corkery, recognised as their moving spirit, was secretary, handled correspondence, helped design costumes and scenery. He supervised the work of Thomas O'Gorman, producer, coach and treasurer, the only CDS member who had been active in the CNTS. Denis Breen recruited and conducted a small orchestra (including Mary Corkery) and composed some incidental music. MacSwiney was a director without specific responsibilities.

A few outsiders who joined the CDS at its inception soon dropped out. Those who remained were already known to each other through the Gaelic League. "The group were mostly teachers of one sort or another; but there were also young tradesmen, clerks, shop assistants". Later some students from University College Cork joined. The most prominent of these recruits was Con O'Leary, who wrote two plays for the Society; his fine voice and commanding bearing made him one of its leading actors. After graduation he went to England, became a Fleet Street journalist, and later helped Corkery publish articles in English magazines.

The Society confined itself to a few simple rules. Only original plays were to be performed; players were not to be borrowed from any other society; no writer was to appear in his own play; players who refused a part were expelled. In practice members were expected to help in whatever came to hand, though some were excused tasks for which they were obviously unfitted. Corkery was excluded from acting by his crippled leg; MacSwiney was too single-minded to make a good actor and too busy to attend rehearsals (even of his own plays); as well as his day work he now taught night classes in accountancy in a commercial school.[22]

The CDS staged eighteen original plays by nine authors. The most prolific authors were Corkery, with five, and MacSwiney with four. The dominant style was the "naturalism" associated with the kitchen comedies and melodramas beginning to dominate the Abbey through the "Cork Realist" imitators of Synge (notably T.C. Murray, Lennox Robinson, R.J. Ray).[23]

The influence of Synge is visible in Corkery's second play, *The Woman of Three Cows* (never staged, probably because of its length). An uneasy mixture of *Riders to the Sea* with *Playboy of the Western World*, it depicts the struggle between a grim matriarch, who rebuilt the dissipated fortunes of the strong farmer Riordans of Acharas after the reckless husband she married for his land ended his career of salmon-poaching, drink and gambling by plunging defiantly on horseback into a swollen ford, and her equally strong and determined grandson who wants to marry the daughter of a poor widow. The old woman dreams of becoming legend by a final heroic gesture – selling the farm and sending the money to her son Fr. Terence who is building a great Church in Sacramento – but the dream collapses when a dying wanderer whom the young man forcibly defends from his cowardly, bullying father is revealed as Fr. Terence, who learned humility after his pride "cast him down from a high place in the Church". Up this point sympathy is clearly with the grandson (the old woman suggests the widow's daughter is after the land, but everything we see of the girl's character contradicts this) but when it becomes clear the old woman is still obdurate her grandson defies her by going salmon-poaching like his grandfather. The old woman emits an imitation of Maurya's lament and is led away to die; it is implied the cycle will repeat itself all over again, which makes nonsense of the portrayal of the girl and ignores earlier hints that the grandson has found spiritual awakening under the guidance of the saintly wanderer. Corkery's confusion shows deep ambivalence towards heroism and conformity; the splendid horseman hurling himself to destruction in defiance of a stifling world became one of his characteristic symbols.

Despite this fatal indecision the writing has moments of Syngean vividness:

> I'd wake up at night with the cold to the small of my back, and there would be his half of the bed as cold as a flagstone and

himself gone, and the old clock ticking away for itself in the
empty room – and then I'd hear a whistle here and a whistle
there – and I'd rise out of my bed and I'd see the torches
moving higher and over across the river, and he'd come back
with the white salmon hanging down his back, and his legs like
two pillars of stone from standing in the running water, so that
I'd have to make down a fire would roast a bull to dry his
things for the morning.[24]

Corkery praised Synge for building an imaginative observation to
give expression to aspects of human nature crushed by everyday life
and excluded from naturalist drama – not sheer escapism, but criticism
of life and visions of its transformation. When the Cork première of the
Playboy (August 29th 1910) produced controversy, Corkery defended
Synge in a lecture to the Cork Literary and Scientific Society. He said
Synge was too sane to trouble himself with "the problems of the modern world . . . the sense of heredity, the bugbear of modern literature . . .
evolution which would make man very much less than the angels";

He saw the passion and colour of life rather than its meaning.
. . . His philosophy deals with the profound and common things
of life – Love, Death, Decay.
     . . . His significance in the world of literature. Ibsen as a man
of genius who set a limit to knowledge. Maeterlinck tilting at
Ibsen with a moonbeam. Synge an earthly Maeterlinck. His
characters exist in a world without institutions, are not troubled by systems; their woes are from without. How Synge
teaches us through the sympathies and antipathies of the heart
(Shelley's phrase). He carries us away from the dreary inter-
course of daily life, gives us holiday where there are fresh
winds, and seagull's wings.

Corkery thought *The Shadow of the Glen* "a folk tale not heightened
sufficiently into dramatic fervour" whose characters hovered uneasily
between tragedy and comedy. *The Tinker's Wedding*, though "without
malice" had "nothing to recommend it except the bravura of its farce . . .
an error of taste". *The Well of the Saints* was "Synge's most philosophic
play. The wisdom of the children of the dark contrasted with that of the
children of the light . . . The grimness of the play; the reflections it stirs".
Riders to the Sea was "Synge's most perfect play", but Corkery reserved
his highest praise for *The Playboy of the Western World*.

Synge's greatest play . . . The people fall in love not with Christy
Mahon the murderer, but with Christy Mahon the romancer.
He lifts them into a world where the old standards do not

apply. The mood of the play; the injustice of examining
passages as if they were part of another mood. . . . The very
wildness of the language the safeguard of the play since it lets
us know what value to set on the views of life presented.

Corkery concluded by calling *Deirdre of the Sorrows* "the opening of a
series of plays at which we can but guess. Its economy of language, its
deeper thought, when compared with what has gone before, hint that
we have lost the best".[25]

This lecture aroused so much interest the Literary and Scientific
Society held a discussion a fortnight later. The audience was apparently
evenly divided; defenders of Synge included Denis Breen and Olive
Brooke Hughes (proprietress of a local social magazine) while opponents compared Pegeen Mike unfavourably with Dickens heroines and
called the Aran Islanders "mongrel Cromwellians". Corkery summed
up by noting the opponents of Synge could not agree what it was they
criticised. He said there was no English-language peasant literature,
that Anglo-Irish literature could not be understood without a knowledge of Irish, and concluded "Mr. Synge's work was as yet the greatest
thing in Irish literature".[26]

In December 1911 a veteran Cork theatre-goer, reminiscing in Olive
Brooke Hughes' magazine *The Irish Outlook*, lamented that "just as
prejudice was being broken down" the Abbey had succumbed to
"Ibsenism" exemplified by the "French decadent" Synge.[27] Corkery
responded with two articles on "Synge and Decadence", complaining
that "our local sufferers from Synge-phobia" knew nothing about
Decadence except the name.

Decadence is an effort to intellectualise emotion; emotion for its
own sake, deep, overwhelming, the decadents would have none
of – they considered it brutal. "Je haïs la passion et l'esprit me fait
mal!" said Baudelaire. Baudelaire, himself, said that modernity
was half of art. In every point Synge's style is directly opposite
. . . we find Synge's characters fiercely alive; while those of the
decadents are puppets: nature with him is wild, rugged, natural;
with them, pretty and artificial: they are given to abstractions; he
avoids abstractions: he believed poetry should deal with the
interests of common life, to achieve this should not hesitate to
become brutal; the brutal was their greatest aversion. Rousseau
and his theories of nature they abhorred; their style is delicate,
complicated, learned with terms drawn from all the sciences, all
the arts; the absence of the modern spirit from Synge's works is
one of his most noticeable characteristics . . . What did he care
about modernity with its dictionary of science? His plays might
have been written three hundred years ago![28]

This over-romantic view of literature did not prevent the CDS staging naturalist plays which were accused of "Ibsenism". The strengths and weaknesses of CDS naturalism are exemplified by MacSwiney's one-act play *The Holocaust*, first performed in December 1910 soon after the Cork employers defeated the ITGWU in a bitter quay strike. It depicts an argument between a cynical doctor and an ailing, idealistic young curate in the bare room where a striker's wife and last surviving child are dying of consumption. As the doctor leaves in despair the father comes in raging at the patronising charity offered by the boss and the complacent Canon. Mother and child die; the father calls down the curse of God on his oppressors, smashes the curate to the floor when he tries to console him, and rushes out to join the socialists as the curate cries feebly "God-forgive!"[29]

Corkery admired *The Holocaust* more than anything else MacSwiney wrote because it was based upon observation. "He had seen what he wrote about, and knew that the sorrows of the poor were commiserated but not really helped. With him injustice was the sin of sins."[30] MacSwiney practised his own precepts a few months later; when his employers humiliated employees who arrived a minute or two late by closing the door for five minutes on the stroke of nine he protested, risking his job. ("Better go back to the lane and live on bread and butter and tea and die of consumption in a few years than weakly submit to injustice that degraded one".) The manager was astonished and backed down. MacSwiney prudently left soon afterwards to teach accountancy full-time; it is said his employers needed two men to replace him.[31]

All his life Corkery remembered the atmosphere at the first performance of *The Holocaust*.

> It is impossible to describe the silence in which the audience followed the play. Here was a piece of drama snatched out of the life of the city; the accents on the stage were the accents they heard about them the whole day long. The priest might have stepped in from the nearest parish church, the doctor from the nearest dispensary. The humble labourer spoke as such men speak on the streets of Cork.[32]

MacSwiney noted in his diary "applause was not pronounced . . . Corkery said they were afraid of it."[33] Some months later, after the poor reception of Corkery's extravaganza *The Epilogue*, critics claimed the CDS had gone into decline because of "Ibsenism", clearly referring to *The Holocaust*.[34] Corkery responded in a lecture on "The Creative Spirit":

> People often say "Don't give us tragedy, don't give us heavy music; we are after a hard day's work and those things are heavy". He thought that was a popular fallacy. He didn't think

there was any refreshment in musical comedy, because the creative spirit was not at work there. Tragedy was entirely different as it must reveal and revelation means something new, and one can see nothing new without being refreshed. . . The lecturer then referred to the literature produced in Ireland written in the English tongue, and said it was scarcely worth talking about . . . because the Irish were not expressing themselves truly, as the Englishman was looking over their shoulder . . . But the people were now beginning to write what they thought, both in Irish and English and he hoped this would continue . . . a literature could not be founded on a lie.[35]

Despite its impact at the time, when stripped of its original context and seen without reference to its author *The Holocaust* is a stilted melodrama. MacSwiney's spokesman, the curate, offers only a vague idealism whose sincerity MacSwiney guarantees by telling the audience he is dying.

The CDS naturalists produced some popular one-act comedies which survived in the Cork amateur repertoire long after the CDS disappeared; Lennox Robinson's *The Lesson of his Life*, D.P. Lucy's *The Passing of 'Miah*, and Corkery's *The Onus of Ownership* – about an inoffensive little man living in rented accomodation with his family who inherits two slum cottages and lives in fear of the ferocious old women who inhabit them[36] – but their "serious" plays, like those of their Abbey counterparts, too often combined unlikely plots, simplistic characters, shoddy writing, and lack of observation.

The CDS suffered material as well as artistic limitations. An Dun was not designed as a theatre. "The stage was miserably small; the dressing rooms a haphazard contrivance behind it". A critic noted it was uncomfortably crowded when seven actors were on stage together. The hall could not accomodate an audience of more than fifty or sixty; the CDS usually lost between £1 and £2 on productions, and kept solvent by subscriptions and occasional appeals to the public for funds.[37] Several promising actors and playwrights left the CDS to seek wider horizons. Lennox Robinson, who already had two plays produced by the Abbey when the CDS first staged *The Lesson of his Life* in December 1909, was an odd man out even before he went to the Abbey as producer. Corkery told Robinson's biographer "he contrasted with us all personally – we were all Catholics connected with the Gaelic League. His education had been otherwise. Still we all liked him, although differing in politics and every deep old attitude."[38] The shy, introspective Robinson formed a close friendship with Corkery which lasted into the 1920s. His play *Patriots* (1912), about an old Fenian returning to his commonsense, unheroic hometown after long imprisonment, was probably inspired by *The Embers*. It was *Patriots* which first showed the young Sean O Faolain the life around him could provide subject matter for literature.

The departure of the Macroom teacher T.C. Murray to become the Abbey's most popular "Cork Realist" was a harder loss, for it was Corkery (they had engaged in controversies in *The Leader*) who saw some articles Murray wrote in dialogue form for the Irish National Teachers' Organisation paper *The Irish Schools Weekly* under the pen-name "Touchstone" and persuaded him to write his first play, *The Wheel of Fortune*, for the CDS. Murray always acknowledged his gratitude to Corkery; Corkery saw Murray, whose naturalism was tempered by a slight lyricism and made no secret of his Catholic faith, as the true heir of Synge.[39]

Only Corkery and MacSwiney among the CDS playwrights made any sustained attempt to produce an alternative to the naturalist style. As well as *The Holocaust* and a slight social comedy, *Manners Masketh Man*, MacSwiney wrote two verse plays based on Gaelic saga, *The Last Warriors of Coole* and *The Wooing of Emer*. They dramatise his own preoccupations. The hunted, starving old warriors who remain loyal to "the dreamer" Crimal whose prophesy of deliverance by a Youth of promise is vindicated by the coming of Fionn are the separatist remnant; the warriors who despaired and swore allegiance to Coole's killer Goll MacMorna are the Parliamentary Party.[40] The conflict between Cuchulain and Emer's jealous father Forgal reflects MacSwiney's desire to see the courageous idealism of youth overcome the obstinate materialism of age and recalls an incident some years previously when he fell in love with a girl whose respectable father refused to countenance a separatist clerk as son-in-law. (MacSwiney then decided he would never marry, since he could not ask any woman to share the life he must lead).[41] His verse was undistinguished; the audience enjoyed the pageantry and ignored the message.

MacSwiney grew impatient with the limitations of the CDS. One of his plays could not be staged because it had five female parts (the CDS had only four actresses). MacSwiney was asked to rewrite it; he gave it six female parts. Another of his plays had to be withdrawn because it required fourteen actors. MacSwiney decided to go on "writing for the larger canvas" in hope of better times; the result was *The Revolutionist*, which he hoped would rival Shakespeare's best.[42] Much of the plot is autobiographical; the hero, Hugh O'Neill, is an idealised version of MacSwiney. In the end, after becoming engaged, O'Neill founds a separatist paper and deliberately works himself to death trying to establish it; his self-sacrifice and the beauty of his dead face show his materialistic friends the truth of his ideals. The play requires an impossibly large cast and eighteen full changes of scenery.[43]

Corkery's non-naturalist plays dramatise his lifelong hesitation between the claims of Romance and Realism. The best is the first, *Hermit and King*, a one-acter written hastily to fill a programme. Colman the aged Hermit lives in the woods with his restless pupil, Rory. Colman is

still haunted by his youthful jealousy of his strong, proud brother
Manus who became King. Manus, hunting with his courtiers, pursues a
miraculous white fawn to the hermitage. Not recognising Colman, he
reveals his weariness with the passing joys of the world, the glories and
horror of battle; he resigns the crown to spend the rest of his life with
the hermit. Colman bids Rory return to the world with the courtiers, for
action is as appropriate to youth as contemplation to age. The play ends
with the recognition and reconciliation of the brothers. The language is
formal, even slightly stilted, but Corkery works in some light relief
about Rory's innocent ignorance of the obsequious formalities of kings.
Corkery's sympathies are clearly with the Hermit, but he takes care to
strike a balance.[44]

The virtues of the play are best seen by comparing it with a later play
based on it. In May 1912 the Leinster Stage Society, an amateur group run
by William and Mary Brigid Pearse, booked the Cork Opera House for
performances to raise money for St. Enda's. Despite support from the
CDS, who showed the LSS members around Cork and came to the
performances,[45] the visit was a disaster; St. Enda's had to make up the
shortfall.[46] In the Opera house the LSS performed *Hermit and King* as a
curtain-raiser.[47] (The CDS supplied other societies with typescripts of
their plays on request; an amateur society in St. Louis, Missouri performed *The Holocaust* after their director, a priest, contacted the CDS
through *The Leader*).[48] The similarities between *King and Hermit* and Padraic
Pearse's *The Master* (1915) – which revolves around the same trio of King,
Hermit, Pupil – suggest the LSS brought home a copy of the script.

In Pearse's play the King is pagan, therefore unambiguously evil; the
pupil Iollan Beag is not an adolescent like Rory but an innocent child
(the hermit's older pupils desert him for the King's feast). Pearse focusses
on the self-doubt of the hermit, who became Christian as much to
outface his old friend and rival as from conviction. (In retrospect the
play can be seen as a last admission of doubt about the morality of the
planned Rising). The King senses his old rival's lack of faith and threatens to kill Iollan Beag unless the hermit apostasises; in the perfect faith
of innocence the child calls on St. Michael for protection and St. Michael
appears. The King is converted; the Master dies in ecstasy. Corkery's
miracle allows the reconciliation King and Hermit have already begun
to desire; Pearse's miracle is an arbitrary intervention which consciously
evades the precept "Thou shalt not put the Lord thy God to the test".[49]

The script of Corkery's next non-naturalist play, *The Epilogue* (May
1911) has not survived, but advance notices show it was consciously
experimental;

> of such a nature as the Society has not yet attempted . . . it is an
> extravaganza in its absence of definite form and in its excur-
> sions into matters not immediately related to its purpose . . .

frankly a play with a purpose . . . a play of ideas. Being an extravaganza, the ideas are not strictly ruled or co-ordinated but will be found to concern themselves for the most part with drama, dramatic ideals, and Cork.[50]

According to a summary by one critic, the play showed the members of an unsuccessful dramatic society lamenting their fate (with much incidental discussion of drama) and finally deciding to proceed to Cork where the CDS is going from triumph to triumph: then a wanderer enters – the secretary of the CDS, who sets about auctioning the Society "properties", costumes of kings and heroes. As general gloom descends, a radiant figure of Hope rises from the property box to predict future triumphs.

The critics were respectful but puzzled; the public showed no interest, and some rowdies made noise during performances. The play was widely misinterpreted as a literal announcement of the dissolution of the Society, and was never revived.[52]

Corkery's last and most ambitious symbolist drama was part of a determined attempt to escape the limitations of An Dun. On August 3rd 1912 the *Irish Outlook* announced the Society had hired the Opera House for a week in December. Rehearsals began in mid-August.[53] On October 18th the CDS issued an appeal listing its achievements and the limitations of An Dun. They announced they had booked the Opera House

to reach the wider field and to place its work on a secure basis . . . The step is a bold one, as the Society is in debt from its former engagements. A small body of subscribers and those directly concerned have hitherto borne the financial burden; but in view of the heavy initial expenditure of the bigger undertaking, the Directors now venture to appeal to all friends of the movement for financial assistance.[54]

The CDS was to perform several of its plays and three new works; two three-act plays (by Corkery and MacSwiney) and the one-act *Drift* by J.F. Lyons. The withdrawal of MacSwiney's political satire *The Man in the Middle* (replaced with a one-acter by Con O'Leary, *The Crossing*) increased the importance of Corkery's *Israel's Incense*.

Nine days before the first performance, the *Irish Outlook* published an interview with Corkery to promote the venture. He claimed to be confident of success.

In any self-respecting Irish-speaking village you will find, perhaps, half-a-dozen poets. . . When Aristophanes made fun of Socrates, Athens . . . was about the size of Cork. . . I remember Miss Alice Milligan throwing it in my face five years ago that

whereas Belfast was a nest of singing birds Cork had nothing to
show ... Belfast has exiled its singing birds. Robert Lynd is in
London; I don't know where Bulmer Hobson is; the Campbell
family is scattered; and so is the Morrow family. But Cork is
beginning to come into its own ... I have had to give full
particulars of our work to Professor Baker of Harvard, the well-
known critic... (*Israel's Incense* is) far and away, the biggest and
most finished piece of work I have ever done yet. And I don't
think it will be found reminiscent of any present-day school of
drama ... I found the phrase in one of Tom Moore's silliest
poems; then I read in Dorothea Townshend's *Life of the Great
Earl of Cork* a story of a certain Thomas O'Brien, a Youghal man,
who sailed for E Brassil; and in this incident and the music of
Thomas Moore's phrase, my play had its origin.[55]

Israel's Incense was very important to Corkery; he apparently associated
it with a moment of inspiration received in the summer of 1912 "sitting
on a rock near Glandore" (perhaps the peninsula of Fylenashouk, associated in his work with emotional revelation).[56] He revised it several
times between 1912 and 1938, renaming it after the central character,
Fohnam the Sculptor. It was published posthumously under this title.

The Prologue reworks *Hermit and King*, qualifying its praise of soli-
tude. Fohnam has withdrawn from the world to live as a hermit in the
woods with his gilly Connud, an old sailor. He works stone splashed
with the blood of quarrymen; the struggle between life and death
obsesses him. The harshness of his statues shocks King Tethra, returning victorious from his wars with King Erc of the Isles; he orders
Fohnam to come to the court and build him a great city. Fohnam
refuses; conflict is averted by the arrival of Queen Alova and her
maidens to accompany the King in his triumph.

This glimpse of court life makes Fohnam restless. That night Eeving,
one of the maidens, returns saying she has been disturbed by his
loneliness; at her urging Fohnam abandons the hut and the sleeping
Connud to flee to the court.

Tethra makes Fohnam Master of the King's Revels, Fohnam works on
the city for three years without the self-discipline to achieve a definitive
plan. He builds and abandons as new ideas strike him; the people are
bled dry by taxation. Tethra defers to Fohnam's artistic temperament,
and does not intervene. Fohnam enthralls the court with marvellous
entertainments; the cries of the poor drifting up from the slums provide
agreeable dissonance. "The sauce to life is death" Fohnam proclaims.

Keltar, Keeper of the Annals, pleads in vain with Fohnam, then tries
to persuade the King to intervene by taking him through the slums to
the quays whence the people flee by night to the lands of King Erc.
Meanwhile Fohnam, who has seduced the Queen with glamorous words

(not from love but desiring to become legend like Diarmuid or Lancelot) arranges to elope with her from the quays by night. He has wearied of Eeving, who pleads with him to return to the woods; after he leaves, she kills herself.

That night Keltar and the King arrive at the quays, the King sickened and dismayed by the slums. He asks if he should have left Fohnam in the woods. Keltar replies that Fohnam should never have gone to the woods or the court. "A sculptor should live among men – the Paraclete is also the Comforter".

King: But your own trade is wisdom, yet you dwell in a Palace.

Keltar: I am not a sculptor. I trade with life only when its cheeks have become pale. "Then the King died and slept with his forefathers".

They hide as a crowd passes, taunting Connud who has wandered the quays half-demented since his master left him, calling out for a crew for a voyage to Hy Brasil. Fohnam and the Queen arrive. Alova is tormented by the sight of women in the slums with "brows like men, mouths like soldiers'"; she cannot heed Fohnam's reply "Forget them . . . shall life have no dung about its roots? Shall we not garden it?" Tethra hears her voice and cries out. Fohnam and Alova hide. Keltar thinks the King is suffering from delusions and leads him back to the palace; but Alova's love for Tethra has reawakened. She refuses to go with Fohnam, declaring she will spend the rest of her life in penitence. As she leaves, Connud wanders past, crying "Hy Brasil". Fohnam follows, sensing a new possibility.

Next morning Tethra crouches on his throne. He has not slept; Keltar's philosophic consolations merely roused him to fury. Outside, Alova passes in a penitential procession. A mob roused by Fohnam, having looted the taverns, besieges the palace clamouring for ships to sail to Hy Brasil. Connud gets into the palace and asks help to separate his picked crew from the rabble and embark them through a secret passage. The King agrees distractedly. As Connud sets sail, news comes that the mob have attacked the procession; Alova is dead. Fohnam bursts in, babbling excitedly of new dreams. He is horrorstricken to hear of the departure of Connud and the deaths of Eeving and Alova, denies his guilt and is killed by Cormac the King's Trumpeter, who loved Eeving. The King orders the body of Fohnam thrown in the gutter, though Keltar pleads to have it taken to the chapel with the others. The King has the palace gates closed, though Keltar asks "My Lord King, do you shut life out because it has sinned?" The King and his retinue leave the stage, broken in spirit. Keltar goes sadly to his desk and records in the annals the story of Fohnam the Sculptor.[57]

The play is striking but incoherent. Fohnam spreads misery and death indifferently for an aesthetic vision, but his opponent Keltar the historian-moralist, though good and wise cannot influence events or touch the human heart. Connud apparently represents the *via media*, the craftsman who conceives a vision and works steadfastly to achieve it; but his vision of Hy Brasil may be a delusion (there is a glaring discrepancy between the half-crazed vagrant of Act II and the cool-headed captain of Act III) and it is not clear if he could have recruited his crew without Fohnam's eloquence. When Fohnam is killed, the land becomes a kingdom of the dead.[58]

Fohnam, Keltar and Connud are aspects of Corkery himself, and the play is crippled by the same deep uncertainty about art and morality, romance and realism, which wrecked *The Woman of Three Cows*. On one level the play can be read as expressing fear that the political and economic triumphs of the Land War were being dissipated by an unimaginative political leadership and a sterile Yeatsean aestheticism indifferent to everyday life and suffering. It makes surprisingly direct reference to the darknesses of contemporary Cork life – emigration, the slums, the prostitutes who walked the quays – but it shows his ambivalence about the aesthetic instinct Corkery praised in his essays as the basis for civic reform. This honest ambivalence was already visible in a notebook entry of 1910:

> Have been reading Brandes' book on Ibsen and examining my conscience – am I afraid of ideas? Am I afraid of the Church? Am I afraid of everything? Yes! Yes! Yes – And this is my unhappiness – I know I shall come to an end without having written my real thoughts! On the other hand, how often I think that such tilting as Ibsen did against the marriage state, against states, against dogma – forced and unreal! There is nothing surer than that if all things were changed into whatever conditions Ibsen wished for, we would still have fresh Ibsens coming along! Art will never lack material – the artist will never live content. Besides it is not possible to think to see the human race live without dogmas and conventions – mankind will always make itself paths and furnish them with signposts.[59]

Israel's Incense confused audience and critics alike, though the acting was praised and the other plays were well-received. MacSwiney lamented in his diary that Corkery had to endure the failure of his play after undertaking all the trouble of organising the Opera House production. Carrying through the productions was a modest success in itself, but the vital breakthrough had not taken place. MacSwiney feared members would become discouraged and drop out.[60]

The appeal for financial support was apparently successful enough

for the CDS to survive the Opera House. There were two more productions, both in January 1913 (a one-nighter in Coachford and a three-day
run at An Dun of two plays by the Crosshaven postman and prolific
amateur dramatist J. Bernard MacCarthy). Throughout 1913 Corkery
held together a dwindling band of members; they held some rehearsals
but did not manage to stage any plays. "We did not fail for lack of
matter; but we saw no way of improving on what we had been doing".
The final blow was the establishment of a Cork branch of the Irish
Volunteers in December 1913 with MacSwiney as second-in-command
to MacCurtain. "Gradually An Dun became a hall for drilling in. Even
our actors took to drilling. Somehow we dissolved". A few members
continued to meet but Corkery turned to other matters – in particular a
novel of Cork life.[61]

Corkery's notebook shows he was working on a novel in 1908. ("I do
not recall a school teacher being introduced into any modern novel. The
modern novel does not deal with the middle class. Have a desire to deal
with the middle class.")[62] This may have been interrupted by the CDS;
in later years he said he began *The Threshold of Quiet* in 1911 or 1912
"without hope of finding a publisher. Put away frequently and taken
up again. I think I must have written every word of it at least half a
dozen times".[63]

The novel depicts the final dissolution of a circle of friends –
white-collar clerks in their late twenties – through slow shock after their
brightest member, Frank Bresnan, commits suicide from secret despair
over his life as a much-admired commercial traveller for tea. The most
prominent character is the introspective Martin Cloyne "one of those
rare people who do their thinking consciously, almost with a certain
enjoyment – having long since become aware of the complexities and
strangeness of the ways of thought, his constant desire, his most yearn-
ing cry in moments of crisis was for more time."[64] The limpid, finely-
textured style of the book, with its slow accumulation of significance
through reflection on passing events, reflects his consciousness. Martin
falls in love with Lily Bresnan, sister of the dead man, but she decides to
enter a convent. In sub-plots young Finbarr Bresnan, shocked into
maturity by the death of his brother, hesitates between the priesthood
and the sea before becoming a sailor, while the friendly erratic jack-of-
all-trades Stevie Galvin hopes for reconciliation with his brother Phil,
who ran away to sea after they quarrelled when Phil pestered Stevie's
girl – but Phil's ship is lost with all hands off the West Cork coast on its
way to Cork.

The novel attempts a comprehensive portrait of Cork. A short
prologue contrasts the casual summer visitor who judges Cork by the
bustling, crowded "flat of the city" with native Corkonians who know
the wide hills above it dotted with convents, monasteries, houses of
refuge "the very fruitage of the spirit of contemplation . . . to us these

quiet hillsides also are Cork."[65] The Cloyne household on the Lough at the southern fringe of the city, the Bresnans on Fair Hill at the northern edge, Stevie Galvin's chaotic lodgings on Morrison's Island in the "flat of the city" seem to offer a cross-section of Cork life; yet from the beginning they are presented as little hidden worlds whose inhabitants meet and talk but have only the most tenuous emotional contact, without any shared medium to articulate their concerns. Their lower-middle-class milieu perches uneasily above the world of the lanes. Martin fears the spontaneous, unpredictable lane-dwellers; the gossip and stir at Frank's wake fill him with nausea when he thinks of the corpse upstairs. Stevie is at ease with the lane-dwellers but his outgoing character leaves him emotionally vulnerable. When the Bresnans' father takes to drink under the shock of Frank's death, Finbarr fears the family will be dragged down into the slums. (The old man catches pneumonia in a drunken stupor and dies). A sense of the past appears only in the drunken maunderings of old Bresnan about the glorious days of his youth when Cork was prosperous. If Cork possesses hidden spiritual treasures, as the prologue suggests, it is unaware of the sources of its life.

The Threshold of Quiet secured Corkery's literary reputation when it was published in December 1917. AE wrote "we take our hat off to Mr. Corkery"[66], Ernest Boyd compared it to Mr. Joyce's *Portrait of the Artist* as a study of Irish urban *anomie*.[67] Later critics are divided on its merits. Frank O'Connor and Sean O Faolain called it the best thing Corkery ever wrote (O'Connor rewrote it in his own manner as *Dutch Interior* (1942)) while George Brandon Saul condemned it as a lacklustre self-pitying tale dominated by religious morbidity.[68]

Saul assumes Martin Cloyne should be identified with Corkery and the reader is meant to reverence his inability to declare his love to Lily Bresnan. Corkery identified with Martin Cloyne to some extent (he described some of his own possessions among the furniture of the Cloyne household, signed his letters to the imprisoned Frank O'Connor during the Civil War "Martin Cloyne",[69] and in the 1950s pointed out 1 Ophelia Place as Martin's house)[70] and is known to have fallen in love with a young woman member of the CDS without ever telling her his feelings (she died soon afterwards of TB).[71] Saul assumes Lily Bresnan is a portrait of this girl; but while this experience probably contributed to the atmosphere of the novel, Corkery told his friend Sean Hendrick that Lily Bresnan was based on another girl he knew whose brother committed suicide in the manner described. (The CDS girl appears as "My Eagle" in two short stories in his second collection, *The Hounds of Banba*.)[72] Frank O'Connor recognised aspects of Stevie Galvin as well as Martin Cloyne in Corkery,[73] and Finbarr Bresnan was partly based on Corkery's memories of boyhood[74]. Furthermore, Corkery had reasons for hesitation (he was lame and had to support dependents) which did not exist for Martin Cloyne.

In fact, Martin Cloyne is portrayed as a coward; though generally perceptive, he uses thought to insulate himself from life. When life breaks in on the even flow of his thought, he panics. He had grown tired of Frank, and allowed him to drift away. As he tries to re-establish his inner equilibrium after the shock of Frank's suicide, he is slowly forced to realise that "dreaming, he had become callous".[75] He has insulated himself from the dangerously spontaneous life, emotions and sufferings of his city. One evening, as he walks the quays with Stevie they encounter a group of sailors and a woman swearing at two policemen with a prisoner. Stevie goes over to ask what has happened – a fight between sailors on leave. Martin, "suddenly aware", stares nervously. It occurs to him that he should feel pity for the woman, but he is too frightened. As they walk away Stevie cries "the poor devils!", thinking of his brother. Martin feels "ashamed of his own narrow range of sensibilities."[76] The incident haunts him for days. At work, he realises that though he deals with cargoes from all over the world

> he had scarcely ever given a thought to the "poor devils" who adventure for them on the seas, who give up their lives to the adventure. Martin began to realise for the first time that he was living in a sea-port town. Turn a corner in the most central streets in Cork city and the tall masts of a sailing ship carry your eyes to the clouds, or the red-banded funnel of a tramp-steamer sends your thoughts to the bunkers below decks; yet you may turn those street corners, day after day, your whole life long, without realising the lot of the "poor devils" who stoke below decks or furl moon-sails on the masts.[77]

Martin cannot reach out to Lily any more than he can reach out to the hidden suffering of Cork. He can only bring himself to visit her when he deceives himself into setting off "without thinking, at a rush, without perceiving where he was going".[78] When he senses Lily is thinking of entering a convent and should be approached immediately, he excuses his cowardice (and unconsciously insults her) by remembering the woman on the quays and telling himself of the responsibility of detaining a contemplative soul in the world.[79] When he hears Lily is going to enter the convent he goes to see her, but loses his nerve at her garden gate and runs away.[80] There is a moment when he almost breaks free of his fears. Talking with Lily about Finbarr, how a boy is a seraph one week and a pirate the next, a chance remark shocks him into speech when he realises she cannot imagine his ever having been a boy:

> You think I was always a clerk ... the middle point between seraph and pirate. . . Destined, destined neither to damnation nor salvation – shut out ... That there's a special limbo for

clerks, where the dishes are neither hot nor cold, lukewarm
rewards for lukewarm people . . . where there are neither wings
nor horns . . . nor incense nor sulphur nor –

For a moment, startled into directness, "they were boy and girl again";
but Finbarr comes into the room, the moment is lost, and Martin
agonises over his behaviour for days.[81]

At the end of the novel it is clear Martin can no longer evade the
truth, and will find redemption through self-knowledge and acceptance of the fate he has brought on himself. He is tragic because his
sensitive, meditative intelligence is so close to the narrative voice of the
novel though Martin would never have put pen to paper.

> There are so many people in the world who feel it almost
> wrong to come up against plain statements of fact! Sensitive
> souls, they do not help the world to progress, but they almost
> make progress worthwhile. They test it: a world that would
> provide them with a suitable medium for working in what a
> world it would be![82]

Corkery hints why Cork cannot provide such a medium when,
describing a desultory conversation between Martin and his friends, he
comments "Time out of mind, perhaps as far back as the disaster of
Kinsale, Ireland has been talking in this hopeless strain".[83]

A scene early in the novel where Stevie, having received a harsh
letter from his brother, wanders along the quays at night crying out to
sleepy English sailors on the ships about Rio de Janeiro[84] shows Corkery
is still wrestling with the theme of *Fohnam the Sculptor*. Stevie is Connud,
the brilliant craftsman driven to eccentricity for want of guidance;
Martin is Keltar, the self-conscious intellectual who cannot deal with
life until it has gone pale in the cheeks; Cork is a kingdom of the dead
where the impulses of the heart and the broodings of genius end in self-
destruction.

There is a character in the novel who takes command of her own
destiny and defies Cork: Lily Bresnan. Her vocation is the moral centre
of the novel.

> Before starting out to write (*Threshold of Quiet*) I remember dis-
> tinctly asking myself what accounted for the fundamental differ-
> ence between life in Ireland and life in England . . . and answering
> that question by the one word – religion . . . I therefore kept the
> religious side of the ordinary Cork Catholic family in view all
> through . . . up to that self-query I can never even have looked at
> English literature as it should be looked at and would be looked
> at by an Irish Catholic of culture that is, as a sort of exotic.[85]

This "examination" may have taken place in 1906, when Corkery wrote that while religion is not vital to every nation and a non-Catholic can be a true Irish patriot "Catholicism is an integral part of Irish nationality . . . Irish literature, speaking broadly, should consist of the thoughts of Catholics for Catholics."[86] In his later critical writings this attitude developed all too easily into an assumption that "Catholic" and "Irish" were synonymous, that Irish Protestantism was not worth discussing and religious developments outside Ireland were irrelevant. This should not obscure the fact that Corkery was not a sectarian name-caller like Moran; he was wrestling with a real problem. If a writer truly believes in such doctrines as the existence of God, Heaven and Hell, the power of prayer, and is writing for an audience who believe all these things, surely the portrayal of life in his works will differ from that given by writers who do not hold all – or any – of these beliefs? If his professed beliefs are not reflected in his works, does he believe them at all?

Some of Corkery's associates at this time – notably Denis Breen and Dan Harrington – were outspoken agnostics.[87] In later life he was reticent about his religious beliefs; he took no interest in many standard devotions and often spoke scathingly of the clergy, including Bishops Cohalan and Lucey ("that fool of a bishop"). Hence many of his acquaintances, including some close friends, believed he was a covert agnostic; but images of the Catholic Middle Ages and contemporary continental Catholicism are so interwoven with his interpretation of Irish history they cannot be detached without destroying the whole fabric. There is a clear relationship between his professed beliefs and his works. Nationalism, religion and art blur together in his writings. He wrote that "nationality is a spirituality"; he compared the artist to the religious contemplative. His developed criticisms of clerical cultural blindness attribute their condition to the after-effects of conquest and colonisation:

> Our educational establishments are of course proverbial for their active discouragement of any tendency towards the arts. Most of those establishments – those that count most in the life of the nation – are conducted by religious orders; whether such establishments in other countries, more especially in countries where the Catholic tradition has never been broken, are so earnestly on the side of philistinism, those who have travelled more than I might say; but it is my own idea that this characteristic of them here is local; that it is in part the outcome of our past.[88]

Similarly, in his early journalism Corkery criticises imported popular devotions by comparison with Early Irish devotional nature poetry. He laments that since "the national treasury of devotion" was lost with the language:

Prose has taken the place of literature, prose oftentimes at its very
worst, with a result that there is a constant craving for what is new
in the forms of our popular devotions, and consequently a callous
neglect of what is old, that is of the native and storm-tried. . . How
dangerous it is for a people, even a very simple religious people, to
live without visitings of imaginative genius! . . . It would be interesting if someone learned enough would write a small book on the
Gaelic idea of these old saints as contrasted with the idea now
prevailing – or shall we say with the absence of idea now prevailing . . . it is an appalling poverty of thought that has in the folk-
mind reduced all these fine heroic, rough-wrought, manly figures
to one dead and foisonless level of sentimental pietism.[89]

Corkery, like many other language activists, apparently saw Irish
almost as a sacred language. He seems to have said his prayers in Irish;
a relative recalls going back unexpectedly to retrieve a scarf after a visit
and finding him saying the Rosary in Irish with his sister.[90]

It seems, therefore, that Corkery's Catholicism was sincere though
idiosyncratic.

Corkery knew many of his readers would be non-Catholic; his portrait of Lily's vocation was a conscious challenge to their sensibilities.
Ernest Boyd, who read the novel for Talbot Press, qualified his praise by
complaining about a passage explaining why Irish Catholic girls enter
convents.[91] (Saul, whose complaint about "religious morbidity" conflates
Martin's *anomie* and Lily's vocation, also objects to this passage).[92]

Corkery carefully distinguishes Lily's vocation from Finbarr's fantasy vocation. "It was not that she shrank from the burden of life; the
worries of the everyday could not disturb a spirit like hers". He stresses
that her pale face has "a richness" which is more than "the mere absence
of colour" just as the blackness of her hair is more than "the mere
absence of light". She is a natural contemplative, possessing "a spiritual
joyousness . . . her faith was such that she could pray at all times".
When her confessor suggests she might become a nun she is attracted to
the idea, but refuses because of her family responsibilities. After her
refusal "her heart was hard and dry . . . she could not pray". She looks
down into the city and sees it as a trap.[93]

Her confessor does not raise the subject again, but after her father
dies and Finbarr goes to sea she tells him of her decision to enter
Kilvirra convent in West Cork. Corkery emphasises her deliberate choice;
at the moment of decision she looks down at the city which is "sharply
detached from the hills".

"Kilvirra", the girl's lips murmured as she gazed at the fleeting
gleam; and Father Cummins thought it a natural thing for her
to say; he had no idea that she spoke to the city, challenging it.[94]

Her vocation is not a capitulation, but a triumph. Martin can only contemplate himself; she will spend her life contemplating God. She has found a point of leverage against the lower-middle-class *anomie* of Cork; but her convent is not (as the prologue might lead the reader to expect), on the slopes of the city:

> Then Martin realised that Cork was empty; and that the dark, bare, sodden hills he had been looking on that day (in West Cork), for Kilvirra is only a little further to the West, were filled with light – a clear light that would shine forever.[95]

During the composition of the novel Corkery had decided the solution to Cork's plight could not be found in the city.

In 1948 Corkery defended himself against the accusation of betraying his artistic vocation by abandoning his exploration of the life he knew best – the life of Cork city – to romanticise a countryside he could never fully understand:

> *The Threshold of Quiet,* my first book, is nostalgic for it looks back to that very self-contained if exotic little world of Cork city that I and mine had been living in for at least a century and a half . . . The book is nostalgic; but it is so with a nostalgia that is very much aware of itself as a thing done with . . . Even before I began *The Threshold of Quiet,* certainly even while writing it in 1911, I was becoming aware of the rootlessness of the life of Cork city . . . had . . . to struggle (with) this sense of rootlessness come upon me . . . to write on within the limits first proposed – that is to continue to accept (it) as a reality, with rootage and returning seasons. (To) become alive, my mind had to move away from the shallowness of that environment . . . Since I have become convinced that the life of Cork city in as much as it is a life apart from what is Irish, is rootless and shallow, I have since never felt any desire to explore it further.
>
> . . . All those critics who are not aware of the fact that Ireland should have its own critical values say it is my best (book). It may well be so, from their point of view. But it is not foundational. To have followed it with others in which the same environment was explored would have been to go weaker and weaker.

He dismissed the novel with faint praise, comparing it to *Knocknagow*[96] (which he believed was kept alive by the people because, despite its artistic failure, it reflected aspects of their life which had not yet received adequate expression). This is too severe. In its careful style, its theme of vocation, its deliberate challenge to those who do not share its outlook, *The Threshold of Quiet* is the *Mansfield Park* of Anglo-Irish literature; but, unlike *Mansfield Park*, it is an isolated achievement. Corkery believed he could go no further in that vein without suffering the fate of Martin Cloyne. He tried to escape from the paralysis of self-consciousness by abandoning the novel for short stories evoking the deep, inarticulate emotions of Gaelic peasants and Cork lane-dwellers. Corkery was searching for new means of expression after the defeat of his attempts to give Cork a civic culture. He accepted the narrower scope of the short story form as the price a hard-pressed Cork school-teacher must pay for continued artistic expression.

> Towards the short story as such I had no special leaning. It is however, a thing one can tackle if he must write at odd moments and in the midst of other work.[97]

At the start of the 1913/14 school year Corkery transferred to St. Patrick's National School near St. Luke's Cross on the North Side; the Corkery household moved from the Lough to 1 Auburn Villas, Ashburton, near the top of Gardiner's Hill.

Two of his pupils left descriptions of this slum school. It had only two rooms; there were about a hundred boys in first class. There were not enough desks; the boys took turns to use those available. It was hideously noisy; the cane was used incessantly. Michael O'Donovan (who became the writer Frank O'Connor) recalls in *An Only Child* the contrast between the stupid, bullying headmaster with his shadowy assistant and the new teacher – choleric, limping and harsh-voiced but light, spare and clean.[98]

During his years at St. Patrick's Corkery wrote occasional articles on education for *The Irish Schools Weekly* under the pseudonym "Le Pinson".

> I am a teacher. I have been teaching for twenty years. During all that time I have never had less than fifty children to teach. Fifty children is a herd. . . (I have spent my career) urging on the sixteen wheels of the tremendous car of bestiality over the pliant and bright little souls of these children. I have after all been but the instrument; the whip was put into my hand and I was bidden drive or die. Yet my conscience is, I say, not wholly clear. I have become a drill-sergeant. Long ago I was a teacher. Then I worked for eternity. Now I work for results.
>
> If I could get people to catch up what I here state, and think on it! But no; walk into our schools twenty years hence and you will find what you may find today – teachers "teaching" herds of children. And it doesn't matter whether you go into primary or secondary schools – into schools conducted by priests or monks or laymen; in this respect they are all equally bad. And

our colleges are no better. Of course it is all a matter of money. And the future will be more parsimonious than the past. What fools these mortals be![99]

"Le Pinson" denounced the rigid discipline which forced the teacher to show the inspector he had *really* worked by correcting even minor errors of grammar and spelling or bad handwriting, so the teacher reduced his workload by rewarding boys who produced neat copies of work already done and punishing those who produced original work with hesitations, awkwardnesses, erasures; thus pupils were reduced to "the level of the machine which manufactures pins".[100] He defended "fal-lals" – non-compulsory subjects like Irish, French, Music and Drawing. He argued that education should not be merely utilitarian. Even the labourer is not merely a labourer; as technical progress shortened working hours, it would become more important to educate for "mans's leisure time: the hours of the evening in which the young man either finds or loses his soul." He was not opposed to "athletics, music-halls, picture palaces" since they reduced drunkeness, but he wanted "such a widespread culture as will put them in their wider perspective. When all is said, that culture is a question of "fal-lals"".[101]

Corkery tried to put his ideas into practice at St. Patrick's. He taught the boys drawing; although the curriculum only gave it half an hour he continually taught them to use their eyes, constantly asking them to recall what they had seen on the way to school until they learnt to notice the life around them. He told them how few people see the world of clouds, their ever-changing light and shades. He hung the classroom with his own paintings.[102] Following his own suggestion in a "Le Pinson" article he bought green and red jerseys and started a school hurling club. On afternoons he took the boys down the Glen to practice, divided them into two teams, and went aside to paint.[103] He taught the boys Irish in an extra class outside normal school hours.[104] Frank O'Connor was mystified, but found (for the first time) a use for his troublesome grandmother – an Irish-speaker, like several other old people in the neighbourhood. Corkery lamented that;

At the close of the week I often find myself reflecting that I haven't given more than a dozen or two dozen words of talk to certain of my pupils – pupils that I am supposed to be educating! Pupils the most valuable from the point of view of intelligence and character! Pupils that any teacher would educate for the love of it if given a crust of bread, a hawthorn bough, and a dash of sunshine! Cut down my mob class and I can meet my pupils as individuals and begin to educate them. I can give more time to each.[105]

Despite these constraints, Corkery managed to help individual
pupils who showed promise. When Seamus Murphy (the future sculptor) got some paper and began making sketches on his own initiative
Corkery took an interest in him and later helped him get into the School
of Art.[106] Frank O'Connor describes how he adopted Corkery as a
father-substitute, and how at Christmas 1913 Corkery awarded him the
only school prize he ever received, a book on Irish history (possibly
bought with Corkery's own money).[107]

O'Connor also describes how Corkery used the set texts to make the
boys patriots.[108] Corkery saw this as an intrinsic part of his educational
methods. In an article on the teaching of civics he declares:

> Our natural affection for our home city or hometown, as we say
> homeland, should be deepened and enriched by learning of
> what that city has meant to our race and country. Thus deep-
> ened, thus enriched, surely our new-found earnestness will
> need but little further coaching to insist that our city's govern-
> ment shall be wise, that its condition shall be healthy, its streets
> cleanly, its appearance comely.[109]

This relationship between progressive educational ideas and nationalism was not unique to Corkery; it can be seen in St. Enda's and the
MacSwiney sisters' fascinating Cork girls' school, Scoil Ite. Under the
Union education was one of the main areas of controversy between
nationalists and the administration. Corkery, like Pearse, complained
that the system he experienced as pupil and teacher trained mechani-
cally for the Imperial Civil Service, with no regard for the needs and
local circumstances of the pupil, and so "hinders the citizen from growing up in natural relationship with his native city as part of his native
country. . . the Imperialist has no home".[110]

Unfortunately these insights were not accompanied by the wider
understanding of contemporary society needed to construct a coherent
alternative system. He sees the good society as essentially static. He
assumed technical skills would always remain the same and could be
acquired outside the formal educational system. In later life he advocated "vocational education" but thought of it as a system of adult
education in the humanities through evening classes. The system he
advocated (including creative writing and the collection, teaching and
publication of local history) was noble; but it was not, by itself, vocational education.[111]

A passage from the article on civics exposes another problem of this
outlook:

> If one does not believe that civics is the result of thinking
> imperially – an effort of nature against such unnatural thinking

– let him study the history of our Irish cities . . . that sense of homelessness is all over the pages of those local histories of ours. They were cities given up to imperial thinking. Their citizens were never at home. They were colonists. They always had an idea that home was elsewhere. And hence what an uninspiring history they left behind them! How unprincipled! And how barren of art they were! Of learning! Of music! Of light![112]

Thus Corkery rejects the whole history of that native city which he said in the same article must be reformed through affectionate under-standing. He is not known to have protested in the late 1920s and early 1930s when "fal-lals" he had defended – Music, Civics, Nature Study – were dropped from the curriculum to make more space for Irish.[113] In the late 1930s Corkery still complained the schools were indifferent to art, but claimed that since the system had now been reformed, these problems were caused by staff brought up under "the old and stupid system".[114] This reference to "reform" can only mean the introduction of compulsory Irish. The Gaelic tradition gave him insights and the confidence to express them, but without sufficient understanding it could become an escape from the indifference of Cork, an imagined panacea to be invoked against all the difficulties Corkery saw and fought but could not overcome. It led all too easily to the sense of displacement Corkery records in a review of an t-Athair Peadar O Laoghaire's *Guaire* where he recalls reading it on holiday in the Gaeltacht and the pain of returning from the pre-conquest world which could produce a folk-tale of such subtle wit to everyday life – "life that is exile".[115] It was not only the colonists who "always had an idea that home was elsewhere". So it was that Pearse, the MacSwiney sisters, and Corkery did not lay the foundations of a new educational system but remained isolated individuals, their educational work remembered only through the pupils they enlightened.

Two periodicals are known to have published short stories by Corkery in this period; the *Catholic Home Journal* of Manchester (Con O'Leary probably helped him to publish here) and the *Irish Review*. He reveals different aspects of his sensibility in each. The two *Catholic Home Journal* stories "The Breath of Life" and "The Child Saint" are idealistic, the latter being an interesting though unsuccessful attempt to handle with subtlety and evocative description a story which might have been a crude and sentimental religious tract, to make articulate the genuine religious emotion which fed on the low-grade religious art he criticised in the *Leader*. Despite some moving passages, they do not make suffi-ciently concrete the hard labour of artistic inspiration and the para-doxes of sanctity.[116]

The three *Irish Review* stories are harsher, more pessimistic. "Alibi or

Home?" describes a ramshackle lodging-house in the Cork slums, with
its own code of practice; one night a sailor, a long-lost acquaintance of
the landlady, turns up unexpectedly, sits morosely by himself (inter-
vening detachedly in the affairs of the regular customers), finally takes
his leave, and is fished from the Lee next morning with the body of the
mate he killed before going ashore. The story fails because the description of the hidden world of the lodging-house and the chatter of the
regulars distract from the enigma of the sailor.[117]

The other stories are amongst the finest Corkery ever wrote. "The
Spancelled" deals with a young widow, rather nondescript, careless
mocked by the neighbours because her miserly husband made a will
depriving her of the bit of land if she married again, and a grabber's
nephew made cunning by sporadic hostility, turned wandering
labourer yet waiting to inherit the bit of grabbed land and make a good
match. They meet when her parish turns out to help save a neighbour's
hay and the passing labourer joins in. He tells her his story on impulse,
to ease his heart; she is too cautious to tell hers. That evening, when he
has a run of luck at cards, "grabber" is flung in his face; his nerve breaks
and he leaves. Some time later the widow goes home, pitying the
wanderer in her heart. She finds him in her house; as he passed he heard
a child crying and went in to comfort it. She panics and threatens him
with a gun.

> In a leap his arms were about her, the gun falling with a rattle
> on the earthen floor. He heard it, half-stooped to seize it; then
> something made him look at the woman's face. Her eyes were
> shut, the mouth wide open and panting; he felt her whole body
> trembling from head to foot. As in very pity he kissed her,
> babbling old-fashioned love-words at her ear.
>
> And so they leaped from their pit of sorrow, as the spancelled
> will until time be over; in no other way is it possible for them –
> this is their philosophy – to revenge themselves on fortune, to
> give scorn for scorn.[118]

The theme might have caused trouble in a magazine other than the
Irish Review (which for much of its existence had an anti-clerical tinge)
though Corkery's handling of the story is perfectly orthodox; he does
not condone their sin but emphasises that they fell through pity and
the unthinking cruelty of their neighbours is more wicked. There is
evidence that in later life Corkery felt uneasy about it. A brief list
of *Munster Twilight* stories in his handwriting contains the comment:
"Easily the best – right through. But suitable?"[119] In 1955 Corkery
refused Frank O'Connor permission to reprint it in an anthology.[120]

These two stories caught the attention of the Editorial Committee.
When Corkery wrote to Thomas MacDonagh in May 1914 asking if

the *Review* could publish "a little volume" of his poems (it had published MacDonagh's *Lyrical Poems* and Pearse's *Suantraidhe Agus
Goltraidhe*) MacDonagh replied that financial constraints made this
impossible but the new Editor, Joseph Plunkett, would welcome any
prose contributions from Corkery.[121] A few weeks later Plunkett himself wrote to Corkery praising the earlier stories, asking for another
and lamenting that the political excitement made it difficult to get
good material.[122] Corkery sent him "Storm-Struck", a story about an
emigrant who returns blind and embittered from the copper mines of
Butte, Montana, to his parents' smallholding at Cuandor (Glandore).
Kitty Regan, the girl he loved, is unhappily married. The blind man
takes to rambling round the cliffs, guided by a little boy. One day,
alone on the headland of Fylenashouk – his favourite resting place –
he is surprised by a thunderstorm. As he is about to panic, a woman
cluches him and leads him back to the road. She sees someone, cries
out and runs away; he recognises the voice of Kitty Regan. That night
he waits in his room, believing he senses her wandering around the
house; he flings open the window and calls to her, and at last cries
himself to sleep "unwilling to confess defeat, unwilling to face the
blank, loveless future" and later seeks solace in bitter jests to
uncomprehending gossips in the pub. "Storm-Struck" was published
in the penultimate issue of *The Irish Review*[123]; the magazine was suppressed after the outbreak of war because of its support for the Irish
Volunteers.

The *Irish Review* also brought Corkery into contact with Pearse,
who was publishing piecemeal in the *Review Songs of the Irish Rebels*,
an anthology of Irish-language political poetry intended to show the
immemorial antiquity of Irish separatism. In February 1913 Pearse
visited Corkery at the Lough. Corkery told him of Maire Bhuidhe Ni
Laoghaire's poem "Cath Cheim an Fhiadh" (about an incident in the
Tithe War of the 1820s) and gave him an article on local traditions about
the battle which he had published in *The Irish Outlook*.[124] They discussed
the MacDonagh translation of "The Yellow Bittern" and Corkery gave
Pearse some money for St. Enda's. Pearse said Mrs. Corkery reminded
him of his own mother, but annoyed Corkery by remarking of the
Lough "That eyesore should be filled in".[125]

Despite these contacts and the example of Terence MacSwiney – who
responded to the outbreak of war by selling his beloved books to
finance a short-lived separatist magazine, gave up his job to cycle
through the country as a Volunteer organiser, sometimes sleeping in
the fields, being tried for sedition and given a nominal sentence in
January 1916[126] – Corkery did not support physical force. He still
believed the need for cultural revival transcended all other issues. (A
few years earlier he had a blazing row with MacCurtain at a Gaelic
League committee meeting after making a sarcastic reference to

committee members who neglected their duties to go drilling boy scouts. MacCurtain, who was involved with the Cork branch of the separatist youth organisation Fianna Eireann, retorted that he felt like a miner who, having worked at the coal-face all day, is scolded by an observer at the mouth of the pit – "I was here all day without seeing you working".)[127]

Corkery was even more distrustful of the Parliamentary Party. He attacked their calls to "forgive and forget" as a betrayal of the Irish national tradition:

> They . . . would reduce the whole nation to the level of a colony; for if our history be jettisoned in what shall we differ from the newest colonials? They dishonour both Gael and Gall.
>
> Behind them and their pinchbeck institutions behold our "Irish" historians – a race of men who had not the imagination to see what a half-tale it was they were labouring at. The result was a repellent book. Take Lecky's *Eighteenth Century*. If that were the whole truth about Ireland in that period – why, jettison it and welcome. But it is not the whole truth. The Gael is not in it. Go below the surface of the eighteenth century – a thing which Lecky with all his learning never did – and one comes on a long-continued battle for principles – and as one realises what steady lights burned amidst the gloom one's heart begins to expand and to hope. I think if I were a Gall, descended from some hard-drinking, rough-riding, duelling wine-smuggling, rack-renting squireen of that time, I still think I should thrill to read of the Gael in that period – his fight for principles, his sweetening of his helotry with skiey lyrics, his music-making, his pride of race, his effort at culture – yes, even were I descended from that member of the Dublin Parliament who thanked God he had a country to sell. But our historians ignore that story. Instead they tell the story of the man who thanked God he had a country to sell – a repellent tale!
>
> They have a lot to answer for – our bat-eyed historians with their muck-rake learning. On them be most of the shame and the blame if flippant featherheads are asking us to jettison our history.[128]

In three particularly vehement articles early in 1916 Corkery denounced the Party as a mindless machine which ignored the importance of cultural nationalism in keeping alive the "kink of nationality" which gave them their raison d'être; they dare not discuss the educational system and "would not be too sorry if the Irish language had been quietly allowed to die". The essential work was done by a few "cranky" journalists and agitators, who refused to disown the past when the war broke out.

> They have had to give up their positions, to fly the country, to suffer jail – without reason given. And all to preserve that national kink of ours. But they have preserved it!
>   Worst of all, the Party have turned round and reviled them – the Party which exists by reason of that kink![129]

Corkery discusses "The Three Irelands", arguing that Orange Ulster ("essentially comic", lacking "the note of spirituality" because "it has never known persecution"(*sic*)) and the nineteenth-century nationalist tradition looking back to Grattan's Parliament are trivial in comparison with "the hitherto hidden Ireland of which the Irish language spoke so intimately".[130] No-one who has come into contact with "the spirit of the Gael" can forget it – "it would be like forgetting himself".

> Our life therefore as a nation depends on our perpetuating our traditions by a continuance of heroic deeds. . . that spirit is abroad in the land. It has always walked the land in wartime. No longer however, as a Poor Old Woman . . . there's many a boy walking the streets of Ireland to-day saying to himself over and over again: "Her holy, delicate white hands have girdled me with steel" . . . And so you need not trouble yourself about the new evangel of forgetfulness.[131]

Thus, writing less than a fortnight before the Easter Rising, Corkery implicitly supported the Irish Volunteers and on some level of his mind anticipated an armed clash with the British; but he does not seem to have felt an immediate threat. He probably expected resistance to an eventual attempt to impose conscription, as did Eoin MacNeill.

Most of his journalism of this period (mainly in *The Leader*, but also in the weekly *New Ireland*) confines itself to cultural themes. An article on "The Peasant in Irish Literature" deserves particular notice. It argues that the body of recent writing about Irish peasant life shows the Irish people are beginning to write about the everyday life around them. It will need vigorous critical sifting, and most of what has been written in English and Irish (by peasant-born writers without literary imagination or superficial writers following fashion) is worthless; yet work of enduring value has already been produced (*Riders to the Sea*, some poems by Padraic Colum). The majority of the Irish nation are peasants, yet they have not found a voice; any attempt to express Irish life must come to terms with the peasant.[132] This article was remembered for some time. Ernest Boyd cited it as the key to Corkery's work, and it gave Frank O'Connor the germ of his theory of the short story as the voice of a "submerged population group".[133]

Corkery stood on the verge of wider literary recognition. In 1915 W.G. Lyon, proprietor of Talbot Press and the Educational Company and publisher of the *Irish Schools Weekly*, visited St. Patrick's selling textbooks and met Corkery. A few months later Talbot Press had accepted a collection of short stories and were considering *Threshold of Quiet*. Lyon christened the collection *A Munster Twilight*; Corkery acquiesced, though he thought the name "too pretty" (perhaps too reminiscent of the Celtic Twilight).[134] A letter from Lyon refers to another manuscript, "Hidden Island" (*sic*).[135] Corkery says he did not begin the book as we have it until 1920; this was almost certainly a selection of his journalism containing, and called after, a lecture on "The Hidden Ireland" delivered to the Cork Literary and Scientific Society on January 25th 1915. (It became Chapter One of the book).[136]

Corkery spent the Easter weekend and Easter Monday of 1916 at his home on the North Side. On Tuesday afternoon he went down into the city centre and learned for the first time that a rising had broken out in Dublin.[137] MacSwiney and MacCurtain had barricaded themselves in An Dun with the city Volunteers. Having gone out to demobilise the county Volunteers in obedience to MacNeill's countermand, they did not get Pearse's final order until Monday night, when the military were alerted and a Cork rising impossible. Their surrender at the end of the week without firing a shot shamed MacSwiney and MacCurtain bitterly, though an enquiry later cleared them of blame.

MacSwiney was sent to Reading Gaol with the other leaders. Con O'Leary wrote to him: "You will be glad to hear that John O'Loughlin, Laurence Kiely and young Daly are in good health and very well. There is no fear of them".[136] The prison censor would not see anything amiss, but MacSwiney would recognise the names of the Fenians from *The Embers* and understand the separatist movement was alive and thriving. Corkery had not imagined such a resurrection for his three deluded fools – or such an use for his theatre – when the CDS staged his first play in 1909.

CHAPTER FOUR

DEEDS AND DREAMS 1916–21

Three letters written by Corkery to the imprisoned MacSwiney in 1916 survive. In July, after the post-Rising negotiations broke down on the contradictory promises of Lloyd George and were finished off by an open letter issued by Archbishop Walsh of Dublin, Corkery wrote from the Irish college at Carrigaholt, Co. Clare:

> Things seem to be waiting. Everyone feels something must happen. It is as if we had neither Leader nor Party. The Party has ceased to exist as a factor in the situation. Archbishop Walsh's letter was the last straw.[1]

The Party had not collapsed as completely as this implies. The little groups and papers which had appeared to claim the heritage of Easter Week could not yet fill the leadership vacuum left by the humiliation of Redmond; they had no alternative leader of national stature. Under these circumstances even D.P. Moran (a violent critic of Redmond's decision to support recruiting for the British Army) advocated continued support for the Party, fearing the country would sink back into the chaos which followed the Parnell split, allowing the British to drop Home Rule altogether. Corkery mentions a friend who suspected the Bishops were deliberately trying to prevent Home Rule, fearing it would undermine their influence. Corkery thought the Bishops spoke as Churchmen rather than Irishmen, but he believed the character of the executed leaders had inspired "self-examination" among the lower clergy, which would produce "a more intense fusion of priests and people . . . influencing even Archbishops and Cardinals. But oh! for a leader! That (thought) is everywhere, in every heart and mind."[2]

For the time being Corkery avoided direct political involvement. His letters to MacSwiney touch on his cultural activities in the second half of 1916 – the Twenty Club, the Munster Players, the publication of *A Munster Twilight*; he also gave lectures to local societies and continued writing for *The Leader*.

The Twenty Club was founded in November 1915 by D.L. Kelleher, the former star undergraduate turned schoolteacher, playwright, minor

53

poet and continental tour guide, who returned to Cork when his occupation vanished in the War. Kelleher and the nineteen other founder
members (including Corkery, MacSwiney and de Roiste) met once a
week in a back room off a side street to discuss a paper. Corkery
recalled these meetings as plagued by "cold feet, bad gas, chairmen,
and poets". They hoped to encourage local writers by publishing a book
a year at their own expense, and did publish one book (a play by J.
Bernard MacCarthy). They also produced at irregular intervals between
1916 and 1918 a magazine *An La/The Day*, containing literary effusions
and comments on local affairs. Corkery thought the Twenty Club a
clearing house for ideas rather than a generator; in a letter to MacSwiney
he contrasts it with the CDS, where a shared interest in Irish gave a
strong sense of identity which helped to hold the society together.[3] It
did not help that at one point Kelleher went off to Dublin to write a
guidebook (prefiguring his later career as a senior employee of the Irish
Tourist Board). *An La* shows increasing sympathy with separatism
(expressed in veiled language to avoid government censorship); the last
issue notes the election of two of the Twenty (MacSwiney and de
Roiste) as Sinn Fein MPs. One local tradition claims the Club was
suppressed, but an essay by Corkery written twenty years later implies
it just faded out. It was peripheral to Corkery, and he to it. The Munster
Fine Arts Society, founded in the 1920s with Corkery as secretary,
claimed descent from the Twenty Club; it held annual exhibitions (usually including one or two Corkery paintings) and survived into the
1960s.[4]

The Munster Players were more significant to Corkery, but again he
remained on the periphery. The CDS rump which continued to meet
after the loss of An Dun had recruited new members and by 1915
formed the Leeside Players who gave occasional performances of
favourite CDS comedies at small-town Feiseanna and local entertainments. "Highbrow" veterans who complained the Leesiders had
abandoned the CDS aim of developing local drama found a leader
when Parker Lynch, a former CDS leading actor, returned from
England. In October 1916 a meeting at which Corkery was present
by invitation (perhaps as mediator) ended with the secession of the
dissidents (including many CDS veterans) and the formation of the
Munster Players for "the promotion of the Irish Dramatic Movement in
this province, the discovery and production of the work of Munster
dramatic writers."[5]

Both companies were dominated by actors rather than playwrights
(both were forced by shortage of material to abandon the CDS rule of
producing only original plays). The Leesiders produced six new plays,
but all were ephemeral comedies by the prolific J.B. MacCarthy. The
Munsters produced eight by members, three of whom were former
CDS writers.

Only one of these plays outlived its parent society; *The Yellow Bittern* by Corkery, based on a story he heard from a woman in the barony of Farney, Co. Louth.[6] The dying poet Cathal Buidhe MacGiolla Gunna, under a priest's curse for his sins, comes to the door of a cabin and is turned away. News is brought that he has collapsed in a nearby hut; a priest enters, having given the last rites, and says a strange woman had everything ready for his arrival and watched over the deathbed. As the inhabitants puzzle over this the strange woman passes in a blaze of light; they sink to their knees in prayer. The appearance of Our Lady on stage has been criticised then and since, but Corkery argued unwillingness to present sacred personages on stage was an unconsciously-acquired Puritan prejudice; an Irish Catholic audience believing in such apparitions should find no incongruity between it and the "realism" of the play. *The Yellow Bittern* became Corkery's most popular play, entered the amateur repertoire, and is still occasionally performed. Corkery was proud it had been accepted as spontaneously as folk-literature, but complained he rarely received royalties from productions.

Neither society had a permanent theatre; they appeared in halls around the city and county, with occasional visits to Dublin. Neither rivalled the CDS achievement; they were divided, some of the best actors and playwrights had emigrated, and it was wartime. They were mainly important for their role in carrying on the CDS tradition. The Munsters disappeared after 1919 and the Leesiders suspended performances soon afterwards due to the War of Independence, but some Leesiders were still trying to revive their group in 1925 and surviving members were active in Cork amateur drama until the 1940s. Thus the Cork Little Theatre tradition can be traced to the CDS.[7]

A Munster Twilight appeared in December 1916 to critical acclaim. "It was published at one shilling and sold in a way that astonished me."[8] Francis Ledwidge wrote to Corkery from the trenches just before his death, praising the book; it reminded him of the old days when they both wrote for *The Irish Review* with MacDonagh and the others. "I would like to say more but I am spancelled".[9] Much of the critical response was due to its handling of the themes of Land, Nationality and Religion with unmistakable talent. For years this type of critic had predicted the emergence of a Catholic nationalist literature of world stature to match the social and political triumphs of Catholic nationalism. Corkery was supplying a long-felt need.

Corkery was modest about his achievement. "About one-third of them will be readable – by such as you – the remaining two-thirds will be for the decent honest folk who revel in Father Thomas Fitzgerald".[10] In retrospect Corkery was no less critical of the stories – a list with brief comments made late in life dismisses most of them – but looked more favourably on their content.

From its matter it is clear to me in retrospect that I had come on a sense of reality. I had discovered where my own roots could find comfort, for it is comforting to have a feeling for all that makes a difference between man and beast – a sense of the past, a sense of terrain as a creative factor.[12]

In a lecture on the short story delivered to the Twenty Club in January 1917 Corkery claims everyone who tells friends an anecdote about a mutual acquaintance is a potential short story writer. Corkery argues that while the novel develops character through incident, the short story writer describes character then uses it to illumine an incident. The anecdotalist does not need to describe the character of the protagonist since it is familiar to his listeners; the writer of short stories is like an anecdotalist enlarging on the story for the only man in the room unfamiliar with the protagonist.[13]

Corkery creates a sense of unarticulated significance around the central anecdote by evocative description, by the unspoken presence of an implied central meaning, and (at times) by the use of an uninvolved first-person narrator. At times this produces an insufficiently – developed anecdote ("The Cry") or an over-schematic allegory ("Joy", despite some fine descriptive touches, is too articulate an account of the confused emotions of the protagonist). At its best this concern with narrative perspectives provides breathtaking results. In "Solace" the eighteenth-century poet Eoghan Mor O'Donovan, weary after a long day ploughing, learns in the evening that he and his family are to be evicted from their few rocky fields. He contemplates the processes of nature "that had happened ever since the beginning of the world, that would continue to happen until the end, whatever woe befell the world of the Gael" and accepts the will of God.

All night he wrestles with words; when day breaks he has shaped a poem which crystallises and transcends all their sorrows.

> Because he had accepted, his face was calm.
> Fearing to awaken his little clan, it was on tiptoe he stepped from the room into the haggard. From a brad he took down a huge, clumsy-handled mall. As if still pursued with the fear of awakening the sleepers, he stepped gently towards the tumble-down cow-house where their one beast – their whole wealth – had passed the night. He undid the wooden bolt, stooped his head, and entered the close-smelling, brown-hued darkness in a gush of lovely sunbeams. The cow was lying lazily on her belly, staring up at him with mild eyes that blinked in the sudden glare. This the poet saw. Without a moment's delay, he raised the mall, swung it and struck one swift, crashing blow at the animal's skull above the eyes. The mall sunk in a little way.

It was withdrawn, swung again, and there was again the sound of crunching bone, less sudden, less loud. A quiver that began at the hind feet travelled through the animal's frame like a wave, another, yet another; then the life went out and there on the floor was a high mass of bones and flesh. The poet went for his butcher's knife to let the blood run from the veins.

A little later he goes back to the hut. "In a voice of authority, and speaking the language of the Bardic Schools, most classical of tongues" he tells his wife and son to prepare a feast for the poets of Munster summoned to hear his poem. His wife "speaking with reverence, however, and as one who would urge a necessary concession, and in the common language of the people" asks if he has thought of the poverty which will follow the feasting; he replies that the song which makes their names immortal makes all their sufferings worthwhile.

The clear-eyed description of the killing of the cow shows Corkery has weighed the cost of inspiration and thus gives force to his praise. Its impact is increased by the last section, presented as an extract from an eighteenth-century account of a journey in Ireland by an Englishman. The traveller, who describes himself as "one in whom curiosity is ever alive, as it seems to be in all those who travel much, more especially if their wanderings take them into foreign lands" follows "several knots of those tatterdemalion figures without whom no Irish landscape seems complete" to "a miserable cabin" crowded with "wild and picturesque figures" listening to an excited recitation by "a huge gaunt man". The Traveller's guide (whom he has described as "a droll-spoken Hibernian") offers to translate the poem into Greek or Latin since he is unsure of his command of English, but finally produces an English version, of which the Traveller can only remember two lines. The Traveller concludes his account by reflecting that "these strong-bodied though ill-clad peasants" would have been better employed ploughing. The reader knows Eoghan Mor ploughed himself to exhaustion yet could not save his family from eviction; in a society where moral blindness calls itself reason, the human urge to create can only be expressed through recklessness.

The traveller is a composite of Arthur Young the agricultural improver, Dr. Smith the historian of Cork and Kerry (who had an eye for the picturesque and met the classically-educated guide) and Lecky (in an article on Lecky Corkery quotes Mrs. Lecky's recollection of his interest in survivals of older ways of life and notes this interest did not extend to the Gaeltacht)[14]; yet in some ways he also resembles the Corkery narrator, who is not a traditional seanachie but an urban visitor recalling his experiences for his friends, a sympathetic outsider observing peasant life like the narrator of *Sketches from a Hunter's Notebook* by Turgenev.

This is made clear in "The Ploughing of Leaca-na-Naomh", whose narrator visits a glen in the Kerry mountains searching for traces of an old Gaelic family. The owner of the only farmhouse in the glen – a large, neglected house – answers his enquiries with a few broken, fearful words. An old farmhand tells him how years ago the farmer was a strong, masterful man, proudly riding to Mass on his stallion Griosach, whose harness jingled with silver bells. Having reclaimed the whole glen in the sweat of his brow, the farmer coveted Leaca-na-Naomh, a large outcrop of fertile land on the side of the mountain overhanging the valley – but who would plough the bed of the saints? He had a labourer, a fool ("they had not yet been cleared away into the asylums"); Liam Ruadh, as strong as the stallion Griosach which played with him. The farmer tried to brain-wash the fool into ploughing the *Leaca*; the fool resisted, then demanded Griosach for the plough. The farmer resisted, then gave in. The fool ploughed the *Leaca* in a fever, on a snowy night, with two stallions fighting in the traces; they went over the edge while the farmer and his men watched from the valley. The narrator leaves, making no further enquiries, sometimes wondering whether Liam Ruadh might have been the last of that immemorial Gaelic family

> no scion of which, if God had left him his senses, would have
> ploughed the Leaca of the Saints, no, not even if it were to save
> him from begging at fairs and in public houses.

Corkery is addressing a favourite theme – "the vanishing of a people's emotion". The farmer's epic struggle to reclaim the land blunted his traditional reverence, led him to violate the *Leaca* and Liam Ruadh and destroy himself. Without a cultural tradition which can shape and express that inchoate reverence, that heroic urge, the Irish are no more than strong superstitious fools riding to destruction (a recurring image). The narrator describes the broken man

> whose features were white with despair; his haggard appear-
> ance reminded me of what one so often sees in war-ravaged
> Munster; a ruined castle-wall hanging out above the woods, a
> grey spectre.

The ruin (another favourite Corkery image) links the man's self-destruction to the destruction of the Gaelic order which would have made sense of his life – and Corkery hints that the narrator himself is diminished by its destruction when the old man says the farmer longed to bring the *Leaca* under the plough:

> "And why not?" I said.
> "Plough the bed of the saints?"

"I had forgotten."
"You are not a Gael of the Gaels maybe?"
"I had forgotten; continue; it grows chilly."

Here is the dilemma of these stories of peasant life. Corkery strips away the ephemeral concerns of the "average" peasant to arrive at the inarticulate pieties of the "typical" peasant, the Gaelic remnants from which Irish national culture can be rebuilt; but is he not projecting his own concerns onto them? By what criterion does he decide what is ephemeral and what essential, when by his own admission he can never know the peasant as he knows the city-dweller?

A Munster Twilight contains several stories with urban settings, notably "The Cobbler's Den", a series of six linked stories which concludes the volume. Some critics argue these represented Corkery's true metier, which he deserted for peasant romanticism. Sean O Faolain, arguing that the influence of Corkery's work on his own work and the work of Frank O'Connor had been exaggerated, excepted the influence of the "Cobbler's Den" stories on O'Connor.[15] This influence presumably lay more in the use of such material than in its handling. In fact, the "Cobbler's Den" stories are constructed in the same anecdotal manner as the peasant stories. There is less emphasis on the isolation of the narrator, but Corkery is engaged in the same task-evoking the atmosphere of a particular little world for an outside audience. He did not abandon this type of urban story; there is one in his third collection *The Stormy Hills* (1929) and several in his fourth and last, *Earth out of Earth* (1939). They have the virtues and limitations of their rural counterparts; they do not, like *Fohnam the Sculptor* or *The Threshold of Quiet*, represent an alternative abandoned because Corkery lacked the resources to develop it further.

Corkery still explored in lectures and articles the problems of Irish culture. He lamented that the vast amount of work devoted to the recovery of the Gaelic past had little effect on the everyday life of the people, that the Gaelic League had given so little attention to organising the Gaeltacht,[16] that writers in Irish had not sought literary models which would help them come to grips with Irish life.

> Is there not a touch too much of the schoolmaster in our Irish writers? Not in all, but in too many. Is there not a certain want of frankness, a fear of being real? Is there not a touch too much of the idyllic?
>
> Because of this desire of ours to turn out a side of things which is perfectly blameless (as if the truth could not be seen through at a glance!) we are not getting up the power or putting forth any of these studies of Irish life which would do more in the end to forward everything Irish than political movements. What would

one not give for a passionately real story of Irish life before the
famine or for a story which – again predicating passionate
reality – would have, say, Egan O'Rahilly or Eoghan Ruadh or
Pierce Fitzgerald or Cathal Buidhe for its central figure.[17]

Corkery argued that such literary models could be found in the
Gaelic past and contemporary European literature. He called on Irish
writers to learn from Russian literature as he had from Turgenev,
arguing that it reflected

> a scheme of life which has much in common with Irish life; and
> at the same time it is a modern literature. It practically did not
> exist before the nineteenth century . . . Pushkin, Lermontov,
> Gogol when they looked from their own eyes on Russia found
> in the first place the cultures of other peoples and languages
> seated in the high places. Looking more intimately at life they
> found a horde of officials, a bureaucracy and behind all this a
> peasant nation.
>   And the one great central fact in that peasant nation was its
> religion: religion coloured every aspect of its life. They also
> found revolutionaries. I need not point out the closeness of the
> parallel.[18]

Corkery complained that Ireland almost never learned about continental writers whose work might provide models for the literary
treatment of Irish life until England took interest in them for some
reason of her own. When the elderly Belgian Francophone poet Emile
Verhaeren came to England after the invasion of Belgium, British
critics hailed him as the greatest living poet. Corkery obtained some
of his work, noted that its imagery showed a sensibility permeated by
Catholicism, and discovered that before the War only four small books
concerning "the greatest living poet" (including translations) appeared
in English.[19]

In "A Plea for the European", a lecture given to the Cork Catholic
Young Men's Society late in 1916, Corkery claimed Ireland was closer to
European culture "still largely what Catholicism has made it" than to
English culture, which was essentially Protestant. Matthew Arnold
was cited among others to prove the most sensitive minds of England
had tried in vain to rouse their countrymen from cultural provinciality
"the product of long years of dissent and mean lodging in selfish
tabernacles". Corkery adduced Arnold's racial theories to prove Saxon
and Celt were so different the English could never rule or even understand the Irish.

Arnold would have been horrified at this dubious use of his dubious
theory, which was meant to justify his own situation as a poet in an age

when poetry had no recognised social position by arguing that while the "vague, dreamy Celts" (including the French – hence Corkery's use of Arnold to claim the Irish were more akin to Continentals than the English) could never govern themselves the competent, complacent Saxon would be unbearable unless his native Philistinism were leavened with a touch of Celtic spirit. (Arnold's mother was of Welsh descent).[20] This vacuous racism is unusual in Corkery's writing (*Synge and Anglo-Irish Literature* (1931) specifically states "race is the product of language, rather than language being the product of race" as part of its argument that the Ascendancy should seek absorption in the Gael; Corkery was free from the anti-semitism which infested Moran, and compared Jews and Irish as exiles from ancient oppressed cultures)[21] but it is one of several vaguenesses in these writings. One of his arguments for the superiority of Russian over English literature as a model for Irish writing was that English writers were preoccupied with "the problems of sex" which were "not the subject of passionate endeavour in Ireland" – as if *Anna Karenina* and the novels of Dostoevski did not exist[22]. He saw European culture as essentially peasant and Catholic; he had no idea of the impact of the Reformation, of secularisation and industrialisation. When questioned about French anti-clericalism, French freemasonry, the paganism of French literature, he could only answer "France is not Europe; neither is Paris France". He did not realise the religious images of Verhaeren were nostalgic evocations of a faith Verhaeren had lost; nor did he grasp the significance of Verhaeren's laments about the disintegration of Belgian rural society and the "tentacular" growth of the towns.

He told Irish writers to learn from international literature; but he said they would learn that only national literature could achieve international fame. "Look at Goethe – how German he is! Look at Molière – how French he is!" He said Irish dramatists, rather than copying foreign models, should for the time being confine themselves to the peasant play – the Abbey's distinctive contribution to world literature (though he admitted the most recent examples were merely stiff "problem plays" and the genre needed an injection of "the heroic spirit").[23] He claimed the quickest way for Ireland to become European was to learn Irish, since this would allow Ireland to choose what interested her from world – and English – literature while bilinguals would have little difficulty in acquiring another language. A deep-seated blindness to change found expression in his praise of Gaelic culture for its failure to produce formal historians. "We have what is far better – a wealth of literature with the sense of history in its every line. Instead of records we have a mass of Art work."[24]

What gave substance to his talk of Europe, despite his evasions, was his attempt to persuade his audience that their emotional responses could and should find deeper and more sensitive expression.

I know a good Irish Catholic father who was greatly shocked at
some religious pictures the *Irish Rosary* published. I need not say
they were pictures of the Old Masters; some of them painted by
the hands of saints. Yet our good Irish Catholic condemned them.
He did not know it, but it was an acquired puritanic and English
outlook on life that spoke through his lips. So also the Cardinal
some time since condemned a little Irish play in which one of the
characters takes the place of the Blessed Virgin. Without wishing
to be more Catholic than the Cardinal, I believe he condemned it,
unwittingly, in accordance with English and puritanic ideals . . .
We have all heard grave discussions, among Catholics, mind you
as to whether the Passion Play at Oberammergau was proper!
And when you take up a little book written about it, you find it
begins with a sort of apology: It is the custom of these good
Catholics and so let us not be rigorous! But St. Philip Neri when he
staged religious plays in the vestry room of his church made no
such appeal. But then he had never heard of the sham piety of the
puritans, never unknowingly imbibed their doctrines. For us who
are of the Tradition all such questions were settled hundreds of
years ago. We should remember this: we too often forget it.[25]

There were obvious political overtones to these denunciations of
English culture: but Corkery still hesitated to commit himself to Sinn
Fein. He was riven by doubts which found expression in *Clan Falvey*, a
one-act play composed in 1917. It is set in the hut of Sean Falvey, a
dispossessed Gaelic noble of the early eighteenth century, reduced to
farming a few poor fields beside a river with the help of his two sons. He
has discovered the poem-book of the O'Falveys in strange hands, spent
their savings (which should have gone to repair the dykes) on redeeming
it, and spends his time reliving past glories and puzzling over cryptic
verses which may prove him The O'Falvey. He keeps his younger son
Donal from the fields to help him with the book; Hugh, the elder son,
must try to save the harvest on his own. Hugh rages at his father, at the
poverty which keeps him from marrying and the book which has
destroyed the O'Falveys. A travelling scholar deciphers the verses which
prove Sean *is* The O'Falvey; the old man is entranced, oblivious to the
news, brought by the local curate, that they are to be evicted. As the dykes
break, drowning their fields, Sean greets the curate as "My Lord Abbot"
come to the marriage of the elder son of The O'Falvey to the daughter of
The MacCarthy Mor. Sean flings open the cabin door, announcing that he
will go to his judgement seat to hear his people squabble over their little
fields; he sees the flood, sees the truth, and collapses in a fit. Corkery
reworks "Solace" and echoes his quarrel with MacCurtain. What good is
cultural revivalism without political action when the nation is being
suffocated here and now through oppression and neglect?

Even after the victory of Eamonn de Valera in the East Clare by-election on July 10th 1917 showed Sinn Fein had produced an alternative organisation strong enough to break the hegemony of the Party and were producing an alternative national leadership (after East Clare Moran finally broke with the Party and endorsed Sinn Fein) Corkery hesitated. On August 10 1917 Liam de Roiste recorded an argument with Corkery in his diary. Corkery denounced Sinn Fein as "politics" and lamented that Ireland had regressed twenty years. Once again the people were obsessed with politics. "The essentials of nationality" had been forgotten.[26]

A fortnight later, writing in *The Leader* under the pen-name "Neuilin Siubhlach", Corkery mocked his own indecision. He laments half-humorously that while the young men are valiant and their patriotic songs have a certain bigness, their speeches and songs are not in Irish. He reproaches himself:

> Poor head! patience awhile. Anyway, 'tis little you have done to bring it to pass; little indeed, far from risking the little life that pulses within you – nothing indeed have you done, except wished, and wished, and wished, and stammered out such broken Irish as must often have made these old poets who you love so well turn over in their unknown and neglected graves.[27]

A week later Corkery jeered at a photograph of the elderly delegates to the Convention, contrasting them with a country lad he saw singing "The Soldier's Song" while working in a hayfield. "He stood . . . erect, a drilled figure, his rake-handle falling into place like a gun".[28] This was his declaration of faith in Sinn Fein.

In the last months of 1917 Corkery wrote a three-act play in praise of revolutionary enthusiasm. *The Labour Leader*, set amidst a Cork quay strike, depicts the struggle between a charismatic Union Secretary and the cautious older members of the Strike Committee. Davna Lambert, the secretary, is a portrait of Jim Larkin – his headlong oratory full of literary allusions, not shrinking from denunciations of his listeners as cowards, his contempt for administrative details like minute-books, cash-ledgers and committee-meetings; his desire to improve the workers culturally as well as economically; but the play also serves as an allegory of the struggle between constitutionalism and physical force. Davna is repeatedly compared to Parnell (a reminder of the Party's original sin in separatist eyes); the most sympathetic conservative, Dempsey, appeals to his long service like a veteran constitutionalist. The play turns on the tension between the attempts of the committee to keep within the letter of the law and Davna's praise of violence as the only way to shock the respectabilities of Cork into abolishing the slums.

Dempsey:	We have an opportunity now of proving to the city, our city, that our union makes for law and not for...
Murphy:	(supporter of Davna): The city! The city! Our city! What part of it is ours? The filth of it. The backyards and the slums.
Clarke:	(ally of Dempsey): But it would not be well to have it against us.
Murphy:	'Tis always against us. Does it turn its back on the unjust employer, on the sweater, on the scab? What sort of houses have we to live in? Kennels! Where do our children play? In the filthy alleys. Where do they sleep? In filthy tenements. You know it. The city!

The conflict comes to a head when Davna decides to rescue an imprisoned striker by force. The committee write to the police but Davna intercepts their letter and appears at the committee-room with a group of bludgeon-men just before a public meeting intended to depose him. After a fist-fight between Davna and a young committee-member (an old friend) news arrives that the railwaymen have come out in support of the strike in delayed reaction to Davna's fiery appeals. The crowd outside are won over, as is Davna's young antagonist; Dempsey and the old guard remain obstinate and are left alone in the deserted committee-room. Inspiration has defeated decorum; for once, Fohnam triumphs over Keltar.

The play is set entirely in the committee-room, with occasional irruptions from the outside world in order to contrast the stifling caution of the committee meetings with Davna's liberating violence. Ironically, this doomed *The Labour Leader* when the Abbey staged it in October 1919; critics found a naturalistic portrayal of a committee meeting as boring as a real committee meeting. Corkery indicates Dempsey is in a continual state of nervous awkwardness, Clarke is ridiculously pompous, and their ally O'Sullivan is a prissy legalist, but his sense of decorum forbade any comic relief broader than mild irony at these failings. (The same sense of decorum led him to believe that while dialect – the speech of the people – gave life and vigour it should only be used sparingly lest the audience be irritated or the characters lose dignity). One of the play's few admirers was the unknown Sean O'Casey;[29] he would not make the same mistake.

The last English-language play Corkery wrote (early in 1918) *Resurrection*, set on the morning of Easter Tuesday 1916, is a straightforward glorification of the Rising. Terence Cantwell, a County Dublin farmer, is an old Fenian made cautious by land purchase. His senile mother, muttering fearfully of Whiteboys, eviction and famine, the dangers of spending on improvements and her father Seamus Mor who stood up to the Yeos in 1798, is a reminder of the long oppression which broke the spirit of the nation. Thus opposition to the Rising is associated with age, cowardice, and souls crushed by oppression; the Rising is presented as the work of young men casting out fear through military discipline, perfect faith (there are several religious allusions besides the title) and renewed contact with immemorial tradition.

Unaware of the Dublin Rising and the involvement of his elder son Michael in the fighting, Terence argues with his younger son Shawn about the Volunteers; he says they are ruining their health, making themselves a laughing-stock, and leaving themselves vulnerable to informers. Shawn retorts that they have no fear of informers;

> No secret societies now, we're after leaving all that behind us
> . . . The Volunteers are a drilled army; they'll fight if the word is
> given. They'll stand still if it is not.

News is brought of the Rising; Terence is told Michael is coming home. The old man thinks his son has turned informer ("there must be a traitor somewhere; there always is") calls this a judgement on his own cowardice, and is overjoyed to find Michael has come back because he is mortally wounded. Terence sends Shawn to the Rising, telling him not to flinch before the firing squad. "There'll be no fear in this house any longer". Shawn opens the door; the dawn has come.

The play is more notable as a political statement than a work of literature; its exclusion of grief from Terence's response to the death of his son weakens its power. The military censor refused permission to include *Resurrection* in a volume of plays by Corkery published in 1919; it was first published in the American *Theatre Arts Monthly* in 1924, later appeared in the *Capuchin Annual*, and was brought out separately by Talbot Press in 1942.

Corkery's support for Sinn Fein soon became well-known despite his use of the pen-names "Richard Mulqueany" and "Newton Grubhlach" for many of his political articles. When the headmaster of St. Patrick's retired in June 1918 and Corkery was not given the post, it was said he had been passed over for political reasons. Corkery resigned his post at the end of the 1917–18 school year; his pupils clubbed together to present him with a wooden bowl hand-carved by his friend the sculptor Joseph Higgins.[30] Corkery became a teacher of Irish and other subjects for the County Cork Technical Instruction Committee – a job involving extensive travel among the small towns of County Cork.[31]

His literary reputation, enhanced by the publication of *The Threshold of Quiet* in December 1917, led the local Sinn Fein organisation to offer him a nomination for Cork City in the forthcoming General Election. Despite a letter from Eamonn de Valera urging him to accept, as a representative of Irish intellect Corkery declined the nomination, suggesting Professors William Stockley and Alfred Rahilly of UCC should be nominated.[32]

Although Corkery began writing some criticism in Irish in 1918–19, notably a lecture on an t-Athair Peadar O Laoghaire which points out the limitations of his work (its wavering between the genres of folk-tale and novel, its neglect of literary form)[33] Corkery resisted suggestions from Terence MacSwiney that he should write exclusively in Irish, since he had not sufficient command of idiom.

> There will be English in this land for the next few hundreds of
> years and we must supply it – we that know a little Irish – or it
> will get its supplies elsewhere.[34]

MacSwiney, who still hoped to write in Irish and believed Ireland would always be two nations unless it was made entirely Irish-speaking as soon as possible, was not convinced. Ernest Blythe, who was imprisoned with MacSwiney in Belfast jail in 1918, recalled his annoyance at receiving a letter from Corkery defending his decision to continue writing in English on the grounds that he could work better and more effectively in English than in Irish.[35]

Despite this difference of opinion Corkery and MacSwiney remained on friendly terms, but MacSwiney's marriage in 1917, his political activities and intermittent prison sentences between April 1916 and January 1919 meant they rarely saw one another. Even when MacSwiney was released after his election to Parliament:

> He was an extremely busy man, always rushing from place to
> place, and one did not care to interfere with his work. We
> would meet occasionally in the streets and have a few words;
> detectives and policemen watching from all corners.[36]

As tension grew and minor clashes occurred between Volunteers and government forces, Corkery wrote a series of six linked stories describing the experiences of a young Volunteer officer, on the run from police after the Rising, travelling around County Cork reorganising the Volunteers. They are set in the period before December 1918, a time of drilling, political demonstrations, and occasional arms raids; the War of Independence is anticipated but has not yet broken out. The series ends with the arrest of the narrator. Three separate stories are set after the outbreak of fighting, but only the last of these, "The Price", depicts the full-scale conflict of ambushes and reprisals. The nine stories were published in 1920 as *The Hounds of Banba*.

It is generally agreed *The Hounds of Banba* is Corkery's weakest collection; Corkery himself thought so in retrospect. Its central vice is the vice of *Resurrection* – an unwillingness to come to grips with the human impact of the revolution. The narrator of the first six stories is supposed to be a man of action, but he shows no distinctive personality at all; he is a nullity onto whom the reader is expected to project his own patriotic emotions. The Volunteers are presented as tightly-drilled, white-faced two-dimensional icons of determination, repelling any touch of violence and disorder – the drunken Irish soldier trying to join the hunger-striker's funeral in "Cowards", the lunatic Colonel MacGillycuddy, apostate descendant of Gaelic chieftains, crazed by the atrocities he has shared in the service of the British Empire. The only serious attempt to come to terms with violence is "A Bye-Product" where a half-wit fascinated by the Volunteers' drilling beats in a police-man's head, takes his gun, and stands guard over his father (who collapsed during a police raid); but Corkery carefully distinguishes this from the real struggle which is "on a higher plane". In his earlier writings Corkery had described the lost years, the cultural constrictions, the survivors' guilt associated with the Land War without denying its justice and necessity.

Even the better stories are insufficiently developed. "Cowards" depicts the conflict between an Anglo-Irish landowner and his national-ist son, who is persuaded to join the British Army on the outbreak of war, loses heart and is shot as a coward; but Corkery is so contemptu-ous of the moral blindness behind Ascendancy loyalties that he ignores their existence altogether and thus cannot adequately portray the conflict. Ascendancy shallowness is more subtly handled in "An Unfin-ished Symphony" where the inane chatter of two young women on their way to a tennis party and the rigid propriety of two withered maiden ladies are contrasted with the deep concealed emotions of the Volunteer narrator on a train journey to his sweetheart.[37] (He is arrested at the station, his love intercepted by the same forces which confine Ireland). Corkery thought this the best story in the volume;[38] but the narrator lacks individuality.

"The Price" which centres on a young woman with a vocation as a nun, recalls some of the symbolic resonances of "The Ploughing of Leaca-na-Naomh" (it is set in a town overhung by a ruined abbey – like Leaca-na-Naomh, a symbol of Ireland overshadowed by its shattered Gaelic past) and contemporary political conflict. (A scene where the heroine challenges the parish priest's refusal to read out the name of Roger Casement in a list of the dead for whom prayers are requested at Mass is based on an incident in Skibbereen Cathedral involving the Redmondite Bishop of Ross). Corkery was dissatisfied with "the miraculous sort of ending" where the heroine, praying at nightfall in the ruined Abbey, sees the Black-and-Tans about to burn the town below as little black figures like an old painting of devils trying to burn a saint of God, and unintentionally frightens away the drunken ruffians

by the sight of her shadow among the ruins. In fact this is quite effec-
tive, but her decision to enter the convent immediately in thanksgiving
(rather than waiting until her parents' death as she had intended) does
not ring true. The pain of renunciation is glossed over; when "The
Price" is compared with the portrayal of Lily Bresnan it is clear the short
story manipulates the theme of religious vocation to shed lustre on the
national cause, rather than handling it in its own terms.

Some critics denounce *The Hounds of Banba* as a betrayal of art for
propaganda; this is unjust. The eruption of events since Easter 1916 left
Corkery groping for his bearings. The separatists he once satirised as
deluded fools had become giants sweeping away the old political land-
marks; everything seemed possible. Two *Hounds of Banba* stories depict
continuity between isolated old Fenians who have kept the faith and
the new generation of rebels; one of these is entitled "The Ember", an
implicit recantation of his caricature of separatists old and new in "The
Embers".

At the end of "The Ember" the young Volunteer who has taken
courage from the old Fenian and received Fenian gold from him to buy
arms for the next Rising, recites for him an old Gaelic verse prophesying
the downfall of England. The old man had not heard the verse before:

> I had given him in perfect form the whole burden and pressure
> of his thoughts. He turned in, wondering how that could be –
> wondering, yet comforted, comforted for ever.[39]

Corkery was working out his justification, suggesting the recovery of
the Gaelic past lay behind the separatist revival; but as yet he lacked the
confidence needed to give his views adequate artistic expression. He
knew he was ageing; his "Neuilin Siubhlach" articles and the epigraph
to *The Hounds of Banba* show him acutely conscious of the gap between
him and the young men of the Volunteers.

> You strike in here, chant your wild songs, and go:
> The chroniclers, with rush lights, stumble after
> And ah! to see them blot the sunrise glow
> Of your bright deeds and dreams, your tears and laughter.

The growth of Sinn Fein brought an enormous upsurge of cultural
activity:

> In 1916 and the following years you met frequently with young
> men who would if they could touch life at all points – it was in
> the air. If I am not mistaken we had then in Ireland more
> publishing firms than ever before or since; weekly papers were
> springing into existence; more books were being written;

our schools of music were looking up; they were shaking off the hegemony of London academies royal and otherwise; art societies were being founded.[40]

As Corkery remarked in retrospect, much of this activity was of little value; but since his early days as teacher and Gaelic Leaguer he had sought out and encouraged talent. In 1908 he had commissioned a bust of himself from his friend, fellow-teacher and Gaelic Leaguer the talented sculptor Joseph Higgins.[41] In 1918 he commissioned a portrait of himself from the young painter William Sheehan, who in 1923 became the first winner of the Gibson Bequest which sent an art student to study on the Continent. Corkery served on the committee which made the award. (Seamus Murphy was to be the third recipient). Despite Corkery's help, Sheehan received few other commissions; he lost the Gibson Bequest through extravagance and drink and died in 1924 at the age of 27 of TB exacerbated by poverty.[42]

Corkery wanted to create a local school of writers who would explore and express the life of Cork through the national spirit which had possessed the young men. He believed he had found the nucleus of such a school in three young proteges on the fringes of the Volunteer movement. Frank O'Connor, Sean O Faolain, Sean Hendrick. O'Connor and O Faolain have left accounts of their backgrounds; how they moved from identification with the heroes of English boys' stories to awareness of their own surroundings, how the independence movement and the discovery of Gaelic culture offered relief from parental pressures, made sense of traces of rural origin visible in their own families.[43]

O'Connor went through several clerking jobs after leaving school at fourteen. He drifted into the Gaelic League with some help from *A Munster Twilight*, and re-established contact with Corkery after an ephemeral magazine published his Irish translation of a French poem. Corkery decided O'Connor showed promise, admitted him to his *salon* (which met once a week in Corkery's house at Auburn Terrace for conversation and gramophone records of classical music) and encouraged him to join the Volunteers.

O Faolain, a scholarship boy at U.C.C., was better educated and more self-confident than O'Connor. He was brought into the Gaelic League at Presentation Brothers' College by Padraig O Domhnaill, the only rebel on the staff, and joined the Volunteers while at U.C.C. O Domhnaill brought him into contact with Corkery, probably in 1918. (O Faolain played the lead in an Irish-language amateur production of *Clan Falvey* in 1919). In later life O Faolain recalled nothing of their first meeting and said his first memory of Corkery was of accosting the older man after Mass one Sunday with a list of Hardy's novels to ask which were the best.[44] Corkery respected O Faolain and held him up as an example of hard work for the erratic O'Connor.

O'Connor remembered how Corkery gave him something of the general education he lacked, beginning his musical education, introducing him to English poetry, lending O'Connor books, introducing him to new authors as the younger man grew ready for them. Corkery took O'Connor on his sketching trips, got him into the School of Art, got him a scholarship to a London art school – which O'Connor turned down for a Gaelic League course for travelling teachers of Irish, believing such a profession ideal for a young writer getting to know Ireland.

O Faolain recalled Corkery's invaluably stringent criticism of their first literary efforts, insisting on rewriting and revision, making them see they must know what they wanted to say before concentrating on how to say it. His distrust of the cult of the masterpiece, his belief that if honest work was produced the masterpieces would come in good time, was well suited to keeping young writers at work without discouraging them.[45]

Sean Hendrick was a later addition to the circle (he joined shortly before the Truce), an insurance clerk with a fine critical mind; his literary promise was never fulfilled but he was prominent in Cork intellectual circles until his death in the early 1970s.

His protégés of these years knew Corkery at his best; a recognised writer with a distinctive style and a fine critical mind drawing on a store of ideas accumulated over twenty years, wide-ranging, confident. O Faolain remembered him speaking of the dangers of provincialism, but thought in retrospect Corkery was insufficiently aware of these dangers.[46]

The conflict intensified as Corkery prepared *Three Plays*, *The Labour Leader*, and *The Hounds of Banba* for publication. Returning from a visit to Dublin in 1919, Corkery encountered MacCurtain on the train; MacCurtain asked to exchange bags in case of searches. Corkery took MacCurtain's bag without asking its contents.[46]

On New Year's Day 1920 MacCurtain's First Cork Brigade launched its full-scale guerrilla campaign with attacks on two police stations. A few weeks later Sinn Fein won the borough elections outside north-east Ulster; MacCurtain became the first Sinn Fein Lord Mayor of Cork, with MacSwiney as his deputy. The new administration promptly declared its allegiance to Dail Eireann and embarked on a programme of civic reform. MacCurtain insisted on presiding over all the committees himself. The Sinn Fein Councillors moved constantly from house to house; at first this was simply an anti-surveillance measure. On the night of March 17th a gunman fired at Councillor William Stockley, Professor of English in University College Cork. Stockley was only slightly wounded (a bullet passed through his coat, grazing his body). He recognised his assailant as a policeman.[47]

Two days later a squad of disguised RIC men shot dead Lord Mayor MacCurtain in front of his wife and children. It is still disputed whether this was a reprisal by local police for the killing of a policeman the previous night or part of a deliberate terror campaign organised by the

British secret service; the blatant cover-up which followed led his friends and colleagues (including Corkery) to believe the second.[48]

MacSwiney was MacCurtain's natural successor. He accepted the nomination in a defiant inaugural speech. He denounced all talk of compromise, saying they could no more compromise with the British than with the Devil, told the minority councillors they were not Sinn Feiners because they had insufficient faith in God, Who allowed the Irish to suffer such persecution in order to prepare them for a noble destiny, compared the liberty for which they fought to the liberty for which Christ died and death for its sake to the sacrifice of Calvary, and finally invoked Isaiah's prophecy on Babylon ("O thou who sittest by many waters, rich in treasures, the time is come for thy entire destruction") against the British Empire.[49]

Soon afterwards P.S. O'Hegarty was horrified to discover MacSwiney planned a spectacular reprisal for MacCurtain's killing, probably a revival of an earlier plan to make up for Cork's quiescence in Easter Week by staging a full-scale Rising in the city. The consequences for the civilian population and the IRA brigade would have been catastrophic; O'Hegarty appealed to Griffith, who vetoed the scheme.[50]

MacSwiney continued the policy of municipal reform during his short mayoralty. Like MacCurtain, he insisted on presiding over all the municipal committees, including a new commission which enquired into the cost of living in order to establish a minimum living wage. MacSwiney believed no-one who needed food and stole it should be convicted of theft. He took an interest in housing; the Sinn Fein corporation undertook three small housing schemes during its existence – the first since 1906. He wanted to remove the element of patronage from public appointments; under the Sinn Fein corporation Seamus Lankford undertook extensive reforms in the local Poor Law administration. (More dubious was MacSwiney's announcement that no-one who could not speak Irish should be allowed to become a teacher or given any public appointment whatsoever).[51] Despite his extensive duties as Lord Mayor and IRA Commandant MacSwiney found time to write to Corkery wishing him luck with an exhibition of paintings in Dublin.[52]

On August 12th the City Hall was raided as MacSwiney presided over a meeting of IRA officers. MacSwiney wanted to fight to the death but was persuaded this would incriminate everyone else at the meeting. (In their joy at convicting MacSwiney the British released the others – including Liam Lynch). It was Corkery who told Mrs. MacSwiney of her husband's arrest.

MacSwiney was tried by court-martial, sentenced to two year's imprisonment for possession of a police cipher, and deported to Brixton prison in London. He refused to recognise the court, saying the Irish Republic was the only legitimate authority in Ireland. From the moment of his arrest he went on hunger-strike, demanding release. Some of his colleagues (including Michael Collins) had doubts about his decision, believing that while the British Government had conceded political status to hunger-strikers in the past they could not release him without exposing themselves to public humiliation.[53]

MacSwiney told his judges he would be free, alive or dead, within a month; so little was known about protracted hunger strikes that it was not realised hunger strikes can survive up to eighty days (though there is a crisis around thirty or forty days). After the first month MacSwiney can never have known how he might die. He lasted 74 days. As the hunger-strike progressed it drew world-wide attention. In Portugal, in Italy, in France, in America there were calls for his release, but the British Government refused. MacSwiney endured with remarkable composure, despite arguments with English prison doctors and feelings of guilt at his longings to return to the hills of mid-Cork.

After his death on October 25th MacSwiney was brought back to Cork and lay in state in the City Hall. His funeral drew the largest crowd ever seen in Munster. The drama critic "Andrew E. Malone" said that despite his shortcomings as a dramatist MacSwiney created one drama which drew the eyes of the world.[54] Some years later his family received a translation of an Arabic poem on his hunger-strike. He became a hero to Indian nationalists; Gandhi praised him (though he believed MacSwiney mistaken in continuing the fast once it was clear the government would not give in). A few years later Corkery found an article he wrote on "MacSwiney as Worker" was reprinted in *Navayuga/Tomorrow*, an Indian labour paper.[55]

Corkery wrote a sensitive obituary of MacSwiney in the December 1920 issue of *Studies* recalling his love of beauty, his self-sacrificing idealism.[56] Terence's sister Annie wrote to Corkery praising the piece, saying he had truly known Terence, and telling him when a parcel of books he sent arrived at Brixton MacSwiney wanted to write and thank him but was too weak.[57] Corkery replied;

> What you say of his longing to be in Ireland only shows how much greater his sacrifice was than the average mind would or could conceive . . . I know how much he loved mid-Cork, every hill of it – and its fine people, and knew quite well that certain of its features would recur to his memory with terrible intimacy. If some people write words about him that jar on you, well, they do so through clumsiness and not through intent. But these clumsy words – including some of my own perhaps – will pass away in quite a short time. We know that he was almost superhumanly perfect – not only as a patriot, but as a man – and history will never have such a glut of men in its pages as to confuse him with the average hero of whom we must accept both good and bad.[58]

Alderman Liam de Roiste TD, an old colleague of MacSwiney in the CLS, who had briefly been a member of the CDS and was on bad terms with Corkery, wrote in his diary that the obituary was inaccurate in details and over-reverent; he described MacSwiney as a single-minded idealist with no thought for others' feelings and no concrete vision of the Irish Republic he wanted.[59] This criticism has recurred since; Michael Collins' biographers note his distrust of MacSwiney's "romanticism"; in *Vive Moi!* O Faolain remarks the lack of concrete detail in MacSwiney's statement of his belief, *The Principles of Freedom*. At times it has been suggested MacSwiney had a death wish. Corkery reacted angrily to this suggestion; he remembered how MacSwiney overflowed with plans for his family, for study, for writing in Irish, and insisted his friend had not wanted to die. *The Holocaust* and his record as Lord Mayor show the abstract idealism of his rhetoric was not incompatible with awareness of social evils and willingness to seek remedies; but he lacked the intellectual tools to integrate them. The gap between his ideals and his everyday work of improvement haunted him perpetually; the hero of *The Revolutionist*, who works himself to death to prove his righteousness, is too obviously a portrait of what MacSwiney thought he *should be* for comfort. Perhaps part of the answer lies in the diaries of Tom Jones, the British Cabinet Secretary which record that during his hunger strike MacSwiney developed TB and was found to have had the disease in latent form for some time.[59a] Did MacSwiney suspect he might die soon anyway?

Corkery remembered MacSwiney as the epitome of the Irish Revolution as he presented it in *The Hounds of Banba*: the desire to reintegrate Cork City, with its petty oppressions and constrictions, into the wounded Gaelic culture surviving in the hills of West Cork; the slow years of preparation, the sudden toppling of powers which seemed immovable, the raising of obscure men to leadership and fame, the triumph over human weakness in the final ordeal.

> On the night of the day on which we had learned of his death I had to go through his city. The streets were of course quite deserted, half lit, and those few who were abroad were hastening to their homes. Suddenly there swept a military lorry down from the hillside barrack. That lorry swept from street to street without reason, just from mere wantonness. And I though of the dead man in Brixton, his agony over. The deep silence of the spirit, the rough rattle of brute strength – symbols of the two parties in the struggle that was being made.[60]

In December 1920 *The Hounds of Banba*, *Three Plays*, and *The Labour Leader* were published; they did not sell well outside Ireland, but the critics praised them. That same month, after an army lorry was ambushed at Dillon's Cross a short distance from Corkery's house, several houses at the ambush site were demolished in reprisal; the following night Crown forces ran riot in Cork, burning part of the main shopping district, the City Hall and the Carnegie Library. The Government claimed the Corkonians burnt their own city.

The Corporation members continued to move from house to house (in May 1921 a priest staying at de Roiste's house was shot dead in mistake for de Roiste). For a time Professor Stockley took refuge in Corkery's house; they became close friends.[61] Corkery dedicated a small collection of poems, *Ui Bhreasail* (1921) to "Professor and Mrs. Stockley, for all they have been and are to Cork".

A visiting Indian nationalist was sent to Corkery to be shown Cork. Corkery noted his visitor seemed almost entirely anglicised, spoke of "Poor India" as something separate from himself, and when asked for a song at a ceilidhe embarrassed everyone by singing an English song. He sent Corkery Tagore's book *Nationalism*.[62]

In 1921 Corkery seems to have began a second collection of short stories about the War of Independence. During the year he published two stories in *Green and Gold*, a story-magazine run by the *Waterford News and Star*. "Sagged" describes the inarticulate rapture of John Bracken, a small farmer's only son, as he wanders his native countryside on the day of his return from prison in England; that night his friends summon him to take part in an ambush. He is wounded and his life is despaired of until the celebrated Commandant (clearly based on Michael Collins) risks his own life to see him and orders him to get better.[63] "The Bequest" describes how the widow of a strong farmer who bought out the local gentry and moved his family into their deserted mansion is found by her two old servants on the night before her last visit to her only son (who is to be hanged in Cork Jail) sitting in the deserted cabin where she spent her early married life. She tells them she is worried the farm will go to cousins who have not the true national spirit and will squander it like the gentry. She returns from her visit to her son radiant with joy. He has told her to make over the land to the Republic; through it he will go on fighting the English "forever".[64]

The first half of "Sagged" with its evocation of John Bracken's inarticulate love for his surroundings, contains some of Corkery's finest painterly prose; but he shrinks from the natural conclusion (to make Bracken die for it in the ambush) and the Kiplingesque Commandant is an irrelevance. "The Bequest" is crude propaganda; the bequest would be unenforceable if the War of Independence failed, superfluous if it succeeded, and the portrayal of the mother as showing unmixed joy defies credulity.

The weaknesses of "The Bequest" are obvious when it is compared with "Morning at Ardnagapall", a revised version prepared later that year. Here the old servants find their mistress in the deserted cottage on the morning her son is to be executed; she tells them she left Cork the previous afternoon because she could not face the crowds of well-meaning comforters. About to return to the house, the old people hear a military convoy on the road, quench the light and shrink down; when it has gone past they take the long way home along the road because the soldiers would shoot at anything moving in the fields. At the crossroads they find a little knot of people around the corpse of a stranger flung from one of the lorries, a young countryman "not more than twenty years of age . . . a boy's face, with soft lips and full cheeks and eyes. His brows were contracted and his lips drawn back a little from the teeth". The old woman takes charge, has the body brought to the chapel, finding comfort in the action.

> Her features since she had gazed on the dead boy in the dust had lost much of the look of concentrated thought and anxiety that had come into them the night her boy was snatched from his bed. Her brows were raised, her features open as a child's, full of sadness still, but neither intense nor passionate. What was personal in her grief had fallen from her. . . The face of the dead boy was as often before her vision as the face of her own boy. She wished she knew the mother of the dead boy. She wished now at this moment she could take her in her arms. That was what more than anything else she wished to do. And she was sure that that mother whoever she was and wherever she was she would find out Ardnagapall and come to her. She had some idea that already she was travelling over the hills to her. She need not be so distracted, she thought: she would find her boy laid out with decency and holiness. She would say to her: my boy, they would not give him back to me.
>
> As if her thought in some way had penetrated the breasts of all present the place became entranced in a wonderful stillness. The spires of smoke were too far away to darken in the least degree the open vibrant vital splendour of the morning. Those fires were in the far background. Around the little chapel was the unstained sunshine, great breadths of it, with the birds singing to it as if their little breasts would burst in the energy of their joy.[65]

Thus Corkery conveys his view that the Irish cause is the cause of the universal human affections; he can plausibly present the pain and suffering of the struggle as transitory in comparison with the ends for which they are endured because he has not evaded their existence as he did in "The Bequest".

Two other typescript stories from late 1921 exist among Corkery's papers. "The Night Watch" is an expansion of an anecdote heard from a commercial traveller who stayed in Millstreet the night after an ambush, when it was feared the town would be burned in reprisal. Looking from the window of his hotel he saw a line of men in the street; the local Volunteers, gathered to defend the town. They stood there all night although it was raining heavily, and only dispersed at dawn.[66] Corkery tries to introduce a note of the transience of human existence reminiscent of Turgenev's story "Bezhin Meadow" by making one volunteer die of pneumonia afterwards; but since this character is not mentioned at all before his death there is insufficient sense of loss.

The other story, "Unsprung" is of the same quality as "Morning at Ardnagapall". Inspired by the story of Kevin Barry, it describes the experiences of the mother of a young medical student and Volunteer from the abrupt news of his arrest to the aftermath of his execution; at the end her friends, and the reader, are still unsure whether she has been awakened to the life around her by her sufferings or gone mad with suppressed grief.[67]

The strength of these two stories, better than anything in *The Hounds of Banba*, is probably a response to the Truce (July 1921). O'Connor and O Faolain have recorded their feelings as the Crown forces withdrew to barracks. A motley army of irregulars had forced a world power to recognise them as negotiating partners.[68] As they appeared openly on the streets, feted as heroes, it seemed Ireland – and Cork – would henceforth be one with the Gael; Corkery could acknowledge the pain and glory of the conflict as part of the national task of building a new civilization on the ancient foundations.

For the rest of their lives that generation of Republicans tried to recapture that moment when a new civilization seemed ready for moulding in their hands. The Treaty Split intervened. The new collection of short stories was stillborn. "Unsprung" and "Morning at Ardnagapall" never appeared in book form.

PART TWO

DONALL O CORCORA 1921–64

CHAPTER FIVE

THE HIDDEN IRELAND 1921–4

Corkery saw the Treaty as a betrayal of the high hopes of the Truce. In an article in the new Republican weekly *Poblacht na h-Eireann* after the Dail ratified the Treaty Corkery compared the Free Staters to Browning's foolish voyagers, who settled with their precious cargo on the barren rocks where they first made landfall, refused to acknowledge "their first fault" even when they learned the happy isles they sought lay just over the horizon, and "perished in their pride".[1] Another article describes sharing a railway carriage with a crowd of farmers' sons, pleasant enough lads without much forethought who become uneasy when one of them absent-mindedly starts singing "Kevin Barry".

> Heavy, heavy days when the evocation of our heroic dead chills us to the marrow of our bones. What have we done! Whereto wandered![2]

Corkery believed only total victory could secure an Irish national culture; any compromise would allow the respectable men with a stake in the country to return to aping English ways, the newly-prosperous farmers to discard what remained of inarticulate Gaelic custom before it could be rescued and used to reconstitute the nation. He was a cultural protectionist, believing if an Irish state could dam the flood of English influence for a few decades a self-confident national culture in Irish and English could be created, ready to meet the world on its own terms. He dismissed the Northern Ireland problem, then and for the rest of his life, by claiming such a culture once created would be so attractive the Ulster Protestants would adopt it spontaneously.[3] Corkery dismissed economic and political arguments for the Treaty as "materialism". A sketch sarcastically entitled "The Stepping Stone" (Collins called the Treaty a stepping-stone to the Republic) described a farmer's young son writing TO HELL WITH DE VALERA AND HIS REPUBLIC on a wall on Election Day 1922 while his father voted for the Treaty.[4]

Frank O'Connor opposed the Treaty because Corkery opposed it. O Faolain initially supported it; then while translating a Gaelic poem he asked himself what the elaborate arguments for the Treaty had to do with the life of the simple country people and joined the Republicans.[5] Corkery and his disciples started a short-lived Republican literary magazine, *An Long/The Ship*, which lasted for three issues.[6] When the Civil War broke out they wrote for the Republican publicity department under Erskine Childers; O'Connor and Hendrick were installed in the *Cork Examiner* as censors.

The Civil War began with the bombardment of the Four Courts on June 28th; within three weeks the Free Staters cleared Dublin of Republican garrisons and launched a major offensive against the Republicans in the south. On a visit to the front O'Connor was captured by a party of Free Staters who were then surrounded in their turn and surrendered after a brief resistance. All his life O'Connor remembered the bullet-pierced head of a dead Free Stater[7]; nothing in *The Hounds of Banba* prepared him for this aspect of the struggle.

On July 21st Corkery wrote to the *Evening Echo* advocating a peace settlement on the lines of Document Number Two, with the removal of the Oath, the Governor-General, and the Royal Veto from the Constitution. De Roiste, who supported the Treaty and was now marooned in Republican-held Cork, remarked in his diary that he agreed with these demands but knew they did not amount to the Republic and did not believe himself entitled to wage war on those who disagreed with him. He recalled sourly how Corkery had jeered at his support for Sinn Fein.[8] A few days later, de Roiste commented that another letter from Corkery was full of references to "the nation", "the rebel tradition" in terms of esoteric abstractions without reference to the responsibilities of government, the consequences of unleashing Civil War, and the behaviour of thoughtless men with arms in their hands.[9]

On August 8th, as the Republican defensive line in North Munster collapsed, Free State troops made a surprise seaborne landing in Cork harbour. After a brief holding action, the demoralised Republicans evacuated the city and fell back in confusion to Macroom. Corkery was out of the city on a painting trip at Inniscarra; Hendrick and O'Connor made their way out to him. Corkery suggested they should go to Macroom to see if they were wanted. The young men hitched a lift on a lorry; Corkery followed to keep an eye on them. The next day the Republicans dispersed to their home districts to fight as guerrillas. O Faolain was recruited for a workshop making bombs; O'Connor and Hendrick worked under Childers on a Southern edition of *Poblacht na h-Eireann*, printed in a Ballymakeera schoolhouse on a commandeered printing press. Corkery went off to finish his painting holiday at Gougane Barra.

A few weeks later, after his return to Cork, Corkery heard rumours that O'Connor was misbehaving, came out and brought him back to the city, hijacking a horse and cart *en route*.[10] O'Connor remained on the run in Cork; soon after his return he objected to a plan to shoot Free State soldiers and their girlfriends on the Mardyke. He went to Corkery for advice. Corkery sent him to Mary MacSwiney T.D., who was surprised O'Connor should have a moral objection to shooting women; but he was told the plan had been abandoned.[11]

The southern edition of *Poblacht na h-Eireann* survived until the end of October. The last issue was devoted to Terence MacSwiney, with articles by Mary MacSwiney, Stockley, and Corkery. Corkery claimed "these dismal days of constitution-mongering" would have been for MacSwiney a martyrdom worse than Brixton. His sensitive idealism made the Irish people aware of their own strength, led them up to the clean fresh mountaintops; but now leaders appealed to material motives "to whistle a herd to the lush pastures in the valleys". They might as well be back in the days of the Home Rule agitation.

> When Terence MacSwiney and his kind began to light up the land with new lamps, the merely worldly-wise, the mediocre, "the average sensual man" were swept aside. When in time those lamps were put out, all those we thought had been put in their place forever, returned. They are now around us sitting in high seats of this city and every city, unabashed, as if they thought we had all lost our memory! ... All these minor corruptions have their origins in that fount of corruption – the false Oath![12]

On November 4th Mary MacSwiney was arrested and went on hunger strike. On November 20th a letter from Corkery appeared in the *Cork Examiner* declaring her action had secured her place in history; to act otherwise would have betrayed the memory of her brother. Four days later Bishop Coholan preached a sermon condemning her hunger strike and "the abominable view" that its abandonment would be a betrayal of her brother; Corkery was not named but everybody understood the reference. Corkery, with Alfred O'Rahilly and Liam de Roiste, later helped to organise a successful petition for her release.[13]

After the demise of his paper Childers made his way to his cousin's house in Wicklow, where he was captured. On November 24th he was executed, under a dubious application of emergency legislation, for possessing a firearm. Soon afterwards the Lee Press, a Cork-based offshoot of his underground publishing operations, produced *Rebel Songs*, a pamphlet of verse by Corkery under the pseudonym "Reithin Siubhlach" (The Strolling Vagabond) dedicated to Childers.[14]

In retaliation for the death of Childers, Liam Lynch ordered the assassination of Pro-Treaty TDs. On December 7th one of his squads shot dead Sean Hales TD (whose twin brother was a Republican commandant in West Cork) and wounded another TD. In reprisal, four

imprisoned Republican leaders were shot without trial on the morning
of December 8th by order of the Free State Cabinet. On December 9th
Corkery wrote to the *Irish Independent*:

> Will anyone show me where is the necessity for further
> bloodshed in Ireland? The present war can be stopped, and
> won, not by either side, but by both, by the united I.R.A. How?
> By simply standing up to England and saying: Your solution of
> your difficulty has been tried by us and found lamentably
> wanting. We refuse to go on paddling our hands in one anoth-
> er's blood. That, we find, is the price we must pay for the
> clauses in your Treaty that concern your King. Wipe out those
> clauses and we are willing to give the Treaty a fair run. . . Does
> anyone think that saying this to England will cause a war at this
> hour of the day? The English will not come back. There will not
> be war. There will be peace.

It was the same proposal, based on Document Number Two, which he
made before the fall of Cork. The Free State government prohibited the
publication of the letter; it appeared only in the Republican underground press.[15]

In February O'Connor was arrested; in Cork jail he saw a young
prisoner who had been "interrogated" – beaten and bayonetted,
reduced to inarticulate moaning, his face like dough. This boy was shot
a few days later. O'Connor was sent to an internment camp at
Gormanstown, where he was exasperated by the idealistic refusal of the
Republican prisoners to recognise their situation, exemplified by a
ballad about a heroic Republican martyr – the boy he saw in Cork jail.[16]

The Civil War ended in May 1923 when the Republican leadership
ordered their forces to dump arms; but thousands of Republican
prisoners remained in detention. In October they began a mass hunger-
strike demanding release; O'Connor saw it as futile and refused to take
part. Corkery, writing to the American litterateur Chester Arthur, made
excuses for him:

> He was in hospital with bronchitis when the strike began, and
> is now as far as I know attending on the others. He was never
> robust.[17]

The hunger-strike broke down after a month; O'Connor describes its
collapse in *An Only Child*. After his release at the end of 1923 O'Connor
was attacked while attending a political meeting in Cork by some
young people who saw him as a traitor; Corkery rescued him.

O Faolain had remained in the hills for some months, experiencing
the demoralisation and physical hardship of the disintegrating Repub-

licans. He returned to the city where he was sheltered by his parents, brought out a clandestine Republican magazine, then went to Dublin as Republican Director of Publicity (everyone better qualified was in jail) until January 1924, when he went back to Cork to finish his M.A.

In May 1924 Corkery put O'Connor in touch with Lennox Robinson, who was recruiting trainee librarians for the Carnegie Trust. O'Connor went to Sligo as assistant librarian; O Faolain, having finished his M.A., spent the school year 1924/5 teaching in Ennis.[18]

Despite his political activities, Corkery kept his job as travelling teacher of art, woodwork and Irish for Cork County Vocational Education Committee; on January 25th 1923 he was appointed clerical assistant to the County Cork Inspector of Irish.[19]

In July 1923 he was one of the lecturers at the first summer school held in University College Cork to train secondary teachers to meet the Irish language requirements imposed by the new state. A participant who wrote an account of the school for *The Leader* said its highlight was "Domhnall O'Corcora's literary criticism."[20]

Corkery gave five Irish-language lectures on contemporary literature. After an introductory lecture giving his views on the general tendency of modern literature he discussed the nature and history of the novel, the short story, the drama and the lyric, ending each lecture with a brief account of the contemporary state of the genre and a critique of recent Irish-language endeavours in the genre.

The lecture on the lyric has been lost; the others survive in manuscript. They are impressive for their time and place. The general remarks on the genres, though idiosyncratic, are often acute. Corkery includes in his discussion Chekhov stories and some Eugene O'Neill plays. ("Only an Irishman or a Jew could have written (*The Emperor Jones*). He knows what slavery is").[21] He showed no compunction in analysing the shortcomings of contemporary Irish-language works.

The overall framework within which these insights are presented is, however, radically flawed. Corkery argues the Renaissance maimed the emergent literatures of Europe by setting up artificial literary models unrelated to the mediaeval Christian popular cultures of the different nations. Thus the Church, by favouring Latin over the nascent vernaculars, unintentionally prepared the way for a sterile neo-paganism. (There is an implicit parallel with clerical hostility to the Gaelic Revival and Republicanism). Gaelic Ireland escaped because higher education was in the hands of the bardic schools rather than the Church, so the Renaissance encountered a mature vernacular culture which could absorb the new influences without being swamped.

Corkery claimed European literature since the Romantics had fought against the spirit of the Renaissance, trying to recapture the mediaeval notes of "Duchas" (tradition/ "homeliness"/nationality) and "Deine" (intensity). Therefore the traditional Gaelic literary "moulds" were the flower of a tradition which, once recovered and fully comprehended, would give free access to the main current of modern literature.[22]

Corkery was trying to do two things at once; introduce Irish-language writers to contemporary literature and intervene in a long-running Gaelic League debate over the revival of eighteenth-century literary metres. From its foundations the League faced problems in the revival of a language which had not been used as a literary medium for over a century and survived only as a group of spoken dialects among remote peasant communities. How could learners of the spoken language be given access to the historic culture? How could the spoken language be preserved from corruption by the speech and writings of inexpert learners whose first language was English (a phenomenon first noticed soon after the turn of the century)?

Only a few eccentrics advocated the revival of Middle Irish as a literary language distinct from the spoken tongue or argued Irish-language writers should confine themselves to the folk-tale format; but almost from its beginning the League was bitterly divided between the leadership, backed by Connacht, Ulster and much of Leinster, who wanted a synthetic standard based on Connacht Irish, and the Munster faction (led by the Dublin-based Keating branch) which claimed the standard should be Munster Irish, the language of the eighteenth-century poets who were the last heirs of the ancient literary tradition. Supporters of the leadership responded by describing the eighteenth-century Munster poets as pedants immersed in dead conventions, who sacrificed sense to sound.[23]

Corkery believed the abandonment of the older forms meant losing contact with the historic literary tradition, leading to the abandonment of literary discipline or indiscriminate adoption of English styles developed for a society very different from Ireland. He believed imitation of English models accounted for the rarity of Irish-language descriptions of peasant life although the majority of Irish people and most native speakers were peasants. (It might just as well be argued the writers assumed their readers were familiar with peasant life). Corkery complained that while the older literature was still handed down and recited in the Gaeltacht, the newer writers never hinted at its existence; he contrasted them with Israel Zangwill, whose *Children of the Ghetto* described the everyday life of its characters without forgetting they were heirs of an ancient culture.[24]

Corkery knew imitation of the old metres had not saved writers like Torna from Tom-Moorean sentimentality[25]; he apparently thought this could be avoided by deeper knowledge of the Gaelic tradition. In a paper which AE praised for its awareness of the need "to shape the language to modern needs and strengthen and perfect it as a means of expression" Corkery gave the 1924 League Ard Fheis his view of the League's task under the new conditions.

To understand what Gaelic culture means; to spread that culture, to deepen it where necessary; to strive against such alien cultures as would swamp it; to introduce from those alien cultures such strains as may invigorate it; and ever and always to smite the Philistine. It is absurd that novels, dramas, poems, books of all kinds, should have been written in Irish by people who knowing Irish in the grammatical sense, know nothing of its literature. Those people, for all their minute knowledge of Irish grammar, are simply writing English literature in Irish.[26]

Unfortunately Corkery's identification of the Gaelic literary tradition with the main current of modern art – the wider framework wherein he discussed the poets of *The Hidden Ireland* – was based on misunderstanding. Many nineteenth and twentieth century artists have praised the Middle Ages as an age of undivided sensibilities; but this image owed more to their own ideals and dissatisfactions than knowledge of mediaeval culture. Corkery drew his idea of the Middle Ages from such sources; his writings show some knowledge of mediaeval art, but otherwise only vague references to scholastic philosophy, Gothic architecture, and Anglo-Saxons.

The Hidden Ireland

As we saw, soon after he joined the Gaelic League Corkery found old people among the Cork lanes with stories and songs of the Munster poets. By 1907 he was writing articles about his discovery of the poets, linking it to an attack on formal history which he saw as a product of the emotional malaise devouring modern Ireland – and Corkery himself. Keltar the Chronicler, the wise man who understands the dead but cannot move the hearts of the living, Corkery's most sympathetic portrait of a historian, is in part a self-portrait. Elsewhere he called historians bat-eyed muck-rakers, ransacking "enemy state papers"[28] to piece together the squalid intrigues of the eighteenth-century Ascendancy, ignoring the noble heritage of the Gael because the Gael left no state papers and leading the descendants of the Gael to believe nothing worth attention happened in eighteenth-century Ireland outside the Ascendancy. He quoted approvingly Standish O'Grady's remark that Irish history seen through state papers was like stained glass windows seen from outside, while Irish history as rendered in literature resembled the same windows seen from within.[29] Corkery saw the Gaelic tradition as subject-matter not for history, but epic – the defining theme of the Irish experience.

For many years Corkery confined himself to short pieces such as the 1915 lecture where he first used the term "Hidden Ireland", "fearing that I was not the man to write it, that I had neither the scholarship nor the leisure"; but as the independence movement mushroomed Corkery came to believe only the hidden influence of the Gaelic tradition could explain its incredible success. "The soul of the Gael is one of the more enduring features of our national life . . . this very fact becomes daily more evident, and all future historians will more and more have to wrestle with it." Concerned that "no one else thinks it worthwhile to write it" and fearing the language was falling under the "meticulous, hard, and acrid" dominance of "grammarians", Corkery undertook to explain the nation to itself.[30]

He read and annotated the Irish Texts Society editions of the poets in country hotels and slow country trains during his journeys as a travelling teacher. In March 1922, writing to C.P. Curran, he mentioned "that blessed book – which never, never will be finished".[31] In later life he recalled the bad oil-lamps in the hotels and the candle-stubs he stuck to the window-ledges of trains, like one of his own poets copying manuscripts by candlelight.

> When I, remembering that my own personal background was such as I have indicated, look back on my undertaking the writing of this book, I wonder at my own temerity. But I simply feel that the thing had to be done; that there could be no rest for me until it was done. . . My *Hidden Ireland* released deep floods of emotion.[32]

The Hidden Ireland frankly admits dependence on the great historians of the literature "whose words I quote so often in these pages. To these I am well content to play the not unnecessary role of *vulgarisateur*".

> All these as well as their students will, of course, find numerous errors after me if they care to look. There are, of course, errors and errors. . . and the propulsive course of epics is not to be hindered even by shoals of errors.[33]

Corkery begins *The Hidden Ireland* with a chapter on the condition of eighteenth-century Ireland.

> It is only weakness to sentimentalise away the filth, the degradation, the recklessness that go with hardship, starvation and tyranny, when these are continued from generation to generation. If we would realise both the staunchness of the martyr and the blossom-white beauty of his faith, we must understand the vigour of the trial that tested him.[34]

Thus Corkery describes a country ruled by an insecure alien Ascendancy, squalid squireens recklessly laying waste their estates "not ever quite sure of their standing in so strange a country", hacking down woods and squandering the proceeds in debauchery, despising the teeming, resentful masses of Gaelic poor whose conditions worsened decade by decade as law and landlords tightened the screw, clearing whole countrysides of poor to make way for cattle, provoking Whiteboy resistance. "Between high and low there was, all authorities agree, no middle class; and consequently a dearth of the virtues for which this class stands".

Corkery illustrates his account with extracts from eighteenth-century Gaelic poems, contemporary observers and later historians; he adds subliminal vignettes of the traces of a murdered civilisation ("broken abbeys, roofless churches, battered castles, burnt houses, deserted villages . . . still raw, gaping, sun-bleached, not yet shrouded in ivy or weathered to quiet tones"), the land itself ravished by the planters, "its half-felled woods hanging like dishevelled garments about it."[35] He does not claim this as an original contribution to social history; he states clearly that it is drawn from the standard authorities. "The facts here gathered are the commonplaces of the social history of eighteenth century Ireland; and the political history of the period explains the causes of the whole frightful disorder". Corkery imagines his readers asking "This we knew already . . . why therefore do you call it the *Hidden* Ireland?" He explains this poverty was not the Hidden Ireland; it hid it.[36]

Corkery describes the few Gaelic Big Houses surviving in remote districts as oases of peace and plenty, built of local materials in a native vernacular style, nestling into the landscape unlike the pretentious, domineering neo-classical mansions of the Planters, possessing "a sense of historic continuity, a closeness to the land, to the very pulse of it, those Planter houses could not even dream of." Corkery claims their inhabitants, through their patronage of the poets, shared an age-old literary tradition producing "unity of mind between the Big House and the cabin".

> The Gaels in the Big House were one with the cottiers in race, language, religion and, to some extent, culture. Those O'Connells, O'Connors, O'Callaghans, O'Donoghues – all the Gaels – were one, it may be maintained, with the very landscape itself. In the poems and stories written hundreds of years, perhaps a thousand years before, the places mentioned were not fictitious; in those same stories were to be found the names of those ancient families as well, so that to run off the family names connected with one of those houses was to call to vision certain districts – hills, rivers and plains; while contrariwise, to recollect the place-names of certain regions was to remember the ancient tribes and their memorable deeds.

How different it was with the Planters round about them!
For them, all that Gaelic background of myth, literature and
history had no existence. They differed from the people in race,
language, religion, culture; while the landscape they looked
upon was indeed but rocks and stones and trees.[37]

Corkery admits the work of the eighteenth-century poets is "poor
and meagre if compared with what their fathers had created in the duns
of kings and grianans of queens" but calls its emphasis on sound a
legitimate exploration of one aspect of language, praises the new genre
it produced (the *aisling* or vision-poem) and presents its Jacobite sentiments, expressed long after the collapse of the last Stuart challenge, as
the product of desperation rather than academic nostalgia.

Corkery claims the ancient literary tradition whose possession marks
off the poets he discusses from the folk-poets of the same period must
have permeated the whole of Gaelic society in its many centuries of
prestige and development.[38] He adduces as proof the fact that despite
their academic nature the works of the eighteenth-century poets were
memorized and handed down to illiterate native speakers in the contemporary Gaeltacht.

In the summer of 1915, in Kerry, about two miles from Dingle, I
heard an old illiterate woman break suddenly into one of them,
changing, however, not without a twinkle in her eye, a word
here, a name there, to make the poem fit in with the fortunes of
the Great War in its early phase.[39]

Corkery claims that throughout the century as Gaelic Big Houses
decreased in number the poets grew poorer and came to rely more and
more on the people, abandoning the aristocratic pride of Aodhagan O
Rathaille for the democratic outlook of Eoghan Ruadh O Suilleabhain
until oppression destroyed the tradition in the first decades of the
nineteenth century.

The language itself was, of course, decaying, declining everywhere almost into a *patois*, and the learning that it enshrined
was shrinking with it, until, in the end, a true peasant's brain
could easily comprehend it. At last we can find no difference
between the songs written by the unnamed poets of the folk
and those written by the true successors of the fili, either in
thought or diction ... their patriotic songs are no better than
the same sort of songs ... the Irish people were beginning to
write in English.
    The Bardic Schools have now been closed for over two cen-
turies, the Courts of Poetry meet no more. The Gaelic literary

tradition is slowly making an end. A poet here and there arises and, stirred by a local catastrophe – as Maire Bhuidhe Ni Laoghaire (Mary O'Leary) by the agrarian troubles of 1822 in West Cork, strikes out a song full of fire and vigour – or emulous of the men of old, writes patiently a few verses in a bardic metre; but the literary tradition is no more, for it has lost the power of creating new forms. . .

The real Courts of Poetry, we may be sure, faded away gently, the poets in one district after another dying out. In some hidden spot, it is likely, some long-established Court did out-live all others, not knowing itself to be the last; on some wintry night, perhaps, its few remaining old gabblers of verse rose up and bade each other good-night, thinking to meet again, think-ing a vain thought. The strange thing would be if, in breaking their little gathering that night, it was given to them to know that it had fallen to their humble and withered labouring hands to roll up for ever the Druidic scroll of the bards, that in closing the door that night they were leaving "the booths of the poets" to desolation for evermore; had that thought struck them one imagines they could hardly have survived the vast and lonely wailing that must have begun to re-echo in their souls.[40]

The Hidden Ireland was well-received when it appeared in 1924, and has remained in print ever since; but it is full of weaknesses. The "propulsive force" of Corkery's evocation, his references to contempo-rary Gaeltacht life, the absence of a chapter on scribes and manu-scripts,[41] the use of anecdotes about extempore composition[42] led readers unfamiliar with Gaelic literature and susceptible to romantic ideas about the Gaeltacht to overlook the distinctions between the pre-con-quest tradition, the eighteenth-century writers, and the folk-tradition.

Corkery claims the tradition of the bardic schools must have reached the whole community because they existed for centuries and enjoyed high status; yet by his own account they were highly exclusive, involved elaborate training and used a special literary language. Corkery explains the aristocratic contempt for the mob expressed by Aodhagan O Rathaille by claiming the tradition only developed a democratic consciousness during the eighteenth century.

If the whole Irish-speaking nation shared the tradition, why did it die while the language survived? Why did the old woman in 1915 not compose a new poem instead of adapting an old one? Why did a separate folk-poetry develop if the whole nation shared the literary tradition? Why were the complex Middle Irish bardic poems not trans-mitted to the twentieth-century Gaeltacht? Could it be that the eight-eenth-century poems were remembered, not because of what they retained of the bardic tradition, but because of what they had in common with the folk-poetry? Why did the tradition not adapt to new circumstances and ideas, find its way into print like other nineteenth-century European vernaculars?

The *Hidden Ireland* soon became a focus of disagreement between Corkery and his former protégés, O'Connor and O Faolain. This tension began to appear when the young men came back to Cork for their 1924 Christmas holidays. They had experienced defeat in a way Corkery had not, were irritated at his continued involvement in Republican politics,[43] and chafed at his view that the writer should spend his life renovating the civic culture of the place where he was born. O Faolain was horrified by the experience of life as a provincial schoolmaster in Ennis and wanted to escape to a fuller life.[44] O'Connor unintentionally made Corkery look foolish in a discussion of Liverpool Cathedral.[45] (Corkery had developed an interest in architecture during the rebuilding of Cork; he wanted the City Hall rebuilt in a style based on Irish vernacular architecture rather than the classical style).[46] A few days before Christmas, Corkery and O Faolain were walking through the city centre when they saw *The Hidden Ireland* in a book shop window. Corkery had not known it was on sale; he bought O Faolain a copy.[47] He may have hoped to win back the younger men by his exposition of the spirit behind the national revolution; instead, he brought their differences to a head.

In *The Irish Statesman* of August 22 1925 Corkery hailed the mediaeval love songs reprinted by T.F. O'Rahilly as *Danta Gradha* as products of "a society which lacked neither culture nor the poise of mind which goes with it", which had not been available to his generation when they were students knowing only the folk-poetry of the later Gael.[48] O Faolain wrote to the *Statesman* using Corkery's review to attack educationalists and revivalists who wanted to impose the "uneducated peasant tradition" of the contemporary Gaeltacht on modern Ireland "which is already in the European current" and calling for a revival of the historic, cultured and intellectual tradition of eighth-to-seventeenth-century Gaelic Ireland. O Faolain does not explicitly include Corkery in his criticisms (he notes Corkery's statement that the eighteenth-century poets are inferior to their ancestors of the intact tradition) but Corkery cannot have been pleased to see the eighteenth century dismissed as "the fag-end of Irish intellectual tradition".[49]

Corkery grew concerned as O'Connor and O Faolain moved into the Dublin literary circle around the *Irish Statesman*, which he distrusted as cosmopolitan and unnational. At Christmas 1925 he wrote to Curran:

> The backwater is very dull. However both Frank O'Connor and Sean O Faolain are now returned having tasted foreign fruit – Ennis, Wicklow and Dublin. They're terrible boys. I'm afraid Frank O'Connor is becoming a Dubliner – as if we hadn't plenty of them.[50]

O Faolain noticed that when he called, Corkery no longer invited him into the house but talked with him at the open door.[51]

The only full-scale dispute between Corkery, O'Connor and O Faolain took place in *The Irish Tribune*, established in March 1926 as a nationalist alternative to *The Irish Statesman* by an alliance of Cork Republicans and dissatisfied Free Staters led by Alfred O'Rahilly.[52] Corkery was a regular contributor during its nine months' existence; he became literary editor in a staff reshuffle after the editor, L.P. Byrne, was dismissed for incompetence in June 1926.[53]

On June 18th the *Tribune* published an article by Hendrick "The Heart Has Its Reasons" declaring the Republican cause transcended mere reason, and an essay by Corkery, "A Landscape in the West". Corkery described the deserted estate of an Anglicised Gaelic landed family, dotted with the ruins of improvements built by one of the family under the inspiration of O'Connell and Young Ireland, and said these improvements came to nothing and the family ultimately disappeared because the man was not prepared to do what the spirit of the nation demanded – "re-establish contact with the mind of his fathers".[54]

The next issue contained a letter from O'Connor accusing Hendrick and Corkery of sentimentalism and muddy thinking. He expressed sympathy for Corkery but claimed he allowed emotion to outrun understanding. O'Connor denounced the mediaevalism of *The Hidden Ireland* as the product of a mind left high and dry, said if the nation did not accept such services as the landlord offered (whatever his tradition) it had only itself to blame if it was left in poverty, and declared the national tradition was not static but the ever-growing sum of national experience, built up by individual contributions and of value insofar as it was acted upon by intellect to create a national philosophy.[55]

Corkery replied that his article was not a mere effusion of sentiment but an appeal to contemporary rich men who had been caught up and inspired by the national movement but fell away in the subsequent reaction. He swept aside O'Connor's distinction between "national tradition" and "national philosophy" without bothering to understand it:

> I can see he has a very immature mind from the fact that having, by implication, given such wrong answers, he blandly writes: "The truth is that we need our national tradition in the making of our national philosophy". If Mr. O'Connor had more control of himself he could, in the light of that statement, have answered those questions correctly. Then, however, he would not have written his letter.[56]

O Faolain entered the controversy with a letter denouncing Corkery as the product of a narrow Ireland fearful for its own safety. He proclaimed that Ireland did not have an intact national tradition, but the makings of one, and that "my generation, which is not Mr. Corkery's generation" would give Ireland a tradition finer than anything contemplated by the likes of Corkery.[57]

O Faolain followed up with a series of articles on the language problem which claimed the language was of value only as a link with the Gaelic past; he called on universities to teach the literary language rather than the contemporary vernacular, which he dismissed as a peasant *patois*, and claimed the money spent on Irish-language summer schools and teacher training would be better spent editing Irish manuscripts and encouraging competent Irish-language novelists. He claimed, bizarrely, that by praising "the decadent drivel of the eighteenth century" *The Hidden Ireland* had done "more to retard Irish education than three centuries of foreign rule".[58]

Aodh de Blacam responded that *The Hidden Ireland* had established the ground rules for future discussion of Irish literature by showing it was a mediaeval literature.[59] O'Connor interposed that while the mediaevalism of *The Hidden Ireland* was a mere fig-leaf covering the literary nakedness of Irish Ireland compared with Anglo-Irish artists like Yeats and Synge the book *was* valuable, not for its principles but for its enthusiasm.[60] Corkery, who had not replied to O Faolain, pounced on the more vulnerable O'Connor: "Some time since I had to point out to Mr. Frank O'Connor that he suffered still from immaturity of mind. Here he's at it again! ... Fools will step in". Corkery declared that national, Christian and mediaeval art are synonymous (presumably because they aim for "intensity") so the *Agamemnon* of Aeschylus can be described as "mediaeval" (which makes the term meaningless[61]).

Thus the only extended exchange in print between Corkery and his rebellious protégés ended in bitterness and incomprehension. Corkery saw them as traitors to the national tradition; they wanted to assert their right to their individual visions of Ireland, and saw the version of "national tradition" purveyed in *The Hidden Ireland* as a stifling fantasy.

In 1938 O Faolain produced a more detailed reply to *The Hidden Ireland* in the prologue to his biography of Daniel O'Connell, *King of the Beggars*. Where *The Hidden Ireland* celebrates anonymous endurance under oppression, fidelity to immemorial tradition as the only hope for the future, *King of the Beggars* celebrates the individual Prometheus leading his people to shake off the slave mentality by defying authority in the name of new ideas from the wider world. O Faolain points out that the Gaelic literary tradition was in fact highly conventional and extremely aristocratic in sentiment.[62] Corkery's picture of the Gaelic Big Houses as oases of peace and plenty is based on praise-poems of the period:

> We may reckon such descriptions as true, for Irish poets were not given to dressing up; they wrote for an entirely local

audience, their own neighbours, who were, of course, as familiar as themselves with the life depicted, an audience, moreover,
not slow of wit or sparing of sarcasm.

Corkery admits eighteenth-century travellers do not mention some
of the activities depicted in these poems, such as chariot races, "steeds
being bestowed upon the *ollamhs* of Fodla", footsoldiers competing in
martial exercises, and "warriors playing at *Fidhchill* of the chessmen";
he attributes their silence to lack of interest in such typically Gaelic
activities.[63] When poets describe the house of a Planter in the same
terms, Corkery sees this as proof that even in the eighteenth century
Gaelic culture could still absorb isolated Planters.

O Faolain shows these descriptions are entirely conventional; the
house of the patron is routinely described as the residence of a hero of
ancient saga, even if that patron is merely a strong farmer or a Church
of Ireland clergyman with antiquarian interests. Moreover, poems
addressed to Ascendancy patrons often explicitly acknowledge their
right to rule. O Faolain denounces the poets as shoddy-genteel
lickspittles, writing conventional paeans to masters who despised them,
confining their resentment to clandestine patriotic songs, insisting with
increasing vehemence on their superiority to the swarming masses of
the poor as they sank inexorably downwards.[64]

This polemic is forceful but partly incoherent; O Faolain simultane-
ously declares the people never took the poets seriously and praises
O'Connell for freeing the people from the paralysing influence of the
poets.[65] Recent scholarship gives a fuller picture of the poets and their
milieu. Michelle O'Riordan has shown that the pictures of the poet as
conscious rebel keeping alive the memory of the Gaelic past or insincere
chanter of conventional praises are both anachronisms. Mediaeval Gaelic
society, like other mediaeval societies, saw itself as essentially static; the
task of the poet was to make sense of change by explaining it in terms of
the past. Poets writing before the Tudor reconquest wrote indifferently
for Gaelic and Norman patrons. The actions of a Gaelic nobleman were
justified by associating them with similar deeds by legendary heroes; a
Norman patron might be given a fictitious Gaelic ancestry or reminded
that the Gaelic aristocrats he displaced themselves ruled by right of
conquest. The poets lost status when the old society was destroyed
because the new conquerors did not want the sort of legitimation the
poets offered their predecessors.[66]

Why did the Gaelic literary tradition survive so long after the defeat
of its original patrons? O Faolain destroys Corkery's claim that it
sustained itself by turning to a democratic audience without explaining
why it survived so long if it was as useless as he maintains. Professor
L.M. Cullen and Dr. Lyne have provided the answer. Both Corkery
and O Faolain assume the Gaelic aristocracy were almost entirely

dispossessed and the Penal Laws reduced Irish Catholics to a homogeneous mass of poverty-stricken peasants with no middle class. In fact, while the Penal Laws remained an arbitrary instrument of terror, they were not fully enforced; a numerous class of large tenant farmers descended from the Gaelic aristocracy survived as middlemen between the new proprietors and the poverty-stricken masses described by Corkery's sources. It was this class who acted as patrons to the eighteenth-century poets, continuing the traditions of their ancestors; their displacement or Anglicisation towards the end of the century brought about the extinction of the tradition.[67]

There is some evidence of peasant deference to the remnants of the old aristocracy as "princes of a people involved in a common ruin"[68] (though Corkery's picture of the Gaelic Big Houses radiating patriarchal benevolence is an exaggeration; all landed aristocrats live off their tenants and the Gaelic Irish were no exception) and the folk-poetry of the period contains millenarian hopes of deliverance; but the eighteenth-century poets cannot be taken as voicing the hopes of the people to the extent Corkery believed.

When all this has been said, *The Hidden Ireland* still exercises extraordinary emotional power. The title with its apt ambiguity (the Hidden Ireland was hidden from the eighteenth-century Ascendancy and is hidden from the English-speaking descendants of the Gael) has become a proverbial description of any neglected or evaded aspect of Irish life.[69] Since most discussions of Irish-language literature are carried on in scholarly literature or in Irish, *The Hidden Ireland* remains one of the few works of popularisation available to casual English-language readers; it has introduced many readers with only the vaguest notions of Gaelic culture to the life and work of Aodhagan O Rathaille, Eoghan Ruadh O Suilleabhain, and their contemporaries. Sometimes it merely produces complacent pride, but it has also inspired the acquisition of knowledge and deeper understanding. Artists like Seamus Heaney and Sean O Riada have acknowledged its influence; some readers experience an enthusiasm akin to religious conversion at their first acquaintance with the book.[70] It is questionable whether its emotional power survives a fuller knowledge of the subject. Corkery expected the book would be superseded by greater treatments of its epic theme, and saw himself as fulfilling "the not unnecessary role of *vulgarisateur*", it is not his fault that no better *vulgarisateur* has yet arisen.

One source of this power is an old-established tradition of literary response to the Gaelic past. In the early nineteenth century poets like Mangan and Callanan produced a distinctive Irish version of the Romantic image of the poet whose inspiration dooms him to destruction in a heartless, materialistic world; they looked back to the assured social position of the poet in Gaelic society, and presented themselves as bards outlawed by the conquest. Like these writers, Corkery drew on the poets' denunciations of the settlers as boors ignorant of poetry to contrast the aesthetic sensitivity of the Gael with the moral blindness of the Planter and contemporary society. His account of the Whitechurch Court of poetry denounces the eighteenth-century "Cromwellian-Williamite city of Cork . . . very busy with putting money in its purse" in terms reminiscent of his *Leader* attacks on contemporary Cork.

> Now that both are such old stories, what one thinks is that it was Whitechurch rather than the city of Cork that had the seed of life within it. That unnative Cork had no past, and was destined to have no future. Its memory is not fragrant; it left no memorials: but to raise the eyes, as I do now, to that wind-swept hamlet on the far-off hillside, is to feel the heart grow warm and the pulse quicken.[71]

The complexities of Corkery's response to the Gaelic past are best seen in his chapter on Brian Merriman. Corkery is shocked at Merriman's lack of decorum but registers the power of the poem.

> The gifts that were his to lay before us the intellect relishes and wishes to retain. . . .
> Taim in achrann daingean na mbliadhnta
> Ag tarraing go trean ar laethibh liaithe.
> In such lines – and he has a number of them – we are conscious of the type of mind that wrote "A Bhean Lan de Stuaim" in the seventeenth century, and "An Cailleach Beara" in the eleventh. This note of devastating bleakness is more truly Gaelic than the soft lyrical tones of Eoghan Ruadh O Suilleabhain.

Corkery accordingly tries to explain away the attitudes expressed in *Cuairt an Mhean Oiche* by arguing, as he argued in defense of *The Playboy of the Western World* in 1910, that it was an extravaganza bounded by unspoken assumptions taken for granted by the poet and his imagined audience.

> The discussion of the absurd as if it were serious and real, is a very Gaelic aptitude, so noticeable that the well-travelled John Synge was likely to think of it as having ousted every other aptitude from that mentality.

Finally Corkery claims Merriman did not observe the decorum of the literary tradition because it was no longer available to him; even had he crossed the Shannon to the old haunts of the Maigue poets, Merriman could have found no ferryman to take him across the wide, dark river of years which "divided him from the bright company which drank and chorused in Sean O Tuama's hostelry in Croom of the Merriment". Instead, he went to Limerick City and the alien town stifled his muse.

> Did he really think to make fame or fortune there as a teacher of mathematics? Or did he nurse the hope of returning to his native places among the Gaels to ease his much-enlightened soul of melodies; putting off that return, however, not noticing how strong is the grip of the years, how violently they draw one on to the days of greyness? There is, surely, after all, more tragedy in his life than in that of Eoghan Ruadh O Suilleabhain; tragedy less flamboyant, certainly, yet, perhaps, as surely springing from some central weakness in himself.[72]

Corkery seems to be projecting his own artistic predicament onto Merriman. When he first visited the Gaeltacht in 1909, Corkery met old people who had seen Maire Bhuidhe Ni Laoghaire (d. 1845).[73] Only one long lifetime separated Corkery from the last remnant of the literary tradition, but no more than his Merriman could he return across the dark river of years which separated him from the intact Gaelic tradition. *The Hidden Ireland* was conceived as an epic celebrating the force behind the triumphant Irish Revolution; in 1924, with the Gaelic League in decline (from 819 branches in 1922 to 139 in 1924)[74] it seemed an elegy for a world that might be lost forever, as Corkery tried to restate the ideals of the Gaelic League for a new generation in his struggle against "The Literature of Collapse".

CHAPTER SIX

THE LITERATURE OF COLLAPSE 1924–31

The Gaelic League had shaped the life of Daniel Corkery and he had seen Ireland transformed by revolutionary idealism. He believed the two merged in one great national awakening, as yet inarticulate but so overwhelming no-one of any sensitivity could encounter it without sensing its power. Those who opposed it must be morally deformed, so dehumanised they could not recognise the promptings of their Irish heart or consciously repressed those promptings.

Corkery denounced "simple-minded bishops of both churches, hot-headed local politicians, philistine editors of local papers and . . . other odds and ends of a dead past" who disputed the possibility of reviving the Gaelic tradition *en bloc*.[1] He jeered at the readers of the *Irish Statesman* as "bank clerks, government officials, tennis-players" who dreamed of English suburban pleasures even when they "found themselves faint and falling in the dry wastes of Aspiration" during the War of Independence, and now revelled in their New Jerusalem. He pointed to the triumph of nationalism over internationalist communism in Italy as proof the world moved on despite West British self-congratulations[2] (though an outraged fascist wrote to the *Irish Statesman* protesting that Corkery libelled Mussolini by presenting him as a woolly sentimentalist creating a homely folk-state, rather than a hardheaded Renaissance condottiere).[3]

Corkery was all the more horrified to find the Civil War brought a reaction against romantic nationalism in literature as well as in life. Corkery recognised the crudity of most of the nationalist literature poured out during the independence struggle, but expected its sentiments would find finer expression when sifted by reflection. Instead, he saw Yeats and AE support the Treaty while veteran romantics fell silent like Alice Milligan or went into exile like Joseph Campbell. (In America Campbell wrote bitterly to a friend accusing Yeats and AE of betraying their inspiration for "the fleshpots" and saying only the "modest, heroic" Corkery remained faithful).[4] New writers appeared who emphasised the violence and horror of the struggle in works ranging from cheap sensationalism for the English market to honest explorations of the cost of conflict. Even old acquaintances from the CDS were caught up in the trend; Corkery denounced a novel by J. Bernard MacCarthy which presented an idiot as the typical Gaelic Leaguer,[5] and criticised *Break O'Day* by Con O'Leary which tried to satisfy both Irish and British audiences by endowing its anti-hero with all the vices attributed by the British to the IRA while emphasising he is not a real IRA man and portraying the real IRA as chivalrous heroes.[6]

In a 1927 essay Corkery denounced the whole phenomenon as "The Literature of Collapse" and wondered whether defeated Germany had experienced the same "cinematic, violent, crude, feminine, cattish, mean" denunciations of national ideals in the name of "the ideals of the daily press, of the average middle-aged man with a stake in the country . . . an ever-increasing volume of words which the historian must later on learn to read backwards if the real temper of the time described in its pages is to be come upon".

Corkery declared that not only were "the novels, the plays, the polemical writings, the reminiscences that have been written in Ireland over the last three or four years" false, but authors and audience must know in their hearts they were misrepresentations:

> In *The Shadow of a Gunman* a poet plays the coward. Poets have – even in our own time, our own land. But really the trumpets that sung to 1916 and all that followed, one seems to recollect that they took whatever was going in the way of executions, hunger-strikings, imprisonments as well as the rest. One protests, for the simple reason that the poet in the little play is there as poet, as a type. . . .
>
> During the seven years from 1916 to 1923 the Irish nation went through a spiritual crisis so intense that only quite a small number of its individuals was not called upon to share in it. The intensity was to be measured not so much by the sacrifices made as by the spirit in which they were made. The death-words of boys, as well as the testimonies of brave enemies who saw them die, are on record. But who that lived through those years needs to be reminded of that spiritual crisis, its intensity, its high-mindedness?. . . These novels have been sent all over the world, the plays have been staged in alien capitals, the political writings reviewed and commended as the last word in frankness. These are the famous books. Other books may have been written, published and thrust aside, or may have been written and never published at all, not being according to market place requirements; but who is courageous enough to suggest that these shy and halting voices may be the true voice, the true record of the new Ireland that has indeed emerged from all the pother?

Why, to suggest as much is to declare that Ireland, the nation, is not sure of itself, looks about timidly, asks itself what is real, what is unreal, and is unable to lift its voice above the timid song of the tit-lark . . . to suggest that all those loud-voiced books that have gone screaming through the world are spurious, are notorious, have in them neither the depth of art nor the courage of art, nor the truth of art. To hold such views is indeed to be heterodox, for . . . those screaming books we are thinking of have been crowned not only by the highest-browed critics in the country, but by the editors of metropolitan and provincial newspapers, and magistrates have quoted them from the bench![7]

Elsewhere Corkery produced more detailed critiques of two writers whom he saw as exemplifying the "Literature of Collapse", Liam O'Flaherty and Sean O'Casey. The selection of this pair suggests shortcomings in his concept of a "Literature of Collapse", for their views on the War of Independence differed significantly. O'Flaherty participated in the protest against *The Plough and the Stars*, declaring that artists should sympathise with the Easter Rising as a heroic gesture. While O'Flaherty emphasises the mindless instinctual violence of the struggle, he does so not to condemn it but to praise it for stripping away bourgeois humanitarian illusions and preparing the way for the rule of a new aristocracy selected by Social Darwinism.[8] This sinister, quasi-fascist interpretation of the War of Independence was profoundly alien to Corkery; but though he despised such "efforts at curdling the blood . . . with whirling adjectives" as *The Informer* ("the cheapest form of melodrama") he praised the lucid bleakness of O'Flaherty's animal stories and admired the portrayal of instinctive love between mother and child in the story "Mother and Son". "The little story is tenderly and beautifully told, and the author of it has the root of the matter in him".[9]

Corkery never felt the slightest respect for Sean O'Casey. He said the Abbey ceased to be a National Theatre in 1922, when it first produced *Shadow of a Gunman*. Corkery attended Abbey performances of O'Casey plays, looked at the applauding middle-class audience, and despised O'Casey for pandering to their prejudices:

To sit among the audience in the Abbey Theatre when one of . . . Sean O'Casey's plays is on the stage is to learn how true it is that the single blot is, *with great gaiety*, attributed to the whole people. To remain silent in the midst of that noisy gaiety, even to fling brickbats about, against it, is, one thinks, to avoid the deeper vulgarity.[10]

Corkery despised O'Casey's attacks on romantic nationalism. "His only philosophy is that sort of humanitarianism which is ready to wound the spirit of man for the sake of a laugh but will protest tragically if anyone else wound the flesh of man for the sake of an idea".

His revulsion against O'Casey was aesthetic as well as political. Corkery saw O'Casey used plot elements from music-hall farce and melodrama "such as the old Queen's Theatre used to specialise in"; he saw, and despised it. He accused O'Casey of sacrificing the development of plot and character for easy laughs and linguistic self-indulgence: "shapelessness . . . one can find no trace of a central ardour at work upon the style of it."[11]

Corkery declared the future of Irish drama belonged in the Synge tradition of the peasant play as carried on by T.C. Murray. He hailed the blend of naturalism, Catholicism and lyricism in *Autumn Fire* (1926) as proof Murray had achieved complete mastery and a foretaste of greater triumphs to come:

> Because he has now perfected his craft, Mr. Murray often achieves
> a sort of hidden tension – the very stuff of drama – that Synge
> only rarely reached and Sean O'Casey knows nothing of.[12]

This prediction was not as far-fetched as it seems now, when Murray is remembered (if at all) for *Autumn Fire* (which in fact was followed by a long slow decline in the quality of his work) and *Maurice Harte*, an earlier play about a clerical student without a vocation driven mad by the pressure of family expectations. In the 1920s Murray was one of the most popular Abbey dramatists and even observers who did not share his outlook acknowledged his power. Sean O'Casey told Joseph Holloway he did not like to watch Murray plays because their unrelieved tragedy affected him too deeply; he inserted humorous touches into his own plays as relief.[13] Thus Corkery's denunciations of O'Casey for breaking the development of plot and character with laughter express a genuine disagreement over literary decorum, though Corkery obscures this by refusing to admit O'Casey has any case at all.

Nevertheless, Corkery tried to produce a sustained response to the "literature of collapse" by articulating in a new collection of stories his own response to the national struggle and its cost, and by reassessing the whole tradition of Irish literature in English around the figure of Synge. In 1910 Corkery held up Synge as the model for a mature Irish literature in English;[14] he still placed his hopes on the Synge tradition as represented by Murray, but he saw O'Casey also drew on Synge. ("The influence of Synge is all over *The Plough and the Stars* as far as the women are concerned.")[15] What weaknesses in the Anglo-Irish literary tradition produced "the literature of collapse?"

The Stormy Hills (1929), Corkery's third collection of short stories, is generally seen as his best. Even Frank O'Connor, increasingly at odds with his old mentor, hailed him as "our best story-teller", the model for the next generation of Irish writers, giving dignity to the anonymous people of an outlawed nation.[16] The most notable dissent, by Sean O Faolain, accuses the collection of "feminine" worship of strength and peddling a romanticised picture of peasants suspiciously resembling the Strong Silent Englishman.[17]

The book certainly has flaws; O'Connor noted some stories were over-schematic and several plots implausible, but remarks significantly: "One may believe or not that such a thing happened, but one is forced to believe that if it happened, it happened so . . . The parallel with life may not be close, but it is exact". O Faolain is judging symbolist art by naturalist criteria, and ignores the note of bleakness which qualifies the romanticism of the book.

> My generation know few happier experiences than this. To return in the height of summer to some far-away Irish-speaking district, to bathe in the local river or sea after the long spin on cycle or in motor-car, to stroll in to the nightly reunion in the college – usually a modest building with felt or corrugated iron roofing – and there to shake hands with half a countryside . . . (to hear the local seanachie recite) a long tedious tale maybe, but I was perfectly content with myself, as who would not, escapted from the hustling, hard and noisy world into a quiet valley of folklore and magic.

Thus begins one story, "The Rivals". The sense of being an outsider in the Gaeltacht is familiar, but the desire to escape from an unendurable world is emerging from the earlier project of drawing inspiration from the Gaeltacht to reform that world, and the narrator speaks of his generation, Corkery's generation, in the past tense.

The narrative persona of *The Stormy Hills* is an ageing observer watching the new generation beginning to come into their inheritance. As he fought the reaction against the ideals of his youth, Corkery realised he was no longer young. A lecture on "Corcaig le linn m'oige" delivered in 1925 to UCC students shows awareness that his audience barely remember pre–1914 Cork, let alone the anglicised city of his youth, and tries to make them realise "what the Gaelic League has done for you."[18] Somewhere between 1918 and 1925 his hair turned white.[19] His acquaintances in later life recall him as possessing the misogyny of an old bachelor, speaking contemptuously of women's intellects. Some thought they saw in this attitude a trace of fear. On his visits to the Gaeltacht during the War of Independence he entertained what seems to have been his last thought of marriage. He was attracted to Madge O'Leary, one of the daughters of the house at Gortafludig, a farm three miles from Gougane; but she was twenty and he was forty-two.[20]

Madge O'Leary believed Corkery commemorated this memory in

the story "Nightfall" where old Reen, a widower returned from New Zealand to find himself a stranger in his birthplace, makes a fool of himself by paying clumsy attentions to a girl already engaged to the son of the house, a former IRA commandant newly returned from imprisonment (presumably after the Civil War). When old Reen tries to impress with a display of dancing as he learnt it in boyhood "before decay had fallen on the local traditions" he achieves a moment of glory, but as his aged limbs begin to flounder the neighbours lose interest: "they had seen better dancers at Feiseanna". Thus Corkery unobtrusively links the trimph of youth over age with the War of Independence and the Gaelic Revival. Old Reen irritates the young people and becomes the butt of neighbours' mockery; yet even while they laugh secretly together at his folly the young people inarticulately realise the preciousness and vulnerability of love under the weight of years.

Corkery believed the future of Irish culture lay with the farmers; could the victors of the War of Independence create a national culture for a distinctively Irish rural civilisation, or would they fail and see the new rulers of the land aping England? He looked with annoyance on strong farmers, beneficiaries of the Land War, supporting Cumann na nGaedheal. His last article for *The Leader*, "The Shepherdless", describes Corkery and a friend visiting West Cork for a *feis* and asking the way in Irish from a farmer's young son – who answers in English. At the *feis* Corkery remembers a young singer he once heard on that platform who died a terrible death during the War of Independence. As the crowd disperses the farmer and his son drive by in a cart; someone whispers "He lives now in a castle". (The sight of farmers living in the deserted mansions of the Ascendancy haunted Corkery). Corkery wonders if the farmer will imitate the former owners of the mansion, the only "cultured" people he ever saw, but puts his trust in the memory of the dead singer as symbol of the power of the Gaelic Revival to overcome "any new alien-hearted Ascendancy that may arise or attempt to arise in this land".[21] In the Fianna Fail weekly *The Nation* Corkery criticised government attempts to improve agriculture for telling farmers to save when they were already so tight-fisted they refused to lay out money even for necessary improvements. The farmers must be given a broader outlook on life, taught "the joy of spending".[22]

Corkery encapsulates these hopes and fears in "The Vanishing Spring". The first-person narrator describes a short holiday on the West Cork farm of his friend Dick Donovan, a War of Independence veteran:

> The city, hill-surrounded as it is, was sweltering . . . It was now the second week in August, and since the beginning of July no rain had fallen to cleanse its sewers. The river, too, was smelling, and my work took me in and out of the dismal

slumland through which it flows. If I had not fled it, there was
nothing before me but a breakdown.

This depth of disgust at the city was new in Corkery (only two of the
fourteen stories in *The Stormy Hills* are set in Cork, and one of these
concerns an old woman lost in memories of her rural childhood) but the
country proves an uncertain refuge.

The narrator revels in the beauty of the scenery as Dick Donovan
drives him along the coast to the farmhouse, but soon realises something is wrong. Donovan is glum and listless; he owns the biggest farm
in the neighbourhood (his own people's land merged with his wife's
inheritance after her two brothers died in the War of Independence) but
it is no better cultivated than the surrounding countryside. Mrs. Donovan
is highly-strung; they have been married several years and the house is
too big for the couple and their few old servants. One evening as they sit
on a headland with their guest watching a liner pass by, she tells her
husband they should buy more land. When he demurs she snaps at him
that any old woman knows *her* people never looked at a field but they
ploughed it; Donovan leaves abruptly to go to a calving. Later the
narrator joins him; they walk along the headland of Fylenashouk and
Donovan pours out his confused fear that his childlessness is a punish-
ment for past land-hunger and present wealth. That night the narrator
cannot sleep; the moonlight which formerly delighted him now
reminds him how it shone on the agonised face of his friend on
Fylenashouk.

The narrator is to leave the next morning. He had noticed Donovan's
wife seemed unusually happy for the past few days "as if there were
some fount of joy within her" but as he takes his leave he notices
Donovan also seems cheerful. The narrator is puzzled until some days
later he receives a letter from Donovan talking of the scenery and listing
improvements he means to undertake. Thus, Corkery implies, after the
post-war interlude of doubt and despair the triumph of nationalism
will allow the cultivation and development of Ireland, the untilled field;
even the narrator, among the stinking slums, finds consolation in the
thought of the new life ripening in the countryside.

The story does not work well as a story, despite some memorable
passages. Corkery sacrifices plausibility to the demands of his allegory;
the suppressed bitterness between husband and wife conflicts with the
denouement. Despite this, the story shows a greater maturity than his
non-fictional discussions of the same subject; by admitting a certain
amount of post-revolutionary guilt and confusion is natural (however
irrational) Corkery gives his view of Ireland an authority absent from
his denunciations of "the Literature of Collapse".

This maturity gives *The Stormy Hills* its lasting power. An awareness
of loss underlies all the stories from the exuberance of "The Lartys", a

celebration of "the joy of spending" where heroic energy and imagination make apparent disaster the material of fresh triumphs in a different sphere, to those stories where Corkery more directly than in his non-fictional writings confronts the possibility that the national revival might fail, that the age-long crushing effort needed for political mobilisation had destroyed the cultural resources needed to underwrite political triumph. In "Carrig-an-afrinn" the old peasant who left the rocky hill-farm of Carrig-an-afrinn to buy the rich, neglected lands of Dunerling East and spent a lifetime reclaiming his new farm (working his wife and elder children to death or madness in the process), now in old age surrounded by his surviving children (their different professions representing different aspects of the new Ireland raised from the clay in living memory by the determination of the peasant) finds meaning for his life and consolation for his guilt in the thought of the Mass-rock on his old farm, just visible in the distance from one corner of Dunerling East. He does not know the Mass-rock has been blasted away to widen the road. In "The Wager" the Gaelic horseman Sean O'Brosnan, forced to risk his life on a drunken whim of his masters can only triumph over his oppressors by hurling to its death the Master's favourite horse – *his* favourite horse which he trained, which trusted him so much it would obey his most dangerous commands. In "A Looter of the Hills" an old woman living with her mentally-handicapped son (a casual labourer) in the Cork slums withdraws into memories of her country childhood after she suffers a stroke and goes blind. Her talk arouses the curiosity of her lane-born son who begins to explore the countryside, bringing back country smells on his clothing, imitating country sounds for his mother, giving her blossoms, hedgerow branches, even a live lamb. In the end he steals a horse and cart to take her back to her native valley; pursuing friends find the bewildered fool sitting in the cart beside his mother who lost consciousness at the sound of her native river, never to reawaken. We are told the son will find consolation in fresh countryside ramblings; Corkery seems to suggest that even if the Gaelic tradition cannot be regained it is better to have drawn consolation from its remnants than never to have seen beyond the Cork slums.

Though they all have striking descriptive passages, "A Looter of the Hills" is the only one of these stories where execution matches design. "The Wager" fails because unlike "The Ploughing of Leaca-na-Naomh" which it reworks (note the contrast between Sean O'Brosnan, who survives through ancestral pride, and Liam Ruadh) it does not emphasise the bond between horseman and horse enough to bring home to the reader the desolation of the victor. "Carraig-an-afrinn" is often praised, but although it *tells* of the harshness which overawes the surviving sons as the half-crippled old man recalls how he worked wife and elder children to death, and the gross peasant language which shocks their more developed sensibilities, Corkery's sense of literary decorum does not allow him to *show* these and thus shields the reader from the full shock of their coexistence with the emotions stifled in the struggle to reclaim the land and only saved from extinction by his inarticulate reverence for Carrig-an-afrinn.

It is often said Corkery was unaware of the survival of pre-Christian beliefs among the peasantry, seeing them merely as creatures of simple piety; in fact he was aware of these beliefs but saw them either as prefigurings of Christianity, implanted in human nature by the hand of God[23] or sinister half-held superstitions held in check by a central, reticent Catholic faith. In *Synge and Anglo-Irish Literature* he claimed that while the peasants showed lighthearted personal affection (which outsiders misinterpreted as irreverence) for God, Mary, and the saints: "When speaking of the fairies a peasant's face grows desolate and sombre, for to him they are evil spirits. It is only to the poets of Dublin town that the fairies are dainty creatures bright in companionship."[24]

In "The Stones" Corkery explores these beliefs more deeply than he ever wanted to do outside fiction. John Redney, a surly, unsociable old farmer in an isolated glen, is ostracised by neighbours who attribute his petty misfortunes to supernatural disfavour at his evil nature. His resentment accumulates until he accepts the role they have prepared for him. There is a local half-belief that when someone is to die his outline is seen as a rock formation among the stony hills. Redney roams the hills searching for his neighbours' images; when a farmer dies he claims to have seen him in the stones. Despite uneasy, half-sincere scepticism the young men agree to go with Redney; on a remote slope where the images of the dead man's family were traditionally seen, he shows them the unmistakable silhouette. They grow uneasy, "would like to hit Redney" but "that was no part of the bargain". Then someone remembers the Redneys were always seen there, and as the old man turns to go he sees his own image in the stones. Redney goes mad with fear, but does not die; thus Corkery indicates he does not believe the superstition, having allowed his readers to feel what it would be like to believe it.

"The Rivals" also touches on such a superstition as part of its larger comic theme of rivalry between two seanachies, a small sharp-tongued cobbler known as the Dreoilin (wren) and a huge, ungainly stonebreaker. Not even visiting scholars can agree which is the better storyteller, but when the stonebreaker dies of a stroke it seems the cobbler has triumphed.

The local graveyard is far up the mountains; the last stage of the funeral procession involves carrying the coffin up from the road along a steep cattle-track. When this point is reached, a fierce gale is blowing. It is suggested under these circumstances they should change bearers halfway ("Twould be a disgraceful thing if anything happened to the dead") but such a thing was never done before and it would mean stopping at the Giant's Grave, a prehistoric monument half-way up the path. "If ever a Christian corpse had been set down above the earth of the ancient pagan this was not the evening for it, for the lonely pillar-stones standing there, weather-worn and bare, seemed the very heart of all the wind-swept mountain about them." Four big men take the coffin silently and move off followed by the mourners, the Dreoilin scrambling among them "and not one of them but noticed how the wind was singing and whistling, *screeching* was the word used by themselves, in the long brown wiry bog-grass and bog-myrtle". Corkery combines the awed admiration of the mourners, the chagrin of the Dreoilin as his rival's funeral becomes legend before his eyes, and descriptions showing a painter's eye for light to present the funeral as a heroic defiance of elemental powers while never making this explicit (just as such beliefs would be voiced only in a guarded manner). The climb culminates in a set-piece description as the bearers, with a last effort, gain the top of the ridge:

> They were moving along in the shelter of a ledge of rock. It overshadowed them; it was black against the sunlight. When they turned the corner of it, mounting up into the sky, gaining foothold on the ridge, the most simple-minded among the mourners were struck with what they saw. The burden before them, the four bearers, having mounted on the ridge, had all in the glaring white milky light that poured on them, against them, from the southern sky become one curiously shaped moving mass of jet blackness; it was as if a cromlech were marching out before them. There was no sun, only a white dazzling light that seemed to be close up against their very faces, hurting their eyes. They saw the burden take on different shapes, according as one corner or another peaked itself into the sky; and between the moving pillar-like legs dagger-like flakes of sky-brightness flashed on them. And the limbs, the coffin, seemed of vast proportions. Size, movement, blackness, glare! It was that vision that the people of, how someone had whispered: "Wonderful!" – and how each and all of them, as they followed on, took up the word – Wonderful! Wonderful! – whispering it to relieve their excited thoughts!

Then they realise – the crowning glory – all four bearers are relatives of the dead man. Peeping comically between their legs into the grave, the Dreolin is glad to pass unnoticed; a few days later he prepares a list of his biggest relatives, only to be told anyone could put *his* coffin under one arm and run up Mushera without drawing breath. Yet he is not entirely comical; Corkery, like the Dreolin a small sharp-tongued story-teller, makes the little man the first to realise the full grandeur of his rival's funeral and hints he may yet "discover some means of matching the stone-breaker in death even as . . . he had matched him in life".

The story is not unworthy of comparison with Seumas O'Kelly's famous novella *The Weaver's Grave*, to which it is indebted; their differences show the different natures of their authors. O'Kelly's old men are faintly ridiculous, their traditional lore mostly obsolete, and with this awareness of obsolescence O'Kelly portrays life and love renewing themselves in a new generation. There is very little of this in Corkery, but he is more deeply aware of the identity problem created by the destruction of Gaelic civilisation, the loss of the language, the presence of an outside audience unfamiliar with Irish life; his works are full of subliminal hints at hidden layers of meaning, carefully-worked atmospheric evocations, allegorical undercurrents, giving them a complexity foreign to O'Kelly's pastoral strain.[25]

There are broader references to Anglo-Irish literature in "The Wager", and the last story of the collection, "The Priest". "The Wager" reverses all the nineteenth-century stories of droll servants cheerfully performing hair-raising feats at the whim of their noble masters; here it is the servant who has the contemptuous self-control of an aristocrat, while the masters are drunken hobbledehoys in crumbling finery and physical decay – "he put his blob of a hand on Sean's shoulder". The central character of "The Priest", Father Reen, whose name recalls the Colonial of "Nightfall" (the first story in the collection) is modelled on Canon Sheehan of Doneraile. His parish, like Doneraile, lies on the fringe of the North Cork mountains and includes a remote mountainy area; like Canon Sheehan, Father Reen has a little garden beside his presbytery where he passes spare hours in meditation.[26] Corkery respected Canon Sheehan though he believed his work was flawed; shortly before his death in 1913 the Canon heard of the Cork Dramatic Society and expressed a desire to meet Corkery and T.C. Murray, but they were too shy to call on him.[27] In 1923 Corkery wrote an article regretting Sheehan had not lived in Cork City, where he might have founded a local school of writers[28]; now, with his own attempt to found such a school frustrated by the defection of O'Connor and O Faolain, Corkery used Sheehan to exemplify the plight of the Irish intellectual.

Father Reen walks in his garden fretting about his remoteness from the life of his parish:

> but then where in the parish was such life to be come upon as he could profitably make use of?. . . There was, speaking from either social or cultural point of view, neither an upper class nor even a middle-class – there was only a peasant class that had only comparatively recently emerged from penury, a class that needed spurring, that needed leadership, and was not finding it. He had long since reasoned out that the time had come for the building up of a middle class, an upper class too, on native lines to take the place of those that had failed; but

often however as the thought came to him he smiled, for he
certainly was not one of those who gets things put to rights . . .
But it was true he was ageing.

He is summoned to Kilmony, the poorest corner of his parish, where
an old man is dying; he rides there in trepidation, for he never attended
a deathbed in Kilmony which was not tormented by the lust of
property. He sees the poor fields of rock and heather, the farmhouses
separated by miles of wasteland hindering

> the growth of any community spirit, which, of itself, would
> little by little induce a finer way of living. My people! My
> people! he thought, so good, so sinless, even so religious, yet so
> hard, so niggardly, so worldly, even so cruel; and again he
> blamed himself for not starting storytelling, or dancing or sing-
> ing or reading or play-acting – anything that would cut across
> and baffle that lust of acquisitiveness that is everywhere the
> peasant's bane . . . he had unconsciously withdrawn himself
> from them, with those hard ways of theirs.

In the farmhouse he finds the relatives waiting in the outside room,
watching each other, the old man within tormented by their surveil-
lance. After a long struggle Father Reen manages to break the chains
riveted by a lifelong struggle with poverty and reawaken long-dulled
religious sensibilities. As the priest leaves the sickroom a relative jokes
about the length of time it took; he silences the man with a glance, goes
out and rides furiously off, tormented by the thought "My people! My
people!"

Like Martin Cloyne, Father Reen is haunted by a sense of powerless-
ness before the subterranean oceans of vulnerability and suffering which
lie beneath the everyday life of his parish; but his vocation gives him a
means of helping fellow castaways and salving his soul. Corkery saw
the writer, like the priest, as a contemplative trying to give his audience
"a new scale of values" and faced in Ireland with the same problem as
Father Reen and Canon Sheehan – isolation brought about by the
scarcity of writers with the same concerns and the absence of an Irish
reading public. (As Eoin O'Mahony remarked in *The Irish Tribune*, AE
and Corkery both claimed to write for the people but the people
preferred *The Red Spy: A Tale of Land League Days* by D.M. Lenihan.)[29]

> Writing is a horrible business. You always have to force
> yourself to it. Years of toil and scarcely any recompense – an
> odd moment now and then, no more. There is only one sort of
> recompense that really floods one with sweetness. It may come
> like this. You throw out your book for all to handle, to twist and

turn. You know beforehand what they will say, practically all of them. You are disappointed again and again. You say – He! Even *he* sees it like that! You try hard to forget it. Now every book you write is of course to yourself an ugly duckling. There is in every one of them some special virtue. There is not one of them but wears a precious jewel in its head. You know it is so. You set it there. The whole toad, body, head, and all, was composed and set to take it – that jewel. Yet none of your critics see it! But once in a half-century or so – this is how it feels anyhow – someone comes in a says – always diffidently I notice – "Do you know, in that story of yours, there is a thing that I have never seen commented on" – and then out comes a phrase or two that lets you know that some too well-controlled energy of yours, some too delicate perception or reflection or balance, was not after all, as you had begun to think, misplaced or mishandled or inept. But as I say, this happens only once every half-century.[30]

Since Corkery's generation were young the rise of an Irish Catholic literature to match the nineteenth-century triumphs of nationalism and Catholicism had been predicted. These predictions were renewed during the War of Independence, and once again disappointed. In the prologue to *Synge and Anglo-Irish Literature*, written in 1929 though not published until 1931, Corkery tried to explain what went wrong. "I begin by saying there has never been an Anglo-Irish literature" he told Curran.[31]

Corkery argued that while Irish-language literature was unself-consciously Irish, Irish writers in English wrote for a foreign audience; most lived abroad and their treatment of Irish life was "imposed . . . by alien considerations". Thus they ignored or despised the central pieties of Irish life associated with Land, Nationalism and Religion. *Synge and Anglo-Irish Literature* is particularly concerned with their attitude to religion. Stockley told an Australian Catholic paper:

The way the Dublin neo-pagan literary school left Catholicism out of their Ireland has long been on Corkery's nerves – just as, for long, he had fierce thoughts about the Hidden Ireland left out of account by Lecky on Ireland's Eighteenth Century.[32]

Corkery explained the blindnesses of Anglo-Irish literature by its history. The first Irish writers in English saw themselves as Englishmen living in Ireland; as the Ascendancy became more conscious of their situation they produced "colonial" writers who exploited the quaint habits of the natives for "normal" English readers. Corkery notes some characteristics of the "colonial mould"; the use of an English traveller as catalyst for explanations of Irish life, the preoccupation with the fall of

the Big House. The first Catholic-nationalist writers in English copied
these conventions, the only model available to them, in their attempts to
express Irish national concerns; therefore, although their work lived
"by Irish suffrage" (whereas true Colonial literature, not written for an
Irish audience lived "by English suffrage") it was neither good art nor
an adequate expression of Irish life.

Corkery claimed the Colonial mould maintained its dominance over
Irish literature in English, although it became visibly inadequate with
the downfall of the Ascendancy.

> For many years past, Anglo-Irish literature has been sitting
> between two stools. When the land is under the stress of a
> national movement the literature makes an effort to seat itself
> on the truly Anglo-Irish stool – the writers make an effort to
> express their own land; but when it is again at peace, the
> literature returns to the Colonial stool – an attitude that pays
> better – with less work besides, for to 'explore' your own land
> for the foreigner, as Donn Byrne did, is far lighter work than to
> express it to itself, as Charles Kickham attempted to do, how-
> ever clumsily.[33]

Thus *all* Irish literature in English is an exotic, like American literature
before Whitman. Even talented writers sprung from the people, like
Padraic Colum and T.C. Murray, find themselves in an almost impossible situation.

> The difficulty is not alone a want of native moulds; it is rather
> the want of a foundation on which to establish them. Every-
> where in the mentality of the Irish people are flux and uncer-
> tainty. Our national consciousness may be described, in a native
> phrase, as a quaking sod. It gives no footing. It is not English,
> nor Irish, nor Anglo-Irish.[34]

The literature an English child reads and learns at school describes
the familiar attitudes and surroundings of his own culture; the Irish boy
reading English literature learns to regard his surroundings as unfit for
literature, since he does not find the familiar events of his neighbourhood described in the literature he is taught to respect. "No sooner does
he begin to use his intellect than what he learns begins to undermine, to
weaken and to harass his emotional nature . . . So does it happen that
the Irishman who would write of his own people has to begin by trying
to forget what he has learnt."[35]

Nevertheless Corkery claims these intellectual strivers have the root
of the matter in them; they are trying to express something fundamental
to human existence.

> Travelling through our quiet midland solitudes in a railway
> carriage I have often thought how different an experience it
> was from walking intimately in those same places, knowing
> whose the cattle were, what fair was to come or had come,
> whose cottage the spire of smoke was rising from in the
> distance; while all the time the nostrils were filled with the
> breath of the earth and the ears with its stirrings.. the half-
> thoughts, the colour that is in memoried words, the pieties the
> ages weave into the very texture of life, the almost unchanging
> idiom of the fireside, the workshop, the ship, the fields – the
> unchanging idiom that remains beneath the inflow of new
> names, always conquering those new names ... It is such
> essences of the landscape, of the people, of life itself, as will not
> pierce a sixteenth-inch pane of glass that makes the difference
> between national and what is now called international litera-
> ture.[36]

The Ascendancy, on the other hand, could only justify their power
by deadening their sensibilities, twisting themselves with contempt to
stifle their natural attraction to "the teeming life" of the natives and
their customs.

> An alien Ascendancy the artist cannot choose but loathe; it has,
> whether Asiatic or Roman or Spanish or British, always been
> streaked with the vulgarity of insensibility. Such an Ascend-
> ancy is *l'étatisme*, the coldest of all cold monsters – freed of all
> the kindly influences of tradition, set loose not to prey on its
> own people, as it even will, but on its enemy – *l'étatisme* there-
> fore at its most callous, because at its most fearful and frenzied.
> Its spiritual growth, one may say, is from insolence to inso-
> lence. In the end it produces extreme types like Sir Henry
> Wilson, at whom, when they unwisely declare themselves, the
> world wonders.[37]

Some Ascendancy writers renounced Ireland altogether and went
to London. Goldsmith retained his homely memories of Irish life; but
most of those writers found themselves emotionally disabled, unable to
acquire the natural emotions of the English.

> From Sheridan to Shaw they either fell back on intellectual
> brilliancy or perished in the void. Their work, therefore,
> and that of all their kind, as one may understand, lacking those
> emotional overtones which are so precious in literature,
> which are indeed the very touch of nature, have something
> of a dry bitterness in them. One reads them in a sort of fear,

uncertain that inhuman laughter may not at any time assault
our ears.[38]

Other Ascendancy writers stayed in Ireland and wrote of Irish life;
but even those who tried to identify with the people found it almost
impossible to shake off instinctive contempt for the natives and their
pieties.

> Many an Ascendancy writer must have wished to present,
> under the form of art, the teeming life he saw about him; many
> must have believed they had done so. But where now are their
> novels or plays? No-one casts the failure in their face; it was not
> from any want of heart or goodness or intelligence or scholar-
> ship or craft they individually failed; it was that the system into
> which they were born made it impossible for them to succeed.[39]

Thus Corkery explains to his own satisfaction the support of Yeats and
AE for the Treaty and the criticisms of the new state voiced in *The Irish
Statesman*. There were exceptions who grasped the Gaelic tradition;
Standish O'Grady, Douglas Hyde ("of course he became a convert to
nationalism in his very boyhood") and, above all, Synge.

> To show how he stands apart from his fellow Ascendancy
> writers it is but necessary to say that he, an Ascendancy man,
> went into the huts of the people and lived with them.[40]

Corkery gives a brief account of Synge's life, arguing that his youthful wanderings in Catholic Europe saved him from the Ascendancy
view of the native Irish as freakish, and that he should be seen as a
nationalist writer.

> In recent years when, owing to many causes, nationalism has
> been under a cloud in Ireland, we find it hinted that he was never
> a nationalist at all, that he did not believe in the Gaelic League
> idea, and that in fact there was no difference between him and
> other contemporary Ascendancy writers in this matter.[41]

Corkery quotes published reminiscences by acquaintances testifying
to Synge's nationalism, and Yeats' statement that Synge opposed his
proposal to establish a company within the Abbey to perform international drama because he feared it would hinder the development of a
distinctive national drama. Corkery claims Synge's lack of interest in
nationalist politics was typical of Gaelic Leaguers and Irish Irelanders
of his generation who "called themselves nation-builders, not state-
builders", and declares "only for the fact that there was a nationalistic

movement in the land . . . Synge . . . never would have come to write
Riders to the Sea".

He proceeds to a detailed discussion of Synge's works. The section
on *The Aran Islands* (which praises the identification with the islanders
shown by the refusal to mention the physical discomforts Synge must
have suffered) was the first discussion of this book as a work of literature in its own right[42], but the main interest lies in the discussions of the
individual plays. Most of the views expressed are simply expansions of
ideas in the 1910 lecture, but Corkery qualified them in such a way that
the book is usually misread as an attack on Synge and a justification of
the *Playboy* rioters.

The most significant change from 1910 is a devaluation of the *Playboy*, now seen as the source of Sean O'Casey and presented as a transi-
tional work marred by irreverence and linguistic self-indulgence. He
sees Synge as big-hearted and fundamentally naive, drawn to the Aran
Islanders by natural attraction but "troubled with the thought that he
could never become more to the islanders than a stranger (because he
had not realised Catholicism was the key to their lives)", raising over
the abyss "the forlorn wail of the tribeless",[43] a folk-dramatist full of
talent but still groping for deeper knowledge of his subject, and with a
tendency to overvalue the daemonic.

> All artists possessed of strong creative power are of course
> tempted towards the imaginative view of life and art; yet to
> yield to such temptation is for them to create art work not only
> narrow in its range but peculiar. The dramatist vacates his
> throne when he asks us to bring with us to his theatre only one
> faculty, not all. We cannot do so, even if we would . . . Are we
> asked to think that the moment our minds begin to refer phrases
> or incidents or appearances in the play to real life, to things
> actually heard, witnessed, experienced; judging them in the
> light of the play, judging the play by them, our minds are gone
> away, become absent-minded as it were?. . . If in the midst of
> our aesthetic trance we begin to see into the life of things has
> our pleasure become impure?. . . Can we see with all our pow-
> ers yet judge not?. . . If we take teaching to include the desire to
> make new judgements, and, furthermore, the ability to make
> them . . . what the dramatist . . . has to remember is that great
> art cannot help teaching, and for him wilfully to prevent his
> own work of art from doing so is to practise abortion or present
> a maimed child to the world, however wildly hilarious that
> child may be.[44]

Corkery's view of art as an expression of the life of the people
implied the people were entitled to judge it by their own experiences

and beliefs. He quotes a passage from *In Wicklow and West Kerry* which contrasts "healthy movements of art" where "variations from the ordinary types of manhood are made interesting for the ordinary man" with decadent art which confines itself to "the freak of nature" as proof Synge held this view.[45] Corkery believed Synge did not deliberately insult his audience, but misunderstood them for the same reason he misunderstood the Western peasants he loved.

Corkery argued that while Synge sincerely identified with the peasants, the religious indifference he inherited from the Ascendancy led him to interpret their spiritual reticence as paganism and their familiar references to God and the saints as conscious blasphemy and irreverence. Thus Synge wrote the *Playboy* as a paean to what he saw as the free, Dionysiac life of the West without realising a Dublin audience "lacking any intelligent means of expression", unused to the high-spirited banter of the West ("what Catholic literature expresses naturally . . . what their own particular branch of Catholic literature expressed naturally when it was intact and not put upon from without")[46] and irritated by long experience of Ascendancy mockery would take violent offense.

In the same way, Corkery argued, religious indifference kept Synge from recognising the bad taste of *The Tinker's Wedding* or understanding that the audience of *The Shadow of the Glen* might naturally wonder how an Irish peasant woman could leave her husband for another man "without the least trouble of conscience", when to their minds this was the biggest issue in the play.

> It is the old inability of Anglo-Irish literature to deal with the facts. How can the people take serious interest in that literature until the questions that arise in their own consciousness, as they read it, exist also in the mind of those who wrote it?[47]

Nevertheless, Corkery argued, the tragic intensity of *Riders to the Sea*, the gnarled humour of *The Well of the Saints* show Synge had the root of the matter in him. He continually questioned and explored his instinctive responses; *Deirdre of the Sorrows* shows he was entering a new phase. "Synge was not yet the Synge he would be, if only he were to live" – but he died.[48]

In analysing *Synge and Anglo-Irish Literature* it must be remembered Corkery was not condemning Synge but assessing him as a model for future writers; he identifies with Synge to some extent, attributing to him his own exhilaration at the discovery of the Gaeltacht, his own sense of isolation from the self-sufficient folk culture of the Gaelic peasantry. Corkery was more disturbed by Synge's extravaganzas than in 1910, but his moral critique still tried to recognise the legitimate attractions of the Dionysiac, to reconcile Keltar with Fohnam.

When all this is said, his picture of Synge is inadequate even when it is remembered he did not have access to Synge's private papers. The account of Synge's life completely ignores his activities as a director of the Abbey, his contacts with Yeats and Lady Gregory, while drawing at length on Corkery's own experiences to discuss the hypothetical influence of the Irish Ireland movement on Synge. Synge was a nationalist, but he despised the Gaelic League and the Irish Ireland movement; his papers contain fragments of a satire *National Drama: a Farce* which depicts an Irish Ireland debating society meeting to discuss national drama after a visit to the music hall, denouncing Shakespeare and Molière as unnational because immoral, ignoring a member who puts forward Synge's own views on national drama, and breaking up in a mad rush for the pub before closing-time.[49]

Corkery's view of Synge as a naive folk dramatist with no coherent philosophy of life is also based on misunderstanding. Corkery finds most of the plays incoherent because he does not understand Synge's outlook. He ignores the influence of Ibsen visible in *Shadow of the Glen* (and even more prominent in the unpublished 'prentice work of whose existence Corkery was unaware) and the less prominent but weightier influence of Darwin. Corkery attributes to Synge a casual religious indifference seen as typical of the dehumanised Ascendancy. In fact, Synge was brought up as a strict Evangelical Protestant and became a committed atheist in his teens after reading Darwin.[50] The passage where Synge speaks of art making variations from the ordinary types of manhood interesting to the ordinary man has Darwinian overtones which Corkery does not see; the "variation" Synge has in mind is a chance mutation which gives its possessor qualities superior to the rest of its species, thereby increasing its ability to survive and propagate itself. (The "freak of nature" mentioned in the same passage is a chance mutation whose possessor is made inferior and thereby doomed to extinction). Corkery sees Martin Doul and Christy Mahon as "variations" whose failings are set against the broad sanity of everyday peasant life; in fact Synge presents them as superior to the inbred, complacent, avaricious, cowardly, cruel everyday peasants around them. Synge was not trying to articulate a vision of life shared by his audience, as Corkery suggests; he had adopted the "modern" tactic of shocking his audience to unsettle their expectations and make them receptive to his views.

In 1910 Corkery praised Synge as a great artist, *the* model for writers trying to create an Irish literature in English. *Synge and Anglo-Irish Literature* repeats that praise, but the downgrading of individual plays reduces Corkery to appealing to what Synge might have written had he lived. Synge is so diminished he cannot bear the weight Corkery places on him.

Corkery urged writers to express Irish values, but he never clearly defined these values. His ideal of a national literature based on the remnants of the Gaelic tradition and the unchanging idiom of field and workshop did not recognise the outside ideas to which Irish intellectuals were necessarily exposed or the economic and social changes transforming the timeless-seeming world of peasants and artisans, although Corkery himself felt the pressures on Irish writers in English.

In a series of articles on the scarcity of significant Irish nationalist Catholic writers, written between the completion and publication of *Synge*, Corkery discusses these constraints more clearly and with greater sympathy for the writers than in *Synge*. After pointing out that any Irish bookshop contained an overwhelming majority of non-Irish books and recalling his own West British education and infatuation with *The Boys' Own Paper*, Corkery gave a list of forty contemporary Irish writers (almost identical to the better-known list of "wild geese of the pen" in *Synge*). He points out that about half of them came from Catholic backgrounds and most of these went to Catholic schools. "Our colleges, therefore, are producing writers, but the writers they produce write neither Irish nor Catholic books". Some imitated English literature from the start, unconscious of any incongruity; Corkery dismisses these with contempt. Other aspiring writers "such as have not been reared up in *really* respectable homes" imitate nineteenth-century romantic nationalist writers and "flounder about, rurally romantic, writing, or rather rewriting, terribly shapeless and almost endless Irish legends . . . all the more terrible and jejeune-seeming because the actual impact of genuine emotion makes the pen wobble in their fingers as they write." Those who escape these pitfalls begin by writing for local papers, then Dublin papers. At this stage their work is "as Catholic and as Irish as one could expect, remembering their unreal education"; but whether they go abroad or remain at home they soon discover the Irish reading public is not large enough to support them and the English are not interested in Catholic or Gaelic themes. This is not merely an economic constraint:

> Let us look at it from the point of view of the writer . . . if he succeed, it is little less than a miracle if he does, in shutting out all thought of a public beyond the seas, if he write really for his own people, he can expect to be judged only by a set of values which is inept, which has never been sifted, or refined, or never written down at all. To know that such a fate awaits his work is not to be stimulated to high endeavour. Who can blame him if he sometimes feels like saying "I'll write for England. The English know where they are. They have a fixed set of values. They judge all work by the same set of values, whether it be French, German, American or Irish. I can make myself a clear vision of such tests as will be applied to my work. If I fail it will not be from not having pitted myself against worthy competitors in an arena where the rules are known".

I think it is too lightly assumed that all such Irishmen as the
late Donn Byrne, for instance, who take to writing for a non-
native public do so entirely from monetary considerations. I
think the fact that they find themselves drawn towards an
arena where criticism has long, long since found its feet, where
it is stabilised, counts as much with them as money or even
fame. It is only writers themselves who understand what a
help or a hindrance it is, that unknown, that unseen, yet half-
comprehended public for whom one writes.[51]

Corkery therefore argued the Catholic colleges should devote themselves to creating an Irish reading public; but he increasingly suspected
this was not enough. Faced with the reaction against romantic nationalism and the decline of the Gaelic League Corkery mourned that "the
overflow of a stronger and richer neighbouring tradition" so stifled the
Irish national tradition that "moments of vision" like the Irish Ireland
movement achieved very little despite enormous efforts.

In those moments of vision . . . the amount of actual art work
created is only relatively large, and its quantity only relatively
good, for the necessary mental equipment is not at hand; the
slow upbuilding of a native art tradition has not taken place,
scholarship has not been fulfilling its duty during the long
preceding hours of gloom, has neither been examining the
national literary moulds, for instance, nor assessing whatever
art work is natively our own; has failed therefore to play its part
in clarifying, strengthening and equipping the national mind
. . . if one shrinks, as one may indeed well shrink, from the
prospect of a series of nationalistic movements, each and every
one of them using up a large amount of national energy in mere
propaganda, one may begin to understand why Ireland is set
on having a language of its own, not only as an indigenous
method of expression, but as a wall of defence.[52]

By 1931, when Cork University Press published *Synge and Anglo-Irish
Literature*, Corkery had abandoned its central proposition – that it was
possible to create an Irish literature in English. At the Catholic Truth
Conference in October 1930, moving the vote of thanks to Alfred
O'Rahilly for a lecture which complained most Irish literature in
English was infected by modern paganism, Corkery declared they
must turn to the Irish language since it had been impossible to write
Catholic creative literature in English for the past three hundred years.
O'Rahilly, who was not prepared to dismiss the English language
as irredeemably un-Catholic, replied that Irish was not immune to
modern paganism.[53]

Synge and Anglo-Irish Literature appeared as part of the contest between Corkery and O Faolain for the Chair of English in University College Cork which marked the final break between Corkery and his ex-disciples. O Faolain's attacks on Corkery in the *Irish Tribune* were so vehement they can hardly have been on speaking terms afterwards. In September 1926 O Faolain went to Harvard on a Commonwealth Scholarship to study Comparative Philology. He travelled on the same ship as Professor Alfred O'Rahilly, Registrar of UCC, who was about to spend a year as visiting Professor at the University of St. Louis. O Faolain impressed O'Rahilly, who told him he might hope for the Chair of English when Stockley retired.[54]

O'Connor remained in Cork until 1928, but while he maintained contact with Corkery their relations deteriorated further after O'Connor casually remarked he had not realised he could miss his new Dublin friends as much as he had missed his old Cork ones. Corkery despised O'Connor's Dublin friends (Yeats, AE and the *Irish Statesman* circle) as a clique of unnational poseurs. They did not quarrel openly, but Corkery made it plain he had chosen his side in the cultural conflicts of the period, and O'Connor was on the other side.[55] In March 1927 Corkery spoke at a mass meeting called to demand a ban on immoral publications (particularly cheap English newspapers); part of the campaign, opposed by the *Irish Statesman*, which led to the 1929 Censorship of Publications Act.[56]

O'Connor was active in the Cork Drama League, an attempt to revive the Little Theatre Tradition; unlike the CDS, it staged Abbey plays and European drama rather than the work of local amateurs. The European plays were suspected of immorality; there were fierce exchanges between O'Connor and Father O'Flynn of the Cork Shakespearean Society in the letters column of the Cork Examiner. Corkery did not intervene, even when his own name was brought into the dispute.[57]

In 1928 O'Connor moved to Dublin as librarian of the Pembroke Library. Corkery visited him occasionally; O'Connor was horrified to hear him declare Irish writers should not draw on foreign literature because the ancient Greeks had not done so, and complained to Hendrick that Corkery betrayed art for abstract ideas.[58] The final break came in 1931 when O'Connor sent Corkery a signed copy of *Guests of the Nation*, his first collection of short stories. Its emphasis on the darker aspects of the War of Independence, its criticism of Republican ideals in the name of "mere humanitarianism", were exactly what Corkery denounced in the "literature of collapse". He never acknowledged the gift.[59]

In April 1929 O'Connor wrote to Hendrick saying AE had shown him a nine-page letter from O Faolain full of denunciations of Corkery; O'Connor remarked they were at each other's throats and mentioned a Chair of English.[60] In his autobiography O Faolain recalls his alarm as he heard Corkery had been invited to give a series of lectures at UCC and received an Honours MA in 1929 for the thesis later published as *Synge and Anglo-Irish Literature*; he realised Corkery was being groomed for the Chair by supporters within UCC. O Faolain could not take Corkery seriously as a potential Professor; he might have been a useful addition to a fully staffed department, but the UCC Professor was the only member of the Department. So far as O Faolain knew, Corkery's only teaching experience was in primary school. O Faolain had NUI MA degrees in Irish and English and a Harvard MA in Comparative Philology; when the chair fell vacant he had two years' lecturing experience in a Catholic teacher training college in England. Above all, O Faolain had the support of O'Rahilly.[61] Unfortunately, O Faolain underestimated Corkery's qualifications and overestimated the value of O'Rahilly's support.

Since 1908 Corkery had delivered numerous lectures to various societies, mostly in Cork but some in other provincial centres and Dublin; his application for the Chair lists some of the more notable of these lectures and offers a full list if required. (He gives a similar selected list of his articles on English literature). Every year between 1923 and 1928, Corkery lectured in the UCC Irish-language summer schools for teachers. He also gave vacation courses for European students at UCD in 1926 and 1929 and courses for Irish teachers at the Dublin College of Science in 1929 and 1930; he was due to supervise a summer course for vocational teachers (in which he lectured on English language and literature) in June 1931. He had worked for the VEC since 1918 as adult education teacher, then county inspector of Irish, and since 1928 "Irish organiser" in charge of Irish-language adult education in County Cork. He tried to remedy one of his main deficiencies by taking a summer course in Old English at Exeter in 1930.[62]

This could not compare with O'Faolain's qualifications and the references he received from eminent scholars; but UCC was a provincial institution, the majority of the Governing Body were non-academics, and Corkery's literary reputation and local eminence might outweigh O Faolain's qualifications.

The enthusiastic reference Stockley gave Corkery shows the outgoing Professor wanted him as his successor.[63] Stockley may have helped Corkery to prepare himself for the position, but Stockley had little influence within the College. After his defeat O Faolain seems to have suspected O'Rahilly of tricking him into applying for the Chair so as to give the appearance of competition to an appointment decided in advance. This would explain why O'Rahilly did not mobilise significant support for O Faolain; but it is a most unlikely suggestion. Why should O'Rahilly have engaged in an elaborate deception over several years in order to provide a strawman, instead of waiting until the Chair was advertised? (In the event, four candidates besides Corkery and

O Faolain were formally considered for the Chair; three more sent in
applications too late to be considered). Despite their contacts in Cork
intellectual circles, Corkery and O'Rahilly were never particularly close.
Corkery did not share O'Rahilly's interest in theology, while O'Rahilly
was never enthusiastic about the Gaelic League; O'Rahilly's fondness
for religious oleographs offended Corkery's artistic taste.[64] Although
O'Rahilly held the second most important position in UCC and led a
faction loyal to him rather than President Merriman, he had not yet
achieved the dominant position within UCC he acquired in the late
1930s and maintained until the end of his Presidency. O Faolain may
have overestimated O'Rahilly's ability to deliver the chair to him. At
one time in the late 1920s he thought of taking up an academic post in
America. It has been suggested his support for O Faolain was seen as an
attempt to impose an unknown protégé at the expense of a well-known
candidate and provoked an adverse reaction.[65] The limitations of the
Governing Body minutes and the loss of O'Rahilly's papers in a fire
prevent exact knowledge, but it seems likely the hesitancy of his letter
to O Faolain (quoted in *Vive Moi!*) came from indecision and inability to
deliver rather than treachery.

The decision to advertise the Chair was taken on March 13th, 1931;
applications closed on April 27th. Both Corkery and O Faolain can-
vassed vigorously (though in theory this was forbidden). On June 19th
the Governing Body made their decision. They voted twice, after hear-
ing that a non-binding advisory vote of the Academic Council (the
heads of departments) gave Corkery ten votes, O Faolain and Kathleen
Ford receiving three each. On the first vote – a preliminary test of
opinion – Corkery received twelve votes, O Faolain three, Ford two and
Eugene Mullan one. The second vote, which was the basis of the recom-
mendation to the Senate of the National University of Ireland, gave
Corkery fifteen, O Faolain two (O'Rahilly and a Limerick county councillor from the same area as O Faolain's mother) and Ford one. On
August 19th 1931 the Senate appointed Corkery Professor with
effect from October 1st on a salary of £600 per annum increasing by
increments of £400 a year to £800. O Faolain was outraged and resentful, though in later years he said had he got the Chair he would have
had to get out within a few years or go to seed.[66]

Soon after the appointment Corkery and his sister moved to
Ballygroman, Ovens, Co. Cork – away from the city. Corkery was 53,
and his best work was done.

CHAPTER SEVEN

OISIN 1931–64

Corkery had a mixed record as Professor of English. He avoided
Academic Council meetings and allowed the administration of the
Department to fall into confusion. He disliked O'Rahilly's association
with "rugbyites" (i.e. players of foreign games and others uninterested
in the Gaelic Revival) but supported him as President against the Gaelic
scholar Cormac O Cadhlaigh in 1943 because he believed O'Rahilly,
though devoid of culture, was better suited to the position.[2]
Corkery's voice was harsh and did not carry well in lectures. Until
the appointment of two lecturers in the early 1940s he had to cover the
whole course by himself and was lacklustre in discussing writers for
whom he felt no sympathy, such as Pope; but on more congenial writers
he was immensely stimulating. He spoke extempore or from brief
notes, closely analysing the text but emphasising its historical background. He avoided explicit proselytisation for his cultural nationalism, though his views were clearly related to his literary tastes. He
despised the "facile Virgilianism" of Tennyson but praised Browning,
Hardy and above all Wordsworth; former students recall his lecture on
"Michael" with admiration. He praised Wordsworth's use of plain
speech to convey emotion. "Always use the Anglo-Saxon words" he
told his students, "they're the pots and pans of the English language",
and regretted the Anglo-Saxons had not been allowed to develop their
national culture in their own way. This Anglo-Saxonism probably influenced his decision to add Hopkins and Auden to the curriculum. Corkery
also brought the work of T.S. Eliot onto the curriculum. He praised Eliot
for freeing English poetry from the influence of Tennyson, and liked to
quote Eliotic pronouncements about "classicism" and "impersonality"
in support of his own view that the artist should immerse himself in the
life of his nation; but he regretted Eliot had not stayed in his own
country and become the American Dante. (When *Notes Towards the
Definition of Culture* appeared Corkery criticised its dismissal of provincial cultures).[3] Corkery preferred the later Christian poems to *The Waste
Land*; less predictably, he admired *Gerontion*. This touch of
unpredictability recurs elsewhere. He might have been expected to

121

dislike Conrad as a cosmopolitan who deserted his native language; instead he responded to Conrad's atmospheric power (his "richly wrought background"[4]) though he justified his interest by claiming Conrad's mastery of a tongue not his own showed it was possible for native speakers of English to produce literature in Irish. Most remarkable of all, although Corkery despised Yeats as a poseur, derided his early work as "candyfloss", hated and feared his cult of the eighteenth-century aristocracy[5], he recognised the power of the late poems. In *Synge and Anglo-Irish Literature*, speaking of "the note of intensity" (which he described elsewhere as distinctly Gaelic, Christian, nationalist and mediaeval) Corkery remarked;

> Mr. W.B. Yeats has schooled himself since Synge's death in the use of this note; and he alone has really mastered it. Whether there is in the themes he chooses a seriousness fundamental enough to demand its use is another question.[6]

Corkery's students recall his lecture on the "Byzantium" poems as one of his best.

Corkery's strongest point was his relations with students. He did not hide his contempt for some he believed were only there because their parents had money, who disliked being given his philosophy of art when they wanted hard facts to reproduce in examinations. Others were repelled by his caustic remarks and his habit of asking individuals sudden questions to detect inattention; but many found him a stimulating mentor once they got over the shock of finding the author of *The Hidden Ireland* was a small white-haired rosy-cheeked man dragging an emaciated leg. Corkery was at his best in small seminars; students found their confusions firmly but unobtrusively clarified, their range of sympathies extended (though it might take them years afterwards to come to terms with his influence and sort out his ideas from their own). Most professors were remote and unapproachable outside class, but Corkery regularly brought favoured students down to Ovens for tea and discussion; he was anxious to influence the new generation, but found them excessively reverent towards him. ("I have no-one to pull my ideas to pieces" he told Hendrick).

His handling of postgraduates was friendly and informal, perhaps excessively so. He was prepared to accept aspiring postgraduates even if their primary degree was not of the standard normally required for postgraduate work. He encouraged research into Anglo-Irish literature (several theses on nineteenth-century Irish writers in English were presented during his tenure of the Chair) but while he discussed topics raised by their theses with postgraduates, he did not examine the drafts before submission. It was said he was not particularly concerned with the quality of the finished text if he knew "obair macanta" (honest work) went into it; not surprisingly, none of these theses were published.[7]

Corkery himself never tried to develop his academic criticism and give it more permanent form. He had only undertaken *The Hidden Ireland*, after contemplating its theme for more than a decade, because he saw nobody else was doing it. *Synge and Anglo-Irish Literature*, which also reflected long-standing concerns, might never have been written but for the need to acquire academic qualifications before applying for the Chair. The amateurish academic culture of the time, which showed little concern with publication,[8] provided no incentive to expand on insights such as his suggestion that some Irishman should write a study of imperialism:

> It is doubtful if we here in Ireland – ordinary people – can write calmly or wisely about nationhood, for the simple reason that we have not experienced nationhood; we certainly have not experienced normal nationhood ... Now, on the other hand, we obviously have experienced imperialism. We obviously have experienced it in a way no Englishman has. What we might then say about it should be of use. A study of imperialism by an Irishman could be nothing else than a study of Ascendancy – alien Ascendancy, for a country might also of course generate a native Ascendancy. Russia would seem to have done so. I have never seen a study of Ascendancy – a study of how being part of an Ascendancy colours the mind of those who uphold it, as also of those others who suffer it. For instance a study of Spenser, Swift, Castlereagh and such folk – lessening down into shorter chapters on Carson, Sir Henry Wilson, Lawrence of Arabia, St.John Ervine, written for the one purpose of determining what such men had in common in their mutual make-up – should prove an interesting book, for truth to say, it seems impossible that any history of Ireland can have validity unless the writer of it comes to his task with a firm grip of Ascendancy psychology.[9]

This sort of approach was neglected by the newly-developing school of Irish history – but Corkery lacked the intellectual tools needed to develop it himself. His failure to develop those insights was also related to his rejection of English. In his chats with favoured students he used Irish as much as possible, although he spoke it slowly and awkwardly.[10] He told one student his books would not last because they were in English; he regretted he had not written *The Hidden Ireland* in Irish. His journalism shows a narrowing of sympathies; in an *Irish Press* article he exalted an t-Athair Peadar (whom he had previously criticised) over Goldsmith, whom he formerly praised.[12] He had once regarded Thomas

Davis as the model "creative statesman"[13] needed to implement cultural nationalism; now, while he still praised Davis for discovering "nationality is a spirituality" he denounced Davis's late advocacy of bilingualism and opposition to the compulsory imposition of Irish on English-speakers as proof Davis had not entirely cleansed himself of the Ascendancy taint. Corkery presented O'Donovan Rossa and the Waterford landowner Philip Barron (who founded a short-lived Gaelic Academy just before the Famine) as more satisfactory precursors of the Gaelic League.[14]

Corkery eventually dismissed his own work as "part and parcel of English literature".[15] Despite this, he continued to write short stories in English in the 1930s, apparently because he felt like doing so. The story "Refuge", where a dying old man in a Limerick tenement finds refuge in re-creating the characters of an old-fashioned Irish romantic novel he wrote in his youth may give Corkery's own view of his position, and of the oblivion awaiting Irish literature in English. In 1939 Corkery published his last collection, *Earth out of Earth*; the title, from a Middle English poem on the vanity of human endeavours, suits their mood of quiet resignation. Like the returned Irish-American in "Understanding" Corkery tried to recapture his old vision for a moment so as to find "peace – even if white in colour and slow in pulse". Several of the stories deal with children or the very old. Twelve of the twenty-three have urban settings; removal from Cork defused the sense of claustrophobia recorded in "The Vanishing Spring". Visitors in his later years were surprised by his affection for the city; he "knew every street" and called the South Mall "the finest street in Europe".[16]

Earth out of Earth, coming towards the end of Corkery's career when he was out of the literary mainstream, has not attracted much critical attention. Saul and Vivian Mercier both dismiss it as lacklustre, but this is too severe.[17] Some of the stories promise more than they perform, and there are one or two unfortunate experiments, but the best of them have a quiet delicacy of observation which won the admiration of Michael MacLaverty, Corkery's closest follower as a writer. MacLaverty particularly praised the three stories seen from a child's-eye viewpoint, and even suggested *Earth out of Earth* was Corkery's best collection because his most "real", least consciously romantic.[18]

Some stories in the collection maintain the "romantic" manner and address old concerns, notably "The Death of the Runner" which reworks the struggle between Fool and Horse used in "The Ploughing of Leaca-na-Naomh" and to some extent "The Wager" to symbolise the emotional maiming forced on the Irish psyche by oppression and the political struggle for freedom.

The Runner is a strange vagrant who wanders the countryside; from time to time he abruptly runs, as if seized by a fit, until he collapses from exhaustion. Everyone knows why he fears water and young colts, yet cannot stay away from either; no-one talks of it. One night the Runner stays at a farmhouse where the farmer, good-humoured with drink, tries to cure him by confronting him with the repressed memory. The Runner was a farmer's son in love with a labourer's daughter; when his father forbade their marriage he rode his father's favourite colt to a pond and in a rage held its nostrils underwater until it drowned. "A queer use for your manhood!" The farmer tells the Runner it's stupid to fear a beast which would now be twenty-five years old, shaggy and grey, without spirit to revenge itself. The Runner goes out silently to sleep in the barn and the farmer boasts he'll be cured in the morning. That night tinkers camp nearby and turn into the river field an old, shaggy grey horse; the Runner comes across it in the early morning, falls into the river and drowns. The farmer goes mad. Corkery is saying *bonhomie* cannot heal the wound inflicted by the loss of the Gaelic tradition; but the improbability of the central coincidence weakens the power of the story.

"There's Your Sea!", the last story of the volume, describes how a young man from a hill farm, who has never seen the sea, has a match made for him in a fishing village between Dungarvan and Youghal. He lives there for a time, but the presence of the sea disturbs him; after finding a drowned cabin boy on the beach during the spring gales he takes his wife back to his own people in the hills.

The sea was part of Corkery's own background through his drowned maternal grandfather and his early memories of exploring the Cork docks. In his writings it stood for wider horizons, adventure, risk; the danger giving the sailor a touch of nobility denied to the cautious townsman or the grubbing peasant. Now he turned his back on the sea.

In the same year as the publication of *Earth out of Earth* the Abbey staged the final version of *Fohnam the Sculptor*. Despite years of revision, he had not resolved the problems of his attempt to portray the artistic vocation. The play failed; Corkery blamed the actors[19] but accepted the style of the play was out of date and reconciled himself to its failure.[20] Thereafter his artistic energies were concentrated on his watercolour landscape paintings and the composition of a play in Irish.

Assessment of his paintings is difficult since no full-scale study has ever been made and most of his paintings are in private hands. Hilary Pyle states his work improved markedly in the mid–1940s, developing a sense of colour reminiscent of the Fauves[21]; paintings from the later years of his life owned by Corkery's nephew and the Cronin family show sensitive handling of light and delight in colour.[22]

Corkery claimed painters alone of Irish artists had developed a distinctive national style which he traced to the middle period of Jack B. Yeats. (He admired Yeats but thought his later style "wilful" though he acknowledged its power). He said they succeeded because they did not have to use the English language as an artistic medium.[23]

The play *An Doras Dunta* is an adaptation of his story "As Benefits Forgot", about an old farm hand turned away after a lifetime of faithful service who goes to sleep in the barn; his unquenched pipe starts a fire which kills him and destroys the farmer's stored crops. Corkery took it through at least ten drafts, consulting his friends about correct Irish idiom.[24] (This was standard among Irish-language writers who were not native speakers.) Corkery told his friend Tomas O Muircheartaigh the language was a bit high-flown but said the story was told him in Baile Mhuirne as something which happened seventy years previously, and claimed the people of Cuil Aodha then spoke a richer Irish influenced by the poets.[25] The play was published in 1953. Corkery was very proud of it:

> It probably is a poor enough play, and the Irish in it is only a poor indication of how I feel the language might be written – even so... (if) even for a little while, it be included among the other works which, coming together, are settling down higgledy-piggledy together little by little, so making a heterogeneous mass on which the younger, more fluent writers of Irish may build more strongly – then this play of mine in Irish I reckon as having more significance than all that I have done in English. After all, what other work except this building up of a new literature in Irish can be said to be of outstanding influence in Ireland today?
>
> Others about me are going the opposite way. Native speakers some of them, educated in Irish, they are taking to English. It is an act of unfaith.[26]

Corkery supported Fianna Fail from its inception and seems to have been happy with its early years in government. A lecture on Tomas MacCurtain delivered in 1934 denounced Blueshirt protests against the effects of the Economic War as "materialism".[27] He remained concerned about the decline of the Gaelic League, however, arguing in 1933 that it should be "given into the hands of young men".[28]

Soon after the enactment of the 1937 Constitution disquiet grew in Irish Ireland circles as the limitations of government policy became clear. After the initial increase in employment created by protective tariffs, industrial growth stagnated; despite one of the largest slum clearance and rehousing programmes in Europe, urban poverty persisted; the drift from the land continued, and the 1938 Coal-Cattle Pact marked the limits of the attempt to replace grazing with labour-intensive tillage; despite a fiercely-pursued policy of restoring Irish through the schools (fully supported by Corkery, who declared "sane education of itself will restore Irish nationhood")[29] the number of native speakers continued to decline; despite censorship of heterodox literature, the long-awaited Irish Ireland literature of world stature had not arisen to replace it. "What is Wrong With our Writers?" Corkery asked in 1938.[30] "What is Wrong With Our Culture?" was the title of an *Irish Rosary* symposium to which he contributed in 1940.[31] Another *Irish Rosary* symposium bore the title "Why We Have Failed". During the 1940s Fianna Fail was challenged by protest parties appealing to its original base of support, while a Gaelic League faction broke away to form the bizarre Ailtiri na hAiseirighe (Architects of the Resurrection) which demanded stricter compulsion to use Irish and the creation of a neo-Gaelic corporatist state. The Ailtiri were strong in Cork and several of Corkery's acquaintances joined, but he remained with the League. Corkery disliked the posturing "Ceannaire" of the Ailtiri, Gearoid O Cuinneagain; when O Cuinneagain claimed the League was not Catholic enough Corkery remarked if the League had been Catholic enough for Fr. O'Growney and an t-Athair Peadar it was Catholic enough for him.[32] Similarly, Corkery stayed loyal to Fianna Fail in 1948; he complained Clann na Poblachta was dominated by Dubliners and Sean MacBride knew Irish but never used it.[33] (Corkery sympathised with Noel Browne over the Mother and Child scheme but thought Browne mishandled the negotiations).[34]

To make matters worse a critique was taking shape which saw many Irish Ireland ideas as misguided or self-deceiving. The Emergency saw the appearance of Patrick Kavanagh's *The Great Hunger* which challenged the romanticisation of peasant life, and *An Beal Bocht* by "Myles na gCopaleen" which ridiculed idealisation of the Gaeltacht. Corkery disliked Kavanagh (though he is not known to have made any comments on *The Great Hunger*)[35] and detested *An Beal Bocht* (after visiting the Gaeltacht in 1942 he wrote to O Muircheartaigh that its people had a natural sense of humour "Myles" would never understand).[36]

The criticism of Irish Ireland ideology was at its most sustained in the writings of O Faolain, which deserve fuller treatment. (O'Connor's contribution to the critique is not discussed here because he was not as systematic a thinker). Since his defeat in the contest for the UCC Chair O Faolain had won recognition as a writer and had most of his fiction banned in Ireland. He wanted to become the Irish Balzac, dissecting Irish society in fiction; he failed because he was too subjective to be that sort of writer, but in the process worked out his own view of Ireland and became a formidable social critic.

Much of this view was worked out in the 1930s in conscious opposition to Corkery. This is most clearly seen in the portrayal of the War of Independence in his first collection, *Midsummer Night Madness* (1932). *The Hounds of Banba* shows the revolution as an "unfinished symphony" with a definite objective, rebuilding the Gaelic tradition through self-sacrifice. *Midsummer Night Madness* portrays it as a "fugue", an individual experience complete in itself, identifying national liberation

with liberation from social constraints – a combination best described
by Conor Cruise O'Brien as "Parnellism".[37] O Faolain presents the
revolution as a necessary adolescent rebellion to be followed by coming
to terms with life – his own terms.

The last story in *Midsummer Night Madness*, "The Patriot", gives O
Faolain's view of the difference between his nationalism and the ascetic
nationalism of Corkery and MacSwiney. The central character, Bernie,
is introduced to separatism as a teenager by the eloquent schoolteacher
Bradley (described as a potential Lord Mayor of Cork). As an IRA man
stationed in Youghal, Bernie courts the dark girl Nora, but they are
separated when the Republicans evacuate the town during the Civil
War. Bernie meets Bradley at a staff meeting in the last squalid days of
demoralisation and disintegration. Bradley has some awareness of the
true situation, but still uses his oratorical power to urge resistance to the
last. Bradley had been hiding with Nora's family; Bernie feels jealous,
but the older man was too preoccupied with politics to notice her.
Bernie is captured under humiliating circumstances; during his imprisonment Nora corresponds with him. They marry soon after his release
and go to Youghal for their honeymoon. After their arrival (and a walk
through the spring fields, life renewing itself around them) they see a
notice of a Republican meeting to be addressed by Bradley and visit it
from curiosity: the speaker is still eloquent though ageing, but they
leave before the end. As Bernie draws down the blind in the window of
their hotel room Bradley's car drives furiously by underneath, the
driver still inflamed by the passion of his speech and blind to his
surroundings; Bernie gazes after his old teacher for a minute then turns
back into the room to Nora. O Faolain implies Bradley's eloquence is
the product of frustration. His pursuit of a sterile ideal blinds him to the
life around him; the life-affirming human affections of Bernie and Nora
are a truer patriotism.

After the first collection there are few direct allusions to Corkery's
fiction in O Faolain's stories. The silenced priest in "A Broken World"
(whose people pay him outward respect while thinking him "cracked")
who found his Wicklow parish divided between poor mountain small-
holdings and the crumbling uncultivated lowland demesnes of the
gentry, tried to make it whole by starting a "land for the people"
movement to throw down the demesne walls and was silenced by his
superiors, is as much a Joycean figure as a kinsman of Corkery's Fr.
Reen.[38] The ex-IRA pigeon fancier in "The End of a Good Man", who
shoots his favourite bird because it constantly refuses to return to its
coop after completing the race until it is too late to claim the prize,[39]
may be a grotesque parody of Sean O'Brosnan in "The Wager" who
preserves his ancestral honour by killing his beloved horse.

The real battle between Corkery and O Faolain was fought in their
non-fictional writings. In the 1930s O Faolain developed his own inter-

pretation of Irish history. Inspired by Frank O'Connor's essay "Democracy and the Gaelic Tradition" he argued pre-conquest Gaelic society was a decadent aristocratic society enmeshed in archaisms, a living fossil cut off from the mainstreams of civilisation, too rotten to be saved even by the great Hugh O'Neill armed with Renaissance statecraft and allied with the Counter-Reformation.[40] With its overthrow it disintegrated or merged into the new Ascendancy which enslaved the silent peasantry as deeply as its Gaelic precursor. The modern Irish nation only began when those ragged slaves dispelled the last Gaelic shadows from their minds, learned pride, and followed Daniel O'Connell into the modern world. O Faolain presented the cult of the Gael as a middle-class pretence of spurious respectability for those who wanted to hide their peasant origins. He attributed the repeated rebellions of Irish history not to the collective struggle of an underground nation for self-definition, but to the Faustian rebellion of individuals against oppression veiled by the pretence of respectability. O Faolain presented himself as the true heir of the War of Independence as represented by the supreme "realist" Michael Collins rather than those irrelevant romatics Pearse and MacSwiney. "All our traditions were of defeat, and victory ended them".[41] Those who tried to revive them were hypocritical "stuffed-shirts", "Celtophiles" who predicted a "national literature" arising from the people "to reflect their Gaelic ideals; but when writers drawn from the people produced a national literature describing the life of the Irish people as it was actually lived in the small fields and narrow lanes, "Professor Corkery and Dr. Devane refuse to recognise the court."[42]

This view of Irish history contains many insights and many historical inaccuracies, but it should not be swallowed whole any more than *The Hidden Ireland*; it is a self-justifying myth. O Faolain wanted to evade any identity he did not create for himself. He juggled identities; among peasants he remembered he was a cosmopolitan, in cosmopolitan circles he thought of himself as the son of serfs. He invented his own religion and called it Catholicism. He rejoiced in the breakdown of social and literary certainties which led to the vanishing of the old-fashioned straightforward Hero and admitted ambiguous characters such as himself to world literature. In his travel books he invented an *alter ego* and debated with him; in his later fiction he displayed the creation of personality through pretence, tact, selective memory, at last escaping from the pretence of reality into the fantasy of a man allowed to live his life over again.

By the 1940s O Faolain had developed this myth of self; the social criticism in *The Bell*, by discrediting the official version of reality, was part of its justification. *The Bell* appealed to the same sort of audience *The Leader* attracted a generation earlier; discontented young men from the provinces, aspiring intellectuals who found in it pungent expression for their own awareness of aspects of Irish life ignored by official nationalism.[43]

Corkery saw this resemblance to some extent; he lamented the numbers "fe smacht an *Bell*" (under the power of *The Bell*)[44] and told his friend and admirer Tomas O Muircheartaigh they needed a magazine like "an tsean *Leader*" (the old *Leader*) to counter it.[45] (*The Leader* still appeared, but most of the original contributors were dead. Moran himself died in 1936; his daughter Nuala took over as proprietor. Corkery had not written for it since 1925; he complained it had gone into decay and most of the contributors were priests.[46] It became a monthly in the late 1940s and survived until 1973). Corkery hoped *An Glor*, an Irish-language weekly edited by O Muircheartaigh, would counteract the views O Faolain and *The Bell* were instilling in the young; he seldom wrote for it himself, but his letters to O Muircheartaigh often mention points which might be useful in replying to O Faolain.[47]

Only once in this period did Corkery try to enter into debate with O Faolain. The May 1942 editorial of *The Bell* denounced the Gaelic League for plunging into politics and losing all concern for civilisation. O Faolain attributed this to the War of Independence, which deflected studious men like Terence MacSwiney into the political struggle. He suggested the League was a sham which should disband, denounced *An Glor* and noted Corkery had just published an article dismissing all nationalist verse in English.[48]

The next issue of *The Bell* contained a note saying it refused to print a reply by Corkery because it was too long (Corkery refused to make any cuts whatsoever) and introduced personalities into what should be an objective discussion.[49] "Nil aon chinnsireacht mar do chinnsireacht fein" (There's no censorship like your own censorship) commented *An Glor*.[50]

Corkery does not seem to have published his full reply elsewhere, but his article "Terence MacSwiney and a Critic" clearly derives from it. Corkery had the advantage over O Faolain of knowing MacSwiney was a dedicated separatist long before he was a Gaelic Leaguer and saw his cultural activities as an extension of his original separatism – but Corkery does not use this knowledge. Instead, he asks if O Faolain would speak of Tom Kettle and Francis Ledwidge as he spoke of MacSwiney and the men of 1916.[51] Corkery did not understand O Faolain's critique; he assumed anyone who questioned the Irish Ireland ideology which shaped his life must be a neo-Redmondite. (This failure to develop is seen in his defence of the moribund Abbey peasant play tradition at this time in the same terms he used twenty or thirty years earlier). Anyone who had once been an Irish Irelander and rejected it could not be in good faith. This attitude was not unique to Corkery (O Faolain regularly accused Irish Irelanders of bad faith) but it was not an adequate response to O Faolain's denunciations of contemporary Irish-language literature to sneer "He should look at his own *literature* and see is it literature or sensationalism".[53] Corkery told O Muircheartaigh Ireland could develop a national literature if she had a distinct language of her own – not even Irish. If Irish writers wrote Kiltartanese the result would be an Irish national literature; "but they'll never do that because then the Americans wouldn't buy their books and where would the Frank O'Connors be then?"[54]

Two pamphlets Corkery wrote at this time, *What's This About The Gaelic League?* (1942) and *The Philosophy of the Gaelic League* (1943) include attacks on unnamed "debunkers":[55]

> A pleasant theory, it seems a joke is being promulgated in Anglo-Irish circles in Dublin: Ireland has two literatures that are one. (Poor old England has only one literature – and that one not two). Ireland, they say, has a literature in English and a literature in Irish – and both are Irish literature. Yeats' work is Irish literature, and Padraic O Conaire's work is Irish literature. So that Ireland is like a two-headed calf; it can cry out its hunger through two throats... The snag, of course, is that the calf, abortionate though it be, owns one throat as surely as the other; when the calf is put out of pain the duplex voice ceases. But Ireland does not own the English language, and so cannot mould it to its mind. The bright young things in Dublin seem to think a language is a megaphone that can be handed round. Another pleasant fiction of theirs is: "It is not possible for any Irishman to write any literature but Irish literature". They say this with fire in their eyes. And an equal fire rages in them if one refuse to accept Swift as an Irishman. The world therefore has been making a grievous mistake for two hundred years, and all because England doesn't know what is, or what is not, English literature . . . Now, who said codology?[56]

One section of *The Philosophy of the Gaelic League*, a reply to *The Great O'Neill*, asserts pre-conquest Gaelic Ireland was not feudal, but "patriarchal" like Old Testament society, and denies that the revival of the pre-conquest literary tradition entails reviving the pre-conquest social order.[57]

In the pamphlets Corkery tries to explain why, as "the generation that raised the flag of Irish Ireland is drawing to an end", those who had grown up since the War of Independence showed no interest in Irish Ireland ideas, did not realise

> how different, potentially and actually, the Ireland that they are privileged to have grown up in is, in spite of its many weaknesses, from the shabby, mindless Ireland of the later nineteenth century

and were therefore susceptible to "reactions, dimmings of vision, dressing up in grandmother's clothes".[58]

Corkery attributed this falling-off to the human losses suffered during the Revolution, the subsequent drifting away of oversanguine Irish Irelanders who believed the work of the Gaelic League was accomplished with the establishment of a new state which could revive the language without their assistance, and the absorption of the most active Irish Irelanders into the political and administrative machinery of the new state. These administrators and politicians remained Irish Irelanders at heart but lost sight of the ultimate aim among the immediate tasks before them and were unconsciously influenced by the arrogant cynicism of the civil service they inherited from the colonial regime.

> In the first twenty years of native government, a great opportunity has been lost, and lost forever. The Shannon Scheme as a keynote of what was to come under native rule differs fundamentally from the municipal theatre the Czechs built, and rebuilt when fire destroyed it, at a time when no sort of native government was theirs.[59]

Corkery believed the inherited Civil Service should have been dismissed *en masse* at independence except for a few officials temporarily retained in subordinate positions to train their Irish-speaking successors, who would thereafter conduct all official business through Irish.

> Let the State here make Irish the language of its Civil Service, and as a matter of fact, it can make English, and English alone, a compulsory study in the schools, without being able to prevent Irish from becoming the language of the country in time. The Civil Service is the pivotal point.[60]

Corkery, like many other cultural nationalists, combined an exaggerated belief in the power of the state to bring about cultural change (encouraged by misleading comparisons with continental movements he believed had revived dying vernaculars, when in fact they developed existing vernaculars as languages of literature and government) with near-total ignorance of the business of administration. He dismisses the achievement of the new state in preserving a functioning Civil Service: "the seals and strings were not tangled up".[61] Even sympathetic critics like M.J. MacManus and Francis MacManus complained his ideas about the Civil Service were "rather too simplified",[62] argued narrowminded Gaelic Leaguers were partly responsible for the decline of the language movement, and compared Corkery to "Oisin bewailing the new times and calling on the Fenians dead for hundreds of years."[63]

In the late 1940s and early 1950s Corkery worked intermittently on a projected book intended to set out his philosophy of nationalism, provisionally entitled *The Romance of Nation Building*. The book was never completed, but its views can be reconstructed from surviving lectures given by Corkery about the work in progress.

Corkery saw the nation as a gigantic collective artefact, consciously created.

> We must rid ourselves of the idea – common enough, unfortunately – that a form is merely a dead mould into which live matter is poured. The matter it is true has life in it, but it is a furtive, rudimentary, unorganised sort of life, life astray in a tangle of incongruous dirt, dirt, for we are told by the scientists that matter in the wrong place is dirt. Of its own energy the form separates the pertinent life from the incongruous adipose dirt about it, leaving it clean, purged of the unnecessary, purged of all that would interfere with its expression of a vital principle – this life we have spoken of – intelligibly and harmoniously. A form is an already organised scale of values.[64]

"A savage tribe" only becomes a nation when some of its members become aware of its distinct identity and create national games, art, customs which collectively express and shape the nation; Corkery calls these *national moulds*. One or more of these moulds may be absent and the nation can still exist; none except perhaps language ("the masterform") is essential. Together they create a civil society, a literature which expresses and enriches the life of the nation, a state adapted to its people's wishes and needs and concerned to serve them.

The nation decays when the state apparatus and its associated high culture lose touch with the life of the nation, declare themselves self-sufficient, and seek to extend their power by conquering other nations. Deprived of their native modes of high culture, state apparatus and social organisation, the national culture of the conquered people declines but its residue and the repulsive nature of an alien Ascendancy prevent their assimilation to the alien way of life.

The alien Ascendancy maintains its power by despising the natives and cultivating a cosmopolitan culture, shallow because cut off from the everyday life of the nation by the pretence that the Ascendancy are no different from their countrymen "at home" though the people, culture, landscape, climate of the conquered nation are completely different from the "home" many of the Ascendancy have never seen.

"At home" the high culture of the imperial nation seals itself off from *its* national life to reflect the hothouse life of the ruling élite; Corkery claims this is why the greatest flowering of English culture was in the Elizabethan age, before the acquisition of the Empire. Corkery argues that only now are the English rediscovering their national roots; they must restore their regional cultures by establishing a Heptarchy of regional parliaments. "That done, England would not continue to terrify human beings with such desolations as Liverpool, Leeds, Wolverhampton, Bristol etc., desolating in as much as not one of them means anything to the human spirit."[65] He quotes as evidence of the rediscovery of England Rupert Brooke's "If I should die, think only this of me" and the speeches of Stanley Baldwin on timeless rural England.

His choice of texts is not as surprising as it might appear. Corkery only visited England twice; his idea of English life was heavily influenced by social critics who portrayed traditional English rural life as a timeless haunt of peace as part of a criticism of urban industrial society. His younger contemporaries the Leavises used the concept of a lost "organic community" of rural craftsmen destroyed by "technologico-Benthamite civilisation" to express horror at the First World War, the Depression, the debasement of the language by advertising, propaganda and commercial mass-literature and as a basis for their defence of unfashionable provincial virtues against the sophisticated *rentier* frivolity of a dilettante metropolitan élite.[66]

This tradition of socio-cultural criticism has often encouraged needed reform (though it can also stir sinister forces) but it is not by itself adequate to provide an alternative framework for society. Corkery's discussion of nationality ignores the effects of class, economic development, and technology. He once considered the possibility that *The Boy's Own Paper* might have instilled in working-class English boys the same confusion and self-hatred it gave him as a boy, but decided their own knowledge of English life would give them a standard for comparison not available to him.[67]

(He was interested in American social realist writers like Clifford Odets because he saw them as nationalists writing about American life without reference to England. He believed American could develop a literature of its own in English because it was big, far away from England and populated by *immigrants* from many lands. Corkery revered Whitman; he despised Henry James and poured scorn on his complaint in *Hawthorne* about the difficulties of the American writer).[68]

He adduced the failure of the Normans to make French the language of England as proof a foreign Ascendancy which maintained links with its original country and refused to identify with the natives could not supplant their language with its own, so English would never supplant Irish. This ignored (amongst other things) the possibility that the invention of printing and the spread of mass literacy might diminish the aptness of the parallel.[69] He told his friends his acquisition of a car was a great blessing (his lameness kept him from riding a bicycle but he could drive a car as well as anyone else)[70] but it does not seem to have occurred to him that this sort of technological development deserved literary expression.

These were all aspects of Corkery's central weakness; an inability to come to terms with historical change. Despite his sophisticated, quasi-structuralist language, Corkery was not a structuralist. Structuralists see an object as the point of intersection of various forms, with no existence apart from them; if the forms change, it changes. Corkery believed the national moulds were produced by a pre-existing national identity which he called "the national tradition", seen as indefinable and unchangeable. (Hence his bizarre statement that national customs are created to express national identity, rather than created for their own sake and then seen to reflect unconscious national characteristics). Corkery denies individual creativity; the human creators of custom are merely instruments of the national tradition, and if customs are destroyed they must be re-created exactly as they were before their destruction, since they alone are adequate expressions of the national identity. Thus the actually existing life of the Irish people is mere "incongruous adipose dirt" which must be purified by the conscious application of the national tradition[71]. It is this conscious re-creation which Corkery has in mind when he speaks of them as "synthetic" and mockingly accepts O Faolain's reference to "the Synthetic Gael".[72]

Since he denies change, Corkery cannot explain corruption. If the state naturally reflects the homely virtues of the nation, why should it become an Ascendancy? It is not surprising that in his correspondence with O Muircheartaigh Corkery laments his ignorance of political philosophy and mentions arguments with Professor James Hogan about the relationship between nation and state.[73] This incoherence is probably responsible for his failure to complete *The Romance of National Building*.

The nearest Corkery came to a final synthesis of his views was *The Fortunes of the Irish Language* (1952) commissioned by the Committee for Cultural Relations. A history of Ireland presented as a history of the Irish language, it repeats many characteristic preoccupations. The coastal towns, seen as little English pales obsessed wth trade, are the villains of its account of the mediaeval period; the peasants are celebrated in its later chapters as "a homogeneous mass... who with all their faults swear by Bentham only in the petty chaffering of the market place." The existence of a Catholic middle class is acknowledged but unexplored; the accounts of nineteenth century nationalist movements ignore conscious leadership and organisation, while emphasising every tenuous link with the Irish language.

Corkery retired from his Chair in May 1947. In July 1948 he became a D. Litt. *honoris causa* by the National University of Ireland. The same year he and his sister moved from Ovens to a new house, "Fanal" in Bishopstown Avenue on the outskirts of Cork, but it cost more than expected. There were financial problems since his relatively short term as Professor meant his pension was not as large as it might have been. The sameness of the suburban houses depressed him; his old friend Denis Breen, who lived nearby, died after a long illness; Highfield Rugby Club opened a passageway beside the house.[74]

In January 1950 Corkery was granted an increase in his pension. In 1951 he and his sister moved to Myrtleville, Crosshaven, Co. Cork – on the edge of a cliff where "not even a crow" could build nearby to disturb them.[75] Their financial position improved further when the incoming Fianna Fail government nominated Corkery and Padraig O Siocfhrada (An Seabhac) to the Seanad in 1951 as a gesture to the Gaelic League. Corkery was enthusiastic at first, but soon became disillusioned when he found most Senators were farmers only interested in the price of cattle; he did not speak during his three-year term and soon ceased to attend except to draw his salary.[76] Old age and remoteness from Dublin may also account for this and for the fact that during his five-year term on the first Arts Council (January 1952 – December 1956) he only attended 15 of 43 meetings.[77]

Corkery still exercised a certain amount of influence on younger writers in English and Irish. Benedict Kiely described him as leader of the school of modern Irish fiction based on "acceptance" of Irish life as opposed to the Joycean school of "rebellion".[78] Francis MacManus (whose trilogy on Donnchadh Ruadh Mac Con Mara was inspired by *The Hidden Ireland*) praised him.[79] Michael MacLaverty told Corkery he was the writer who most influenced him.[80] Corkery and MacLaverty corresponded for a while about literature and teaching (Corkery's views about the impossibility of Irish literature in English were not mentioned) and MacLaverty persuaded the American publishers Devin-Adair to publish a selection of Corkery stories, *The Wager* (1950) but their relationship grew more distant after MacLaverty asked Corkery's opinion of his new novel *The School for Hope* and was saddened when the reply confirmed his own doubts.[81] Donnchadh and Sile Ni Cheileachair, who attended an Irish-language course for writers given by Corkery at Cuil Aodha[82], dedicated their short story collection, *Bullai Mhartain* "Do Dhonall O Corcora, a mhuin linn". (To Daniel Corkery, who taught us). To the last, Corkery was anxious to meet and influence the young, believing the future lay with them. From time to time during Corkery's last years an t-Athair Tadhg O Murchu, the well-known Cork Gaelic Leaguer, would bring a promising student to Myrtleville to meet the great man. Corkery influenced the policy of the Gaelic League through his friendship with Tomas O Muircheartaigh (1907–67) civil servant, gifted amateur photographer, and language activist heavily influenced by Corkery's opposition to bilingualism. (Corkery illustrated the futility of bilingualism by claiming nine bilinguals in the same room as a monoglot would find themselves using his language).

They corresponded extensively in Irish from 1937 to 1962.[83] O Muircheartaigh was the moving spirit behind *An Glor* and its successor, the monthly *Feasta*. His term as President of the Gaelic League (1955–9) was dominated by an abortive attempt to establish an Irish-language theatre in Dublin. Corkery wrote an enthusiastic essay hailing the project as a sign of the continuing vitality of Irish Ireland and the international renaissance of nationalism which was breaking up the colonial empires.[84] O Muircheartaigh was deeply affected by the failure of the project, which is believed to have contributed to his early death.[85]

Corkery's influence was strongest in Cork. Sean O Riordain said its intellectuals lived in his shadow as Dunquin lived in the shadow of Sliabh an Iolair.[86] Murphy and Hendrick, whom he respected becaue they stayed in Cork, respected him despite differences of opinion and kept in touch even after his move to Crosshaven. (When Murphy opened his studio in the early 1930s Corkery, maintaining his old role as a local patron of the arts, gave him one or two early commissions, notably a bust of Corkery now in the Crawford Art Gallery).[87]

During the War when petrol rationing forced him to stay in Cork during the week he became involved with An Ciorcal Staidear, a discussion group set up by some young Gaelic Leaguers, which met one evening a week to hear and discuss a paper in Irish. Corkery usually spoke last, summing up the discussion and adding some comments; occasionally he gave a paper. The members, like most of his younger acquaintances, thought of him as Donall O Corcora rather than Daniel Corkery.[88]

A paper on Irish poetry given by Corkery in 1947 to An Ciorcal Staidear had unfortunate repercussions. At this time most contemporary Irish poetry was written by non-native speakers whose grip of Irish syntax and idiom was uncertain, using English poetic modes awkwardly transposed into Irish. Corkery saw this problem – and suggested as remedy the revival of eighteenth-century Gaelic metres, the last product of the intact literary tradition.[89] After the lecture Corkery told a mutual friend, Clara Ni hAnnrachain, he was not surprised at the absence of Sean O Riordain because O Riordain knew nothing about Gaelic prosody; when he heard this O Riordain began studying Gaelic prosody and triggered a period of writer's block.[90]

O Riordain's diary shows his ambivalence towards Corkery; at times he accuses Corkery of killing Irish poetry and blames him for his agonising periods of writer's block, mocks his confident pronouncements and obsequious disciples; but he visited Corkery regularly, recorded some of his conversations in the diary, wrote a poem for a 1951 Corkery issue of the UCC Gaelic miscellany *An Siol*, and paid tribute after Corkery's death in the diary and his *Irish Times* column.[91]

The conversations recorded by O Riordain and the articles Corkery continued to write for the *Irish Press* and *Feasta* well into the 1950s show his mind still alert and idiosyncratic. He praised Mairtin O Cadhain's collection of short stories *An Braon Broghach*, calling it the work of a remarkably gifted author with a deep instinctive knowledge of his country; but while Corkery admitted the power of certain descriptive passages in *Cre na Cille* the novel was too experimental for his taste.[92] (He told O Riordain the work of Joyce would not endure because it was freakish.)[93] O Cadhain later expressed respect for Corkery's attempts to expound the philosophy of the Gaelic League and criticised the League leadership for ignoring them.[94]

Corkery admired Maire Mac an tSaoi and wrote a sensitive essay on her poem "Inquisito 1584"[95] but disliked Mairtin O Direan whom he believed excessively influenced by Dublin Literary fashions.[96] He remarked cryptically that there was only one Irish Catholic novel, *Castle Rackrent* – and a Protestant wrote it![97] He generally would not have the names of O'Connor and O Faolain mentioned in his presence, though he once told O Riordain that O'Connor was a born writer despite his flaws while O Faolain was not and would never be a writer.[98] One day in the mid–1950s, on a visit to Cork, he unexpectedly passed O'Connor in the street. "Well, if it isn't Mr. Frank O'Connor, who only writes for American magazines now" he said, and walked on. It was their last meeting.[99]

Corkery passed through the last years of his life in a mixture of hope and apprehension for Ireland. He was perturbed by the continued failure to revive the Irish language. He wrote a bitter article in *Feasta* denouncing the Irish people for celebrating the Moore centenary and ignoring the tercentenary of Seathrun Ceitinn.[100] He wrote in *The Fortunes of the Irish Language* that Ireland might lose her soul and become "an enlarged replica of one of her mediaeval trading stations." He proposed the establishment of a Department for the Irish Language under a minister whose first loyalty was to the language, equipped with the emergency powers given to the War Ministry in wartime; this led to an exchange with an t-Athair Eric Mac Finn, who pointed out that such a Department could not be independent of the rest of the Government in the way Corkery suggested.[101]

Corkery distrusted Lemass, believing no Dubliner should be Taoiseach because they did not understand the rest of the country.[102] Looking back after de Valera retired he thought de Valera had subordinated the language movement to political considerations and recalled ruefully how Stockley once told him "You have no idea how *political* he is."[103] He had been critical of the ultra-Republicanism of his younger friends but now began to say "Maybe you're right; 'tis the young men will finish the job". During the 1956–62 border campaign he thought the Government should support the IRA if they recognised the Government.[104] At times he seems to have felt his work had been futile. James N. Healy, who came to inquire about the CDS for an exhibition on the theatrical history of Cork, was snubbed and told nobody would be interested in it nowadays.[105] Corkery once took a friend to the Lough to show him the house of *The Threshold of Quiet*; after seeing the house Corkery looked around at the new suburban houses and said "They've ruined my setting."[106]

At the same time he saw the collapse of the colonial empires as proof of a world trend towards nationalism. He told readers of *The Irish Press* the redrawing of Indian provincial boundaries according to language was a sign of this trend and contrasted the Anglicised Indian who visited him during the War of Independence with a young engineer he had just met who was much more distinctively Indian without being any less up-to-date as an engineer, and even knew a few words of Irish.[107] He admired the Israelis and their revival of Hebrew. He took an interest in proposals for Church use of the vernacular. A friend who visited Northern Spain was asked about the Basques. At a dinner held by his friends to mark his eightieth birthday in 1958 he said he was sorry he would be leaving the world so soon when it was getting so interesting.[108]

Corkery rarely spoke of the Troubles in private, telling his relatives "Those times are best forgotten" and suggesting MacSwiney should not have been allowed to die because he was too valuable[109]; but his last published works included introductions to two War of Independence memoirs and biographies of MacCurtain and MacSwiney. He saw these as essential to remind the new generation of the ideals behind the Revolution and counteract the debunkers.[110]

He spoke of new projects, did some research on Gaelic life in the eighteenth century (apparently with the idea of writing a social history to complement *The Hidden Ireland*)[111], thought of writing a study of *Seadna*.[112] He gave his last public lecture, on sculpture, at a Seamus Murphy exhibition.[113] He continued painting almost to the end of his life, although his eyesight began to deteriorate in 1950 and in the early 1960s he became almost wholly blind. His mind remained clear, but in the last two or three years of his life he began to forget names and lose the thread of conversations. As he and his sister grew older they found it increasingly hard to look after themselves in their remote house. They spent the winter of 1963 in Passage West with their unmarried niece, Maureen Corkery. Shortly before they went to Passage West for the winter of 1964, Corkery told a visiting friend they would not be able to keep up Myrtleville much longer. "It's the painting I'll miss the most" he said.[114]

Corkery liked Passage West and the company of his relations, though he was slightly irritated at the name of the street where his niece lived – Victoria Terrace. (A proposal has since been made to rename it Corkery Terrace). Every day he went for a walk along the sea front. On 31st December 1964, after returning from his daily walk, Daniel Corkery sat down, complained of a pain in his side, collapsed and died almost immediately.[115]

He was buried at St. Joseph's Cemetery near the Lough, where his parents are buried. Seamus Murphy carved a plain headstone as Corkery desired, inscribed with a small Celtic cross, DONALL O CORCORA 1878–1964, and the name and dates of his sister Mary who was buried there after her death in 1965.

The newspapers published respectful obituaries and some reminiscences by friends and acquaintances. Radio Eireann broadcast two commemorative programmes after some prompting. Some Gaeilgeoiri complained his death had not received sufficient attention, a view encouraged when Sean O Tuama rang up Radio Eireann to enquire about the memorial programme and was asked by a junior staff member "Who was Daniel Corkery?"[116]

His papers went to UCC, where they suffered some vicissitudes before the library was reorganised in the 1970s. The survival of acquaintances, the modest, enduring reputation of his own work, the publication of *An Only Child* (1962) and *Vive Moi!* (1965) ensured Corkery a place in the history of Irish culture; but he had outlived most of his contemporaries and with them the memory of the invigorating shock of discovery provided by the early Irish Ireland movement which inspired, shaped and limited his career. Only one anonymous obituarist recalled Corkery had once written essays under the pen-name "Lee" for *The Leader*.

NOTES

All items are by Corkery unless otherwise stated. The Corkery Papers in UCC have been catalogued since these notes were completed.

PREFACE

1.	E.g. comments on Corkery in Terence Brown *Ireland: A Social and Cultural History 1922–85* (rev. ed. Dublin 1986); Seamus Deane *et al.* (eds.) *Field Day Anthology of Irish Literature* (Dublin 1991).

CHAPTER ONE

1.	George Brandon Saul *Daniel Corkery* (Bucknell University Press, 1973); interview with Bill and Mary Corkery 17–8–1988.
2.	Letter from Professor Aloys Fleischmann to author 16–5–1989.
3.	"Corcaig le linn m'oige", MS lecture in Box 92, Torna Papers, UCC. Translation by Patrick Maume.
4.	"Reflections in Suburbia" *Leader* September 29 1906 p. 89–90.
6.	"Corcaig le linn m'oige" *op.cit.*; notes attached to "Building a Nation" TS lectures in Box 4 Corkery Papers UCC.
7.	Maura Murphy "Nineteenth-Century Cork" in D.W. Harkness & Mary O'Dowd (eds.) *The Town in Irish History* (Belfast, 1981); Michael Gough "Socio-Economic Conditions and the Genesis of Planning in Cork" in Michael J. Bannon (ed.) *The Emergence of Irish Planning 1880–1920* (Dublin, 1985); Andy Bielenberg *Cork's Industrial Revolution* (Cork, 1991); Eddie Lahiff "Class Struggles in the South of Ireland 1880–1922" (unpublished paper delivered to UCC Socialist Society March 1989).
8.	Davis & Mary Coakley *Wit and Wine* (Dublin, 1986).For Callanan's works see *Gems of the Cork Poets* (Cork, Barter, 1883). Note particularly "Gougane Barra" and the first verses of "The Recluse of Inchydoney" for anticipation of favourite Corkery themes. Corkery makes a brief, critical reference to Callanan in his review of an t-Athair Peadar O Laoghaire's autobiography *Leader* October 16 1915 p. 234–5. I am also indebted to an unpublished paper on early nineteenth century Cork intellectuals by Mr. Philip Hannon, delivered at UCC in 1988. Tom Moore's "O Blame Not The Bard" also uses the same theme.

9.   "On a Hilltop Near Cork" *Leader* December 21 1901 p. 278, "Corcaig le linn m'oige" *op.cit.*

10.   Drafts of autobiographical radio talk, Box 19 Corkery Papers UCC.

11.   G.B. Saul *Daniel Corkery op.cit.*

12.   "The South Mon and Myself" MS lecture, L370 Cork Municipal Museum Archives; "Our First Duty" *Irish School Weekly* August 1st 1914.

13.   D.W. Miller *Church, State and Nation in Ireland 1899–21* (Dublin, 1973); Barry Coldrey *Faith and Fatherland* (Dublin, 1988).

14.   "Ourselves and Literature – II" *Standard* December 13 1930 p. 8.

15.   Autobiographical radio talk drafts, Box 19 Corkery Papers op.cit.

16.   W.T. Rodgers & Bernard Donoghue *The People Into Parliament* (London, 1965).

17.   Autobiographical radio talk drafts *op.cit.*

18.   "My First Glimpse of the Gaeltacht" *An Gaedheal* December 1937 p. 6–7.

19.   Autobiographical radio talk drafts *op.cit.*

CHAPTER TWO

1.   "Thoughts on the Cork Exhibition" *Leader* September 14 1901.

2.   X (D.P. Moran) "Confessions of a Converted West Briton" *Leader* September 1, 1900; D.P. Moran *The Philosophy of Irish Ireland* (Dublin, 1905); Donal McCartney "Hyde, D.P. Moran and Irish Ireland" in F.X. Martin (ed.) *Leaders and Men of the Easter Rising* (London, 1967); (P.S. O'Hegarty) "D.P. Moran" *Dublin Magazine* April–June 1936 p. 103; Louis J. Walsh obituary of D.P. Moran *Leader* February 22 1936; William Dawson "Arthur Clery" *Studies* March 1933 p. 77–88. For the clashes between Joyce and the future *Leader* contributors see Richard Ellmann *James Joyce* (rev. ed. Oxford University Press 1988) p. 70, 96 and Arthur Clery *Dublin Essays* (Dublin, 1920). For the influence of Finlay and Magennis see Daniel J. O'Sullivan *The Literary Periodical and the Anglo-Irish Revival* (Ph.D. UCD 1969) chapter on *The New Ireland Review*; John S. Kelly "The Fall of Parnell and the Rise of Anglo-Irish Literature" *Anglo-Irish Studies* II (1976) discusses the tendency of Parnellites to compensate for their minority status by adopting cultural nationalism.

3.   "Imaal" (J.J. O'Toole, d. 1927) is probably the John O'Toole thanked for help and advice in the foreword to *The Hidden Ireland*.

4.   "Cork Council Chamber" *Leader* January 3 1903 p. 310–2.

5.   "The Cork School of Art" *Leader* February 15 1902 p. 408–9.

6.   "On a Hilltop Near Cork" *Leader* December 21 1901 p. 278; "The Art Question" *Leader* January 25 1902 p. 361–2; "St Patrick's Day in Cork" *ibid.* March 29 1902 p. 70–1; "The Frenzy of Imitation" *ibid.* May 31 1902 p. 215.

7.   "A Night and a Day" *Leader* July 19 1902 p. 328.

8. "Continental Cork" *Leader* May 22 1909 p. 302.
9. "Jim Larkin" *Leader* July 20 1910 p. 472–6.
10. "The Trades Congress and Ireland a Nation" *Leader* June 12 1909 p. 399–400.
11. "The Trade Unionist in Irish Politics" *Leader* April 17 1909 p. 254–5. The series which contains this article is sometimes mistakenly attributed to Thomas MacDonagh (e.g. Denis Donoghue (ed.) W.B. Yeats *Memoirs* p.177n.)
12. "Dublin Cameos II – The Dubliner" *Leader* July 28 1907 p. 364–5.
13. Corkery notebook Box 28 Corkery Papers P. 47–8 (August 10 1907).
14. "A Night in Rochestown" *Leader* January 27 1906 p. 380.
15. "A Growing Evil" *Leader* May 28 1904 p. 217; "The Vanishing of a People's Emotion" *Leader* May 26 1906 p. 217–8.
16. "Is Moral Force Dead?" *Leader* June 27 1908 p. 295–6.
17. Corkery notebook *op.cit.* p. 24–5.
18. "A Growing Evil" *op.cit.*; "The Vanishing of a People's Emotion" *op.cit.*
19. "My First Glimpse of the Gaeltacht" *An Gaedheal* December 1937 p. 6–7.
20. "The Art Question" *op.cit.*
21. "A Night and a Day" *op.cit.*; Diarmuid O Murchu obituary of Corkery *Agus* February 1965 p. 4–6; interview with Diarmuid O Murchu 21–5–1989.
22. "My First Glimpse of the Gaeltacht" *op.cit.*
23. "The Memory of Our Poets" *Leader* September 14 1907 p. 56–7.
24. "Nature Study at the Cork Exhibition" *Leader* August 15 1903 p. 406–7.
25. "On a Hilltop Near Cork" *op.cit.*
26. Corkery interview in "Death of a Lord Mayor" broadcast Radio Eireann 21–11–1960 (RTE Sound Archives).
27. Corkery notebook *op.cit.* p. 63 20–8–1907.
28. G.B. Saul *Daniel Corkery* op.cit. p. 21.
29. Frank O'Connor *An Only Child* (1962; Pan edition 1971) p. 163.
30. "Irish Drama in Cork" *Leader* November 2 1907 p. 169–70.
31. Corkery notebook *op.cit.* p. 56 12–8–1907.
32. *Cork Examiner* December 6 1904; ibid. November 21 1905; Corkery to Tomas O Muircheartaigh 14–11–1958 Corkery papers Box 16 Folder 5; Liam Ruiseal *Liam Ruiseal Remembers* (Cork, 1978) p. 9–11; "Father Matthew in Irish" *Leader* August 10 1907 p. 396–8; Corkery introduction to Flor O'Donoghue *Tomas MacCurtain* (Tralee, 1958) p. 7–8; Corkery notebook *op.cit.* p. 64 21–8–09; interview with Clara ni hAnnrachain 10–12–1989.
33. "The Bonny Labouring Boy" *Irish Rosary* November 1903 p. 853–5; "The Bowlers" *Irish Rosary* September 1903 p. 664–8.

34. "An American Wake" *Leader* July 4 1903 p. 314–6; "The Story of a Lane" *ibid*. December 9 1905 p. 254–5.
35. "The Joy of Marching"*Leader* July 26 1902 p. 338–9.
36. "Cantillon's Symphony" *Leader* December 15 1906, p. 284.
37. (Anon.) "A City Ruskin" *Q.C.C.* June 10 1905 p. 55–6.
38. "The Criticism of Irish" *Leader* November 7 1908 p. 279–80.
39. E.g. "Commercial Sculpture" *Leader* August 23 1902; letter from T.C. M(urray) *ibid*. September 6; defence of Corkery by "S.R.P." *ibid*. September 20; "Big Pennyworths" *ibid*. September 27; T.C.M. replies, *ibid*. October 4; "About Coloured Statuary" *ibid*. October 11; Robert Elliott replies to T.C.M. *ibid*. October 18. This controversy concerned gaudy religious statues, with Murray arguing artistic merit was irrelevant if they produced devotion and Corkery replying that only the deep thought induced by genuine art could affect the heart.
40. Interview with the late Leon O Broin 21–3–1988.
41. "Irish Drama in Cork" *Leader* October 5 1907.
42. "Eoin" "A Captious Critic at the Munster Feis" *Leader* October 12 1907 p. 119–20.
43. "Buadhthain" "The Irish Drama at Cork" *Leader* November 2 1907 p. 169–70.
44. "Irish Drama in Cork" *Leader* November 2 1907 p. 169–70; "Peculiar Propagandism" *Leader* November 16 1907 p. 202.
45. "Siobhan" "Irish Drama" *Leader* November 23 1907; "Irish Drama" *ibid*. December 7 1907; "Siobhan" "Irish Drama" *ibid*. December 21 1907; "Irish Drama" *ibid*. January 4 1908.
46. *The Bell* April 1947.
47. "The Want of Ornament" *Leader* June 6 1903 p. 236–7; "Industry "Alone" and Art" *ibid*. August 22 1903 p. 420–2; "Ornament" *Leader* September 5 1903 p. 30–1.
48. "Nollaig" *Leader* December 14 1907 p. 269–70. Corkery is discussing why customs such as the carol-singing described by Hardy in *Under the Greenwood Tree* are not found in Ireland. (He does not notice the custom is abolished during the course of the novel).
49. "England a Nation" *Leader* December 14 1907 p. 269–70.
50. "The Gaelic Leaguer and Politics" *Leader* April 3 1909 p. 140–2.
51. "A Moral Force Movement" *Leader* July 4 1908 p. 310.
52. "The Idea of Empire" *Leader* July 11 1908 p. 329–30.
53. "A Moral Force Movement" *op.cit.*
54. "The Play's the Thing" *Leader* September 12 1903 p. 44–6.
55. "Mid-Autumn" *Leader* September 24 1904 p. 77–9.
56. "The Irish Literary Theatre in Cork" *Leader* December 31 1904 p. 311.
57. Ibid.
58. "Mr. Yeats in Cork" *Leader* December 30 1905 p. 313–4; interview with Bill and Mary Corkery 17–8–1988.

59. "Dublin Cameos V – Some Institutions" *Leader* August 24 1907 p. 7–8.
60. Corkery notebook *op.cit*. 15–8–1907. p. 59.
61. *Ibid*. 19–8–1907 p. 62.
62. Minutes in Corkery Papers Box 28, published in Robert Hogan & James Kilroy *History of Irish Drama – II: The Years of Synge 1905–9* (Dublin, 1978); Barry Hogan "Heroic Days in the Dun Theatre" *Cork Examiner* 8–9–1956.
63. Copy in Corkery Papers Box 23 published in Hogan & Kilroy *op.cit*. p. 262–3.
64. "Davis and the National Language" in M.J. McManus (ed.) *Thomas Davis and Young Ireland* (Dublin 1945) p. 14. For Rossa's state of mind at this time see Terence MacSwiney Diary December 10 1905 P 48c/102 MacSwiney papers, University College Dublin archives.
65. *The Embers* was published in Robert Hogan & Richard Burnham *Lost Plays of the Irish Renaissance III: The Cork Dramatic Society* (Proscenium Press, New Jersey 1984). The MS and TS scripts in Corkery Papers Box 25 contain slight but significant variations from the published text.
66. "Drama" "Drama in Cork" *The Leader* October 29 1910 p. 250.
67. *Cork Constitution* quoted in Hogan & Kilroy *The Years of Synge op. cit*. p. 323.

CHAPTER THREE

1. "The Spirit of Ballingeary" *Leader* July 31 1909 p. 562–3.
2. Liam de Roiste "History of Colaiste Na Mumhan" TS lecture in Liam de Roiste Additional Material, Cork Archives Institute.
3. "Terence MacSwiney" TS in MacSwiney Papers P48c/179(2) UCD.
4. MacSwiney Papers P48c/1 (1); P48c/6/67.
5. MacSwiney Papers P48c/105/76.
6. Terence MacSwiney Diary December 6th 1902 MacSwiney Papers P48c/99.
7. *Ibid*. June 27th 1903 P48c/99; January 20th 1907 P48c/103.
8. *Ibid*. September 18th 1905 P48c/100.
9. *Ibid*. October 1909 P48c/104.
10. *Ibid*. October 31st 1903 P48c/99; February 25th 1906 P48c/102.
11. *Ibid*. March 28th 1906 P48c/102.
12. Liam de Roiste in MacSwiney Papers P48c/108 22–9.
13. MacSwiney diary P48c/100 July 7th 1904.
14. *Ibid*. P48c/102 February 8 & 9 1906.
15. *Ibid*. P48c/102 P. 35–43. Apart from the sources for specific quotations listed in previous notes, this account of MacSwiney is based on P.S. O'Hegarty *Terence MacSwiney: A Memoir* (Dublin, 1922); Moirin Chevasse *Terence MacSwiney* (Cork, 1961).

16. Autobiographical radio talk draft, Box 19 Corkery Papers.
17. Corkery interview in "Death of a Lord Mayor" RTE Sound Archives (broadcast 21–11–1960).
18. "Terence MacSwiney: Lord Mayor of Cork" *Studies* December 1920 (reprinted in Chevasse *op.cit.*).
19. Autobiographical radio talk draft, *op.cit.*
20. "Terence MacSwiney" MacSwiney Papers P48c/179(2).
21. Corkery interview with Etienette Beuque, MacSwiney Papers P48c/9/25–7.
22. Introduction to projected publication of four plays by MacSwiney, MS G 1057 Cork Municipal Museum; Liam Ruiseal *Liam Ruiseal Remembers* (Cork, 1978); Liam Ruiseal "Daniel Corkery and the Cork Dramatic Society" *Cork Examiner* January 6 1965 p. 4; "Terence MacSwiney" TS radio talk, MacSwiney papers P48c/179(2).
23. (Robert Hogan) "Cork Realists" in Robert Hogan (ed.) *Macmillan Dictionary Of Irish Literature* (London, 1980) p. 173.
24. *Woman of Three Cows* unpublished MS Box 23 Corkery Papers.
25. *Cork Free Press* October 28 1910 p. 10 col. 3.
26. *Cork Free Press* November 11 1910 p. 10 col. 3.
27. "Malvolio" "Memories of a Cork Theatregoer" *Irish Outlook* November 18th & 25th 1911.
28. "Synge and Decadence" *Irish Outlook* December 16th 1911, p. 7, December 3rd p. 4–5 (not listed in J.M. Levitt *J.M. Synge – A Bibliography of Published Criticism*). The December 16th issue is not in the *Irish Outlook* file in the National Library of Ireland, but there is a copy in the UCC library.
29. Unpublished TS in MacSwiney Papers.
30. "Terence MacSwiney" P48c/179(2) MacSwiney Papers.
31. MacSwiney Diary February 25th 1911 P48c/104.
32. "Terence MacSwiney" P48c/179(2) MacSwiney Papers; Corkery interview in *Death of a Lord Mayor* broadcast 21–11–1960 (RTE Sound Archives).
33. MacSwiney Diary January 17th 1910 P48c/104.
34. Anonymous review of *The Epilogue*, *Cork Free Press* May 20th 1911 p.8; Letter from "Wagner" *Cork Free Press* May 22nd 1911.
35. "The Creative Spirit" *Cork Free Press* December 12th 1911 p.3.
36. *The Onus Of Ownership* and *The Lesson of his Life* are published in Burnham & Hogan *Lost Plays of the Irish Renaissance III: The Cork Dramatic Society* op.cit. The late Mr. James N. Healy, who had a TS of *The Passing of 'Miah*, kindly allowed a photocopy to be taken for the UCC Archives.
37. Hogan & Kilroy *Years of Synge* op.cit.; Introduction to MacSwiney Plays MSG 1057 Cork Municipal Museum; MacSwiney Diary December 4 1910, December 25 1912 P48c/104; appeals for funds in *Cork Free Press* November 30 1911 p. 8, October 18 1912 p.3.

38. Letter from Corkery quoted in Michael J. O'Neill *Lennox Robinson* (New York, 1964) p. 53.
39. T.C. Murray to Moirin Chevasse 25–8–50, MacSwiney Papers P48c/207.
40. *The Last Warriors of Coole* is reprinted in Burnham & Hogan *Cork Dramatic Society op.cit.*
41. Chevasse *Terence MacSwiney op.cit.*
42. MacSwiney Diary P48c/104 January 22nd 1911, December 25 1912.
43. Terence MacSwiney *The Revolutionist* (Dublin, 1914).
44. Published by Corkery in *Three Plays* (Dublin, 1920).
45. Desmond Ryan *Remembering Sion* (London, 1934).
46. Ruth Dudley Edwards *P.H. Pearse – The Triumph of Failure* (London, 1977) p. 166–7.
47. *Irish Outlook* May 4th 1912 p.10.
48. Letter from priest in *Leader* February 11th 1911 p. 631–2; Corkery reply *Leader* February 18th 1911 p. 6; Corkery interview *Irish Outlook* November 23rd 1912.
49. *The Master* in P.H. Pearse *Collected Works: Plays, Stories, Poems* (Dublin, 1917). See also Raymond J. Porter *P.H. Pearse* (New York, 1973) p. 104–8.
50. Advance notice *Cork Free Press* May 15 1911 p. 2.
51. Anonymous review – cutting in cuttings collection, Corkery Papers – marked *Exam. May 20th.*
52. *Ibid.; Cork Free Press* May 20th 1911 p.8.
53. *Irish Outlook* August 24th 1912.
54. *Cork Free Press* October 18th 1912 p.3.
55. R(obert) C(ooney) "This Week's Portrait – Mr. Corkery" *Irish Outlook* November 23 1912 p.1–3.
56. Corkery to Tomas O Muircheartaigh 23–6–1946 Folder 2 Box 16 Corkery Papers. Cf. the reference to Fylenashouk in "Seagull, O Seagull" *Ui Bhreasail* (Dublin, 1920).
57. *Fohnam the Sculptor* was published in 1974 by Proscenium Press, New Jersey (G.B. Saul ed.)
58. In Celtic mythology "Tethra" is the ruler of the kingdom of the dead.
59. Corkery notebook *op.cit.* August 17th 1910.
60. MacSurney diary P48c/104.
61. *Cork Free Press* January 4 1913 p. 11, January 30 1913; *Irish Outlook* March 22 1913, May 24 1913; interview with James N. Healy; Corkery obituary for Con O'Leary *Cork University Record* Easter 1959 p. 24–6.
62. Corkery notebook *op.cit.* August 24th 1908, August 30th 1908, January (8th?) 1907.
63. Letter from Corkery quoted in Vivian Mercier *Realism in Irish Literature 1916–40* (Ph.D. Trinity College Dublin 1944). p. 69.

64. *Threshold of Quiet* (Dublin, 1917) p. 220. All page references to 1944 edition.

65. *Ibid*. p.3–4.

66. *Irish Homestead* November 3 1917.

67. E.A. Boyd *Ireland's Literary Renaissance*. (rev. ed. London & Dublin, 1922)

68. G.B. Saul *Daniel Corkery op.cit*.

69. Frank O'Connor *An Only Child op.cit*.

70. Interview with Diarmuid O Murchu *op.cit*. 21–5–1989.

71. G.B. Saul *Daniel Corkery op.cit*.

72. Interview with Seamus de Roiste (who received this information from Hendrick who was told it by Corkery) 8–5–1989.

73. *An Only Child op.cit*.

74. Corkery letter quoted in Arthur Fedel *The Miracle and the Quaking Sod* (MA UCD 1951) *op.cit*.

75. *Threshold of Quiet* P. 220.

76. *Ibid*. p. 162–3.

77. *Ibid*. p. 170.

78. *Ibid*. p. 222.

79. *Ibid*. p. 163–4.

80. *Ihid* p. 222.

81. *Ibid*. p. 135–6.

82. *Ibid*. p. 175.

83. *Ibid*. p. 11.

84. *Ibid*. p. 93.

85. Autobiographical lecture drafts, Box 19 Corkery Papers; letter quoted in Vivian Mercier *Realism in Irish Literature op.cit*. p. 69.

86. "Catholicity and Irish Nationality" *Leader* May 5 1906 p. 174–6.

87. James Matthews *Voices: A Life Of Frank O'Connor* (Dublin, 1983) p. 252–3; Frank O'Connor An Only Child *op.cit*. p. 152–3, 163. Breen received the last rites before dying (Corkery to Muircheartaigh 21–9–1950).

88. "The Twenty Club" MS lecture Box 92 Torna Papers UCC.

89. "A Word in a Book" *Leader* October 9 1915 p. 211–12.

90. Interview with Bill and Mary Corkery.

91. E.A. Boyd letter Box 2 Corkery Papers.

92. G.B. Saul *Daniel Corkery op.cit*.

93. *Threshold of Quiet* p. 46, 120, 127.

94. *Ibid*. p. 237.

95. *Ibid*. p. 310.

96. Autobiographical radio talk drafts Box 19 *op.cit*.

97. *Ibid*..

98. Frank O'Connor *An Only Child op.cit*. p. 112–6.

99. "Juggernaut in Education" *Leader* February 26 1916 p. 61–3.

100. "The Bugbear of Corrections" *Irish Schools Weekly* September 6th 1916.
101. "A Plea for Fal-Lals" *Ibid*. May 10th 1913 p. 231.
102. Seamus Murphy interviewed in Donncha O Dulaing (ed.) *Voices of Ireland* (Dublin, 1984) p. 55–6.
103. Seamus Murphy "Daniel Corkery – An Appreciation" *Irish Times* January 2 1965 p. 12; "School Clubs" *Irish Schools Weekly* May 10th 1903.
104. *An Only Child op.cit.* p. 112–6.
105. "The Three R's?" *Irish Schools Weekly* May 27th 1916.
106. Interview with Mairead Ni Mhurchu.
107. *An Only Child op.cit.* p. 112–6.
108. *Ibid*.
109. "Civics" *Leader* September 18th 1915 p. 135–6.
110. *Ibid*.
111. *Irish Tribune* July 2nd 1926 p. 8; "The Deeper Plough: a word to Macra na Feirme" *Irish Press* November 11th 1949.
112. "Civics" *op.cit.*
113. Terence Brown *Ireland: A Social and Cultural History 1922–85* (new edn. Dublin 1986).
114. "The Twenty Club" MS lecture in Box 92 Torna Papers.
115. "Guaire" *New Ireland* September 25 1915 p. 318. The story is not a folktale but a modernisation of a literary romance.
116. "The Child Saint" *Catholic Home Journal* April 7th 1916; "The Breath of Life" *ibid*. May 26th (cuttings in Torna Paper Box 81).
117. "Alibi or Home?" *Irish Review* June 1912.
118. "The Spanceled" *ibid*. March 1913.
119. 3 small pages of comments on *Munster Twilight* and *Hounds of Banba* Box 23 Corkery Papers.
120. Matthews *Voices op.cit.* p. 321.
121. Corkery to MacDonagh May 29th 1914 with MacDonagh pencil notes MS 20, 642. Thomas MacDonagh Papers, National Library of Ireland.
122. Plunkett to Corkery July 10th 1914, L313 Cork Municipal Museum.
123. "Storm-Struck" *Irish Review* July/August 1914.
124. "The Battle of Keim-an-Eigh" *Irish Outlook* December 4th & 11th 1916.
125. Pearse letter to Corkery in Seamus O Buachalla (ed.) *Letters of Padraic Pearse* (Dublin, 1980); "Songs of the Irish Rebels" *Leader* January 19th 1918 p. 589–90; interview with Clara Ni hAnnrachain 10–12–1989.
126. O'Hegarty *MacSwiney op.cit.*; Chevasse *MacSwiney op.cit.* Corkery's first cousin Patrick Corkery was also active in the Volunteers, and later in the War of Independence; his health was undermined by a

hunger strike and he died young. (Information from Bill and Mary Corkery).

127. Corkery introduction to Flor O'Donoghue *Tomas MacCurtain* (Tralee, 1958).

128. "The Jettisoners" *Leader* September 25th 1915 p. 157.

129. "The Kink of Nationality" *Leader* March 18 1916 p. 134–5. For this article (and some others in 1916) Corkery uses the pseudonym "Richard Mulqueany".

130. "The Three Irelands" *Leader* April 1st 1916 p. 183–4.

131. "Forgive and Forget" *ibid.* April 15th 1916 p. 233.

132. "The Peasant in Irish Literature" *New Ireland* December 4th 1915 p. 57.

133. Ione Malloy *Corkery, O'Connor and O Faolain; A Literary Relationship in the Emerging Irish Free State* (Ph.D. University of Texas 1979).

134. Autobiographical radio talk drafts, Box 19 Corkery Papers op.cit.

135. Lyon to Corkery 1–1–1916, Box 2 Corkery Papers.

136. "The Hidden Ireland" *Cork Free Press* January 26th 1915 p. 6. A list of articles for the proposed selection (drawn up a few years later) in the cuttings collection, Corkery Papers shows Corkery used the pseudonyms "Le Pinson", "Richard Mulqueany" and "Neuilin Siubhlach".

137. Notes by Corkery P48c/179(3) MacSwiney Papers.

138. Con O'Leary to MacSwiney July 15 1916 P48b/191 MacSwiney Papers.

CHAPTER FOUR

1. Corkery to MacSwiney n.d. (July 1916) MacSwiney Papers P48c/306.

2. *Ibid.*

3. *Ibid.* Despite some omissions by transcriber, the context shows the meaning of this sentence.

4. Anonymous obituary of D.L. Kelleher *Cork University Record* Easter 1958; Professor Thomas Dillon "Memories of D.L. Kelleher" *ibid.* Easter 1959; "The Twenty Club" MS lecture Box 92 Torna Papers; Sean O Faolain *Vive Moi!* (London, 1965) p. 136–7; National Library of Ireland file of *An La*; Corkery to MacSwiney September 10th 1916 P48b/207 MacSwiney Papers; G.B. Saul *Daniel Corkery* op.cit. p.32.

5. Corkery to MacSwiney n.d. (autumn 1916) P48b/49(2)–(4).

6. Arthur Fedel *The Miracle and the Quaking Sod* op.cit. p.17–18.

7. Interview with James N. Healy 18–1–1990; Barry Hogan "Heroic Days in the Dun Theatre" *Cork Examiner* 8–9–56, "A Gallant Effort Begins to

Wilt" *ibid.* 15–9–56, "Splinter Groups; Offshoots of the Parent Body" *ibid.* 22–9–56; J.A. Swanton "Memories of the Leeside Players" Christmas Number *Cork Weekly Examiner and Holly Bough* 1963 (I am grateful to the late James N. Healy for giving me copies of these articles); Michael Farrell "Drama in Cork" *The Bell* December 1941 p. 214–20; Robert Hogan, Richard Burnham & Daniel P. Poteet *History of the Irish Theatre IV – The Rise of the Realists 1916–20* (Dublin, 1979). Occasional references to a third group of "Cork Players" (e.g. MacSwiney to Corkery 15–6–18, L313 iii Cork Municipal Museum) are the product of confusion; both groups used this term to refer to themselves.

8. Autobiographical radio talk drafts Box 19 Corkery Papers.

9. "A Critic and Terence MacSwiney" *Irish Press* June 29 1942.

10. Corkery to MacSwiney n.d. (Autumn 1916) 48b/49 (2)–(4) MacSwiney Papers.

11. Notes on *Munster Twilight* & *Hounds of Banba* Box 23 Corkery Papers.

12. Autobiographical radio talk drafts *op.cit.*

13. "The Short Story" MS lecture to Twenty Club 20–1–1917, Box 92 Torna Papers.

14. For Dr. Smith see "Irish Intellectuals" *Leader* January 22 1916 p. 590–2 and his description of Killarney quoted in Luke Gibbons "Romanticism, Realism and Irish Cinema" in Kevin Rockett *et. al.* (eds.) *Cinema and Ireland* (1988 edn., London) p. 204. For Lecky "W.E.H. Lecky; "Successor of the Four Masters" " *Catholic Bulletin*; August 1916 p. 442–4. Corkery rarely wrote for the *Catholic Bulletin*; he found their financial treatment of contributors unsatisfactory. (Corkery to MacSwiney (late Augumn 1916) P48b/489(2)–(4) MacSwiney Papers).

15. Sean O Faolain "Daniel Corkery" *Dublin Magazine* April–June 1936 p. 49–61.

16. "The Gaelic League in the Gaedhaltacht" *Leader* August 28th 1915 p.63–4; "The Position of Irish Culture" *ibid.* July 8th 1916 p. 469–70.

17. "Russian Models for Irish Litterateurs" *Leader* May 27th 1916 p. 325.

18. *Ibid.*

19. "Europe Ahoy!" TS Torna Papers Box 81; "Emile Verhaeren" *Irish Monthly* February 1921 p. 45–50.

20. Lionel Trilling *Matthew Arnold* (New York, 1938); Park Honan *Mathew Arnold* (Toronto, 1981).

21. "An Ursgeal" MS lecture (summer 1923) Box 81 Torna Papers.

22. "Russian Models for Irish Litterateurs" *op.cit.*

23. "The Irish Peasant Play: A Defence" *Irish Weekly Independent* Christmas Number 1917; "Drama: International Or National?" MS Box 81 Torna Papers.

24. "What Shall We Read In Irish?" *Leader* May 26 1917 p. 372.
25. "A Plea for the European" MS lecture to Cork Catholic Young Men's Society (late 1916) Box 81 Torna Papers.
26. De Roiste Diary 10th August 1917 MS 31, 148 (1) National Library of Ireland.
27. "Outcry – but no Gaelic" *Leader* August 25th 1917 p. 59.
28. "Youth and Age Cannot...." *Leader* September 1st 1917 p. 81.
29. Garry O'Connor *Sean O'Casey – A Life* (London, 1988) p. 131–2.
30. Seamus Murphy "Daniel Corkery – An Appreciation" *op.cit.*; MacSwiney to Corkery 15–6–1918 L313 Cork Municipal Museum.
31. G.B. Saul *Daniel Corkery op.cit.*; Cork County Technical Instruction Committee minutes 20–6–1918, 18–7–1918 (I am grateful to Traolach O Riordain for providing me with these references).
32. De Valera to Corkery August 14th 1918 L313 iii; Corkery to De Roiste 24–8–1918 U271/C157 De Roiste Papers Cork Archives Institute.
33. "An t-Athair Peadar" MS lecture Box 92 Torna Papers; lecture reported *Fainne an Lae* April 26 1919. Corkery collaborated with his cousin Seamus O hAodha on an Irish-language school play *An Clochar* (Dublin 1919), an Irish-language adaptation of Chaucer's Prioress's Tale (relocated to a girls' convent school outside Cork in AD 1000, with Cork Vikings as villains). *An Clochar* is probably mostly the work of O hAodha, an established Irish-language writer (it was republished under his name alone in 1935).
34. Corkery to MacSwiney (mid-autumn 1916) P48c/489 (2)–(4) MacSwiney Papers.
35. MacSwiney to Corkery 13–4–1917 L313 Cork Municipal Museum; Earnan de Blaghd *Gael A Mhuscailt* (Dublin, 1973) p. 197.
36. Corkery answers to Etiennette Beuque, TS P48c/7/25–7 MacSwiney Papers.
37. Corkery hints but does not state that they are Ascendancy; I owe this point to Patrick Buckland *Irish Unionism 1886–1921: Vol I Southern Unionism* (Dublin, 1973).
38. Notes, Box 23 *op.cit.*
39. This passage was added after this story was published in the Boston *Shamrock and Irish Emerald* March 1919 (cuttings file, Corkery Papers).
40. "The Twenty Club" *op.cit.*; cf. also *An Only Child* p. 147–8.
41. The bust remained in plaster until after Corkery's death, when it was cast in bronze. Two copies were made; one is in UCC, Mairead Ni Mhurchu (daughter of Joseph Higgins) has the other.
42. Mary Leland "Interview with Seamus Murphy August 1975" *Cork Review* No. 4 (Seamus Murphy Issue) 1980; chapter on "The Gibson Bequest" in Peter Murray *Illustrated Suummary Catalogue of the Crawford Art Gallery* (Cork, 1991) p. 9–11. Mairead Ni Mhurchu has the portrait.

43. *An Only Child* (London, 1962); *Vive Moi!* (London, 1965).
44. O Faolain interview with Andy O'Mahony 26–7–71, RTE Sound Archives.
45. *An Only Child op.cit.*; Murphy interviewed in O Dulaing *Voices of Ireland op.cit.*; Paul A. Doyle *Sean O Faolain* (New York, 1968) p. 136n.
46. Corkery introduction to O'Donoghue *MacCurtain* op.cit.
47. *Old Ireland* April 26 1920 p. 464, Kathleen Keyes MacDonnell *There is a Bridge at Bandon* (Cork 1972).
48. Corkery answers to Etiennette Beuque questionnaire P48c/7/25–7 MacSwiney Papers.
49. Speech given in full in Chevasse *MacSwiney op.cit.*
50. Chevasse *MacSwiney op.cit.*; T. Ryle Dwyer *Michael Collins, The Man Who Won The War* (Cork, 1990). p. 85.
51. Chevasse *op.cit.*; Siobhain Lankford *The Hope and the Sadness* (Cork, 1980); Michael Gough "Socio-Economic Conditions and the Genesis of Planning in Cork" in Michael J. Bannon (ed.) *The Emergence of Irish Planning 1880–1920* (Dublin, 1985).
52. MacSwiney to Corkery July 24 1920 L313 Cork Municipal Museum.
53. T.P. Coogan *Michael Collins* (Dublin, 1990).
54. "Andrew E. Malone" (L.P. Byrne) *The Irish Drama* (Dublin, 1928).
55. Undated cutting in cuttings file.
56. "Terence MacSwiney: Lord Mayor of Cork" *Studies* December 1920.
57. Annie MacSwiney to Corkery 4–1–21, L313 Cork Municipal Museum.
58. Corkery to Annie MacSwiney 11–1–1921, P48c/3/36 MacSwiney Papers.
59. De Roiste Diary No. 36, 24 February 1921. De Roiste Papers U271 Cork Archives Institute. This entry may have been revised after De Roiste and the MacSwiney family took opposite sides in the Civil War.
59a. Tom Jones *Whitehall Diary Vol. III; Ireland* p. 37
60. "Terence MacSwiney" TS P48c/179(2) MacSwiney Papers.
61. "Professor W.F.P. Stockley 1859–1943" *Capuchin Annual* 1948 p. 257–67.
62. "A Story of Two Indians" *Irish Press* September 27 1953 p.2; "What is a Nation?" *Sunday Press* October 16 1953. The copy of *Nationalism* is in the UCC library collection of books owned by Corkery.
63. "Sagged" *Green and Gold* March 1921 p. 69–73.
64. "The Bequest" *Green and Gold* December 1921 p. 322–7.
65. "Morning at Ardnagapall" TS Box 81 Torna Papers.
66. Diary for week ending September 17th 1921, Box 28 Corkery Papers; "The Night Watch" Box 92 Torna Papers.

67.   "Unsprung" TS Box 81 Torna Papers.
68.   *Vive Moi! op.cit.; An Only Child op.cit.*

CHAPTER FIVE

1.   "Their First Fault" *Poblacht na h-Eireann* January 31 1922 p.4.
2.   "Even in Our Ashes" *ibid*. February 14 1922 p.2.
3.   "The Winning of "Ulster" " *Leader* July 22nd 1916 p.517–8; "The Difference" *Capuchin Annual* 1943 p. 164–7.
4.   "The Stepping Stone" MS Corkery Papers Box 17.
5.   Ione Malloy *Corkery, O'Connor and O Faolain; A Literary Relationship in the Emerging Irish Free State* (Ph.D. University of Texas, Austin 1979). p.31; *An Only Child op.cit.* p. 167.
6.   Saul *Corkery op.cit.*; Matthews *Voices op.cit.* Both these saw all three isues; there is no file in NLI or UCC, and I have only seen one issue (No. 1, May 6th 1922) Cork City Library.
7.   *An Only Child op.cit.* The standard account of the Civil War is Michael Hopkinson *Green Against Green* (Dublin, 1989).
8.   De Roiste Diary July 21st 1922. (Cork Archives Institute).
9.   *Ibid*. July 24 1922.
10.   *An Only Child op.cit.* Chapter 17.
11.   *Ibid*.
12.   "The Light-Bringer" *An Phoblacht* (southern edition) Terence MacSwiney Issue October 25 1922 p.2.
13.   Corkery letter, Cork Examiner November 20 1922; Coholan Sermon *ibid*. November 25 1922; De Roiste Diary November 22 1922 (Cork Archives Institute U271/A/47). De Roiste noted that the petition was hindered by local outrage at the shooting of a soldier and a girl by Irregulars.
14.   *Rebel Songs* is very rare; I was unable to locate a copy in time to use it in this study. For a brief description of its contents see Saul *Corkery* op.cit. P. 40–1. For the Lee Press see Patrick J. Twohig *The Dark Secret of Beal na mBlath* (Cork, 1991) p. 75.
15.   Corkery letter in *Poblacht na h-Eireann War News* No. 117, 18th December 1922. (File in Cork Archives Institute).
16.   *An Only Child* op.cit. p. 191–206.
17.   Corkery to Arthur 2–11–23. This letter is reprinted in Matthews *op.cit.* p. 386–7; its source is given as "TS, Corkery Papers". There is no trace of the TS in the Corkery Papers but the original is pasted into an autographed copy of *Ui Bhreasail* presented to Arthur (in my possession).
18.   *An Only Child op.cit.* p. 191–216; Frank O'Connor *My Father's Son* Chapters 1–2; *Vive Moi! op.cit.* p. 163–71.
19.   G.B. Saul Corkery *op.cit.* p. 41; VEC minutes.

20. Finn Mac Eoin "Irish Emancipation" *Leader* September 8th 1923.
21. "An Drama" MS lecture Box 92 Torna Papers.
22. "An Bothar Ceart" MS lecture Box 92 Torna Papers. The idea about the bardic schools recurs in *The Hidden Ireland* (1924; all page referencs to 1967 edn.) p. 98.
23. Raymond Porter *P.H. Pearse* op.cit. p. 51–2, 146.
24. "An tUrisgeal" (The Novel) MS lecture Box 92 Torna Papers.
25. Corkery to MacSwiney P48b/489 (2)–(4) MacSwiney Papers.
26. *Irish Statesman* July 5th 1924.
27. "Mediaeval Irish Poetry" *Irish Tribune* August 27 p. 22–3; "Fair, Fine-Wrought Speech" *Irish Tribune* n.d. (in Corkery Papers cuttings collection). The four surviving lectures in Box 92 Torna Papers are "An Bothar Ceart" (The Right Road), "An tUrsgeal" (The Novel) "An Gearrsceal" (The Short Story), "An Drama" (The Drama). A fifth lecture "An Liric" (The Lyric) has been lost.
28. "Our Star of Knowledge" *Irish Statesman* June 14th 1924 p. 427–9.
29. "Ireland Under Elizabeth" *Leader* August 22 1903 p. 424–6.
30. *The Hidden Ireland op.cit.* p. 5, 7.
31. Corkery to Curran 28–3–22 Curran papers CUR L 203 UCD Special Collections.
32. Autobiographical radio talk drafts Box 19 Corkery Papers.
33. *Hidden Ireland op.cit.* p. 6.
34. *Ibid.* p. 24.
35. *Ibid.* p. 26, 41.
36. *Ibid.* p. 36.
37. *Ibid.* p. 47. This passage reflects Corkery's lifelong fascination with the idea of dinnsheanchais (Gaelic lore of place-names), a culture allowing a whole countryside to be read like a manuscript.
38. *Ibid.* p. 94.
39. *Ibid.* p. 135.
40. *Ibid.* p. 153, 124.
41. This point is made by Aodh de Blacam *Irish Tribune* July 30th 1926.
42. *Hidden Ireland* p. 155, 188 have anecdotes about extempore composition; references to oral transmission on *ibid.* p. 24, 54, 165 etc. can lead unwary readers to believe all the poetry discussed was orally transmitted.
43. *Vive Moi! op.cit.* p. 186–8; Corkery describes going to Limerick with Professor Stockley to canvass for the Republican candidate at a by-election in 1924 in his obituary for Stockley "Ireland loses a Realist" *Irish Press* 6th July 1943.
44. *Vive Moi! op.cit.*
45. *My Father's Son op.cit.* (page references to Pan edition) p. 17.
46. *Hidden Ireland* p. 47; "Town Halls That Are Still-Born" *Irish Statesman* December 6th 1924, with reply by "Architect" (?Curran) "Architecture in Ireland" *ibid.* December 27th 1924; Corkery to

Curran (December 1925) CUR l 208 Curran Papers; "A Problem for Cork City" *Irish Independent* 15 April 1929 p. 2; "The New City Hall for Cork" *ibid.* 17 April 1929; "The New City Hall For Cork" *ibid.* 20 April 1929.

47.   Corkery to O Muircheartaigh 23–5–42 Folder 1 Box 16 Corkery Papers.

48.   "Love Songs in Irish" *Irish Statesman* August 22nd 1925.

49.   Sean O Faolain "The Best Irish Literature" *Irish Statesman* September 5th 1925.

50.   Corkery to Curran (December 1925) CUR L 208 Curran Papers.

51.   Ione Malloy *op.cit.* p. 37.

52.   Contacts between Republicans and Free Staters in the Cork Gaelic League (de Roiste Diary No. 53, 6 July 1925, Cork Archives Institute) led to the formation of a joint "Irish Ireland" group, An Cumann Aontachta, to oppose the Boundary Commission report. (De Roiste diary no. 54, 21 December 1925; *Leader* October 31, November 7, 14, December 8 1925, January 23 1926). The group only lasted a few months but led to the foundation of *The Irish Tribune* (De Roiste diary No. 54 30 April 1926). This was intended as a nationalist rival to the *Irish Statesman* (L.P. Byrne to W.P. Ryan, LA11/F/70 W.P. Ryan Papers UCD). Byrne attributed his sacking as editor to his refusal to act as a tool by Cork businessmen who wanted Protection (Byrne to Ryan 4–6–1926 LA 11/F/73) but it was clearly meant to be Protectionist from the beginning and O'Rahilly's claim that Byrne was dismissed for incompetence is more plausible (O'Rahilly to Ryan 14–6–26 LA/F/36 Ryan Papers).

53.   Alfred O'Rahilly to W.P. Ryan 14–6–26 LA/F/36 W.P. Ryan Papers UCD.

54.   "A Landscape in the West" *Irish Tribune* June 18th 1926 p. 20–1.

55.   Frank O'Connor, *Irish Tribune* June 25 1926 p. 17–18.

56.   "A Landscape in the West" *Irish Tribune* July 2nd 1926 p. 22.

57.   Sean O Faolain "The Spirit of the Nation" *Irish Tribune* July 23rd 1926 p. 23.

58.   Sean O Faolain "The Language Problem" *Irish Tribune* July 9th, 16th, 23rd, 30th 1926. The remark about *The Hidden Ireland* is in the July 23rd article.

59.   Aodh de Blacam *Irish Tribune* July 30th 1926.

60.   Frank O'Connor *Irish Tribune* August 13th 1926.

61.   "Mediaeval Irish Poetry" *Irish Tribune* August 27th 1926 p. 22–3. I owe the point about the difference in Corkery's responses to O Faolain and O'Connor to Ione Malloy *op.cit.*

62.   Sean O Faolain *King of the Beggars* (Dublin, 1938) p. 23–37, which draws on Frank O'Connor "Democracy and the Gaelic Tradition" *Ireland To-day* July 1936 p. 38–40.

63. *Hidden Ireland* p. 53 ff.
64. *King of the Beggars op.cit*. "Proem: 1691/1775".
65. Maurice Harmon *Sean O Faolain – A Critical Introduction* (rev. ed. Dublin, 1980) p. 209–10.
66. Michelle O'Riordan *The Gaelic Mind and the Collapse of the Gaelic World* (Cork 1990).
67. L.M. Cullen *The Hidden Ireland; Reassessment of a Concept* (Gigginstown, 1988); Gerard Lyne "Dr. Dermot Lyne, a Catholic landowner under the Penal Laws" *Journal of the Kerry Historical and Archaeological Society* 1975, "The MacFinin Dubh O'Sullivans of Tuosist and Kenmare" *ibid*. 1976, "Land Tenure in Kenmare and Tuosist" *ibid*. 1977, "Landlord-Tenant Relations on the Shelbourne Estate" *ibid*. 1979. Corkery's portrayal of the towns as pure Ascendancy enclaves has also been undermined by such work as Gerard O'Brien (ed.) Maureen Wall *Catholic Ireland in the Eighteenth Century* (Dublin, 1989) but it is not discussed here since it is not directly relevant to the literary tradition.
68. L.M. Cullen *op.cit*. quoting Arthur Young.
69. It has even been adopted to describe an association of Irish country house hotels! The Hidden Ireland Ltd. *The Hidden Ireland* (Dublin, 1988 and subsequent editions).
70. This experience is described by Seamus Heaney "Forked tongues, Celts and incubators", in Robert Bell, Robert Johnstone & Robin Wilson (eds.) *Troubled Times: FORTNIGHT Magazine and the troubles in Northern Ireland 1970–90* (Belfast, 1992) p. 113–6. Note the emphasis on the elegiac aspect of *The Hidden Ireland*.
71. *The Hidden Ireland* p. 125.
72. *Ibid*. Chapter 9 "Brian Merriman".
73. "An t-Athair Peadar O Laoghaire" MS Box 92 Torna Papers; "Mo Sceal Fein" *Leader* October 16th 1915 p. 234–5.
74. Breandan S. MacAodha "Was this a Social Revolution?" in Sean O Tuama (ed.) *The Gaelic League Idea* (Cork, 1972) p. 29.

CHAPTER SIX

1. "Love Songs in Irish" *Irish Statesman* August 22nd 1925.
2. "Visions National and International" *Irish Statesman* March 22nd 1924, p. 46–7.
3. Joseph Hone "Of Visions" *Irish Statesman* April 19th 1924 p. 172. Hone was the official biographer of W.B. Yeats.
4. Norah Saunders and A.A. Kelly *Joseph Campbell: A Critical Biography* (Dublin, 1988). p. 105.
5. "The Literature of Collapse" TS Box 81 Torna Papers.
6. Con O'Leary *Break O'Day* (London, 1926); "A Novel of the Civil War" *Irish Tribune* September 3rd 1926 p. 20–1.

7.   "The Literature of Collapse" *op.cit.*

8.   Liam O'Flaherty "Fascism or Communism?" *Irish Statesman* May 8th 1926; Letter from Captain Jack White *ibid.* May 22nd 1926.

9.   "Liam O'Flaherty" *Irish Tribune* July 16th 1926 p. 20–21.

10. *Synge and Anglo-Irish Literature* (Cork, 1931) p. 181. Page references to 1955 impression.

11. Review of Sean O'Casey *Five Plays* broadcast by Radio Eireann January 19th 1935 TS Box 19 Corkery Papers.

12. "The Genius of T.C. Murray" *Irish Tribune* March 19th 1926 p. 21–2.

13. Robert Hogan & M. O'Neill (eds.) *Joseph Holloway's Abbey Theatre* (Southern Illinois University Press, 1967) p. 220.

14. This view was more commonly held at the time than is generally realised. Yeats' agent complained about young men who exalted Synge, the dramatist of Irish peasant life, above the haughty Yeats (J.M. Hone *Life of W.B. Yeats* Pelican edition London, 1971, p. 224) and the "realist" tradition which dominated the Abbey after 1910 claimed descent from Synge.

15. Review of O'Casey *Five Plays op.cit.*

16. Frank O'Connor review of *The Stormy Hills, Irish Statesman* October 26 1929 p. 158. This contains the first statement of the theory of the short story writer as voice of a "submerged population group" developed in *The Lonely Voice* (London, 1962). I owe this point to Ione Malloy *op.cit.*

17. Sean O Faolain "Daniel Corkery" *Dublin Magazine* April–June 1936, p. 56–7.

18. "Corcaig le linn m'Oige" MS Box 92 Torna Papers.

19. The Sheehan portrait shows it black in 1918; Maighread Ni Mhurchu remembers it white in 1926.

20. Patrick J. Twohig *The Dark Secret of Beal na mBlath* (Cork, 1991) p. 72–3, 75. (Source given as reminiscences taperecorded by Madge Clifford before her death in 1988).

21. "The Shepherdless" *The Leader* September 26th 1925 p. 190–2.

22. "The Joy of Spending" *The Nation* December 13th 1930 p. 2, 13.

23. Corkery notebook August 17th 1910 Box 19 Corkery Papers.

24. *Synge and Anglo-Irish Literature op.cit.* p. 115.

25. For O'Kelly see Vivian Mercier *Realism in Irish Literature op.cit.*; G.B. Saul *Seumas O'Kelly* (Bucknell, 1974).

26. H.J. Heuser *Canon Sheehan of Doneraile* (New York, 1917) Canon Sheehan "Lenten Time in Doneraile" in *The Literary Life and Other Essays* (Dublin 1921) p. 192–3 has a description (far less bleak than Corkery's, indicating the difference between the two writers) of Toreen, the original of Kilmony.

27. D.L. Kelleher "Canon Sheehan, Philosopher and Friend" *Capuchin Annual* 1952.

28. "The Neglect of Canon Sheehan" *Irish Independent* May 30th 1924.

29. Eoin O'Mahony in *Irish Tribune* December 24th 1926 p. 20.

30. Autobiographical radio talk drafts Box 12 Corkery Papers.

31. Corkery to Curran 25–5–29 CUR 205 Curran Papers.

32. Quoted by "Viator" "Persons and Places" *The Standard* May 10th 1930 p. 5.

33. *Synge and Anglo-Irish Literature op.cit.* p. 10.

34. *Ibid.* p. 14–15.

35. *Ibid.*

36. *Ibid.* p. 86, 237. Corkery praises Synge for disliking "all that modernity connotes" (*ibid.* p.78).

37. *Ibid.* p. 39.

38. *Ibid.* p. 38.

39. *Ibid.*

40. *Ibid.* p. 27.

41. *Ibid.* p. 43. Note how Corkery blurs the distinction between the Yeats circle and Unionist writers by lumping them together as "Ascendancy".

42. Richard J. Finneran (ed.) *Anglo-Irish Literature; A Review of Research* (New York, 1976) p. 357.

43. *Synge and Anglo-Irish Literature op.cit.* p. 55.

44. *Ibid.* p. 71–3.

45. Quoted *ibid.* p. 127, 168.

46. *Ibid.* p. 166.

47. *Ibid.* p. 132.

48. *Ibid.* p. 209, 227.

49. Declan Kiberd *Synge and the Irish Language* (London, 1979); Anne Saddlemeyer (ed.) *J.M. Synge – Collected Works III – Plays Book I* (Oxford, 1968).

50. David Greene & Edward Stephenson *John M. Synge 1871–1909* (London 1959, rev. ed. 1990); Edward Stephenson *My Uncle John* (London, 1974).

51. "Ourselves and Literature – IV: Our Writers" *The Standard* February 14th 1931 p. 9.

52. *Synge and Anglo-Irish Literature op. cit.* p. 243.

53. Conference report *The Standard* October 18th 1930 p. 2.

54. *Vive Moi! op.cit.* p. 209, 257–9.

55. *My Father's Son op.cit.* p. 45, 53–4.

56. *Cork Examiner* March 21st 1927 p. 7–8.

57. Matthews *Voices op.cit.* p. 43–53.

58. O'Connor to Hendrick n.d. (July 1929) Cork Municipal Museum.

59. Matthews *Voices op.cit.* p. 78.

60. O'Connor to Hendrick 13–4–29 Cork Municipal Museum.

61. *Vive Moi! op.cit.* p. 257–9; O Faolain application for Chair of English (15 April 1931) File 2637 Secretary's Office, UCC Archives.

62. Corkery application for Chair of English (27 April 1931) File 2637 *op.cit.* (The application does not mention the honorary B.A. denounced by O Faolain in *Vive Moi!*; O Faolain seems to have misunderstood Corkery's receiving permission to undertake a MA without having a BA); G.B. Saul *Corkery op.cit.*

63. Testimonial in Corkery application op.cit. Maurice Harmon "The Chair at UCC" mentions a furious quarrel between Stockley and O Faolain during the contest.

64. Corkery to O Muircheartaigh 4–10–43 Folder 1 Box 16 Corkery Papers.

65. File 2637, Secretary's Office UCC; UCC Governing Body Minutes UC/GB/10 15 June 1931 p. 132, 19/7/1931 p. 140, 6/11/1931 p. 143; Maurice Harmon "The Chair at UCC" and Dermot Keogh "Democracy run riot" in Sean Dunne (ed.) O Faolain issue *Cork Review* (1991); *Vive Moi! op.cit.*; interview with Professor Aloys Fleischmann 10–5–1989. It is sometimes suggested Bishop Coholan voted for Corkery, but Coholan was not present at the meeting which decided the appointment.

CHAPTER SEVEN

1. Interview with Professor Aloys Fleischmann 10–5–1989.

2. Corkery to Tomas O Muircheartaigh 4–10–43, 16–10–43 Folder 1 Box 16 Corkery Papers.

3. "The Case of Mr. T.S. Eliot" *Irish Press* March 24th 1941.

4. Daniel Corkery to Michael MacLaverty August 1954, quoted in Sophia Hillan King "Quiet Desperation; variations on a theme in the writings of Daniel Corkery, Michael MacLaverty and John McGahern" in Myrtle Hill & Sarah Barber (eds.) *Aspects of Irish Studies* (Belfast, 1990).

5. Corkery to O Muircheartaigh 15–9–1937 Folder 1 Box 16 Corkery Papers; *What's This About The Gaelic League?* (Dublin, 1942) p. 9.

6. *Synge and Anglo-Irish Literature op.cit.* p. 212n.

7. Sources for Corkery as Professor; interviews with T.J. McElligott (20–6–1988), Desmond Brennan (13–4–1988), the late Professor John Barry (27–2–1989), Dan O'Donovan (9–5–1989), Maighread Murphy (26–5–1989), Seamus de Roiste (8–5–1989); information from Professors John A. Murphy, David O'Mahony, John Cronin, Cornelius O'Leary; Sean O Tuama "Daniel Corkery, cultural philosopher, literary critic: a memoir" in Birgit Bramsback & Martin Croghan (eds.) *Irish and Anglo-Irish Literature; Studies in Literature and Culture* (Uppsala, 1988); T.J. McElligott *This Teaching Life* (Gigginstown, 1988); *Recollections of Daniel Corkery* Radio Eireann programme broadcast 7–1–1965, *Donal O Corcora Remembered*

broadcast 3–3–1965 (both in RTE Sound Archives). I am grateful to Professor O Tuama for giving me a copy of his paper before publication.

8. J.J. Lee *Politics and Society: Ireland 1912–85* (Cambridge, 1989) p. 544.
9. "The Book I am Writing Now" MS radio talk, Box 4 Corkery Papers.
10. Interview with T.J. McElligott 20–6–1988; interview with Diarmuid O Murchu 21–5–1989.
11. T.J. McElligott *This Teaching Life op.cit.*
12. "The Grave at Castlelyons" *Irish Press* September 18th 1939.
13. "Had Davis Lived" *Leader* November 20th 1915 p. 347–8.
14. "Davis and the National Language" in M.J. MacManus (ed.) *Thomas Davis and Young Ireland* (Dublin, 1945) p. 114–23; *The Fortunes of the Irish Language* (Dublin, 1954) p. 116.
15. Interview with Arthur Fedel quoted in Fedel *The Miracle and the Quaking Sod* (UCD MA 1951).
16. Information from Bill and Mary Corkery.
17. Saul *Daniel Corkery op.cit*; Mercier *Realism in Irish Literature op.cit.*
18. Michael MacLaverty *In Quiet Places* Sophia Hillan King (ed.) (Dublin, 1989) p. 125–6. Fedel *op.cit.* also defends *Earth out of Earth.*
19. Interview with T.J. McElligott 20–6–1989. For the play's faults in performance see Robert Hogan ed. *Joseph Holloway's Abbey Theatre* vol. 3 (Proscenium Press, 1970).
20. Corkery to O Muircheartaigh 23–6–1946 Folder 2 Box 16 Corkery papers.
21. Hilary Pyle, *Irish Art 1900–50: An Exhibition at the Crawford Art Gallery* (Cork, 1975) p. 23.
22. I am grateful to Maighread ni Mhurchu, Bill and Mary Corkery, John and the late Mary Cronin for allowing me to see their Corkery paintings.
23. "Jack B. Yeats Once More" *Irish Monthly* September 1945 p. 363–7. (Corkery to O Muircheartaigh 3–11–1954 records his gratification when Yeats visited a one-man show of Corkery paintings in Dublin); (Sean O Faolain) "Ulster" *The Bell* July 1941 p. 11. For a discussion of the Irish School of landscape painters see Brian Kennedy "Irish landscape painting in a political setting, 1922–48" in Myrtle Hill & Sarah Barber (eds.) *Aspects of Irish Studies* (Belfast, 1990).
24. Corkery to O Muircheartaigh 22–3–1946, 26–9–1946, 6–2–1947, 11–11–1947, 25–11–1947 Folder 2 Box 16 Corkery Papers. In the same way, O Muircheartaigh consulted Corkery when translating *Riders to the Sea* (Corkery to O Muircheartaigh 18–10–1941 Folder 1 Box 16).
25. Corkery to O Muircheartaigh 23–5–1946 Folder 2 Box 16 Corkery Papers.

26. Autobiographical radio talk drafts Box 12 Corkery Papers.

27. *Ibid*.

28. "What's Wrong With the Gaelic League?" *An Caman* December 9 1933 p. 7.

29. "The Twenty Club" MS Box 92 Torna Papers.

30. "What is Wrong with Our Writers?" *Irish Press* August 19th 1938, p. 8.

31. "What is Wrong With Our Culture?" *Irish Rosary* February, March 1942. (Corkery's contribution is in the February issue).

32. Corkery to O Muircheartaigh 1–9–1942 Folder 1, Box 16 Corkery Papers; Interview with Diarmuid O Murchu 21–5–1989.

33. Corkery to O Muircheartaigh 6–11–1947 Folder 2 Box 16 Corkery Papers.

34. Corkery to O Muircheartaigh 15–5–1951 Folder 3 Box 16 Corkery Papers.

35. Corkery to O Muircheartaigh 16–7–47 Folder 2 Box 16 Corkery Papers.

36. Corkery to O Muircheartaigh 9–4–42, 18–8–42 Folder 1 Box 16 Corkery Papers.

37. "Donat O'Donell" (Conor Cruise O'Brien) "The Parnellism of Sean O Faolain" *Maria Cross* (London, 1950).

38. Sean O Faolain "A Broken World" in *A Purse of Coppers* (London, 1937).

39. "The End of a Good Man" in *Teresa and Other Stories* (London, 1947).

40. Sean O Faolain *The Great O'Neill* (London, 1942).

41. Sean O Faolain *An Irish Journey* (London, 1941) p. 297. This rejection of the past is not based on post-colonial servility as alleged in Corkery to O Muircheartaigh 26–7–1947 (Folder 2 Box 16 Corkery Papers) and Richard Kearney (ed.) *The Irish Mind* (Dublin, 1985) p. 36, but on the desire to create a new world out of nothing, free from the constraints of the past. The idea that a violent independence struggle frees the colonised by destroying colonial dominance *and* the remnants of traditional culture is quite common among anti-colonial writers (cf. Frantz Fanon); this view can be criticised, but hardly for servility.

42. Sean O Faolain "Commentary on the Foregoing" *Ireland Today* October 1936 p. 32 (reply to Dr. James Devane "Is an Irish Culture Possible?" *ibid*. p. 21–31).

43. This account of the 1940s crisis of traditional nationalism is indebted to Terence Brown *Ireland: A Social and Cultural History* (new edn. 1986) Ch. 6.

44. Corkery to O Muircheartaigh 23–3–42 Folder 1 Box 16 Corkery Papers.

45. Corkery to O Muircheartaigh 26–8–41 Folder 1 Box 16.

46. Corkery to O Muircheartaigh 30–1–43 Folder 1 Box 16.

47. Corkery to O Muircheartaigh 1–4–43 Folder 1; 16–7–47, 26–6–47 Folder 2 Box 16.
48. (Sean O Faolain) *Bell* editorial May 1942; Corkery's article is "What is Wrong With Irish Culture?" *Irish Rosary* February 1942 p. 92–4.
49. Anonymous note, *The Bell* June 1942 p. 157.
50. For Corkery's immediate response to the editorial see Corkery to O Muircheartaigh 19–5–42 Folder 1 Box 16.
51. "A Critic and Terence MacSwiney" *Irish Press* Monday June 29th 1942 p. 2.
52. "Peasant Plays and the Abbey" *Sunday Independent* June 8th 1947.
53. Corkery to O Muircheartaigh 20–2–1942 Folder 1 Box 16.
54. Corkery to O Muircheartaigh 9–4–42 Folder 1 Box 16; the idea of an Irish literature in Kiltartanese recurs in *The Philosophy of the Gaelic League* (Dublin, 1943) p. 10.
55. Corkery told O Muircheartaigh he did his best to annoy the *Bell* people in the pamphlets (Corkery to O Muircheartaigh 1–12–1941 Folder 1 Box 16).
56. *What's This About The Gaelic League?* op.cit. p. 24–5.
57. *The Philosophy of the Gaelic League* op.cit. p. 12–13; Corkery to O Muircheartaigh 30–1–1943 Folder 1 Box 16.
58. *What's This About the Gaelic League?* op.cit. p. 12.
59. *Ibid.* p. 19, 14.
60. *Ibid.* p. 18, 16.
61. *Ibid.* p. 18.
62. M.J. MacManus, *Irish Press* 8–4–1942. MacManus later asked Corkery to help counter the damage done to the image of Ireland abroad by O Faolain (MacManus to Corkery 18–1–1948 Box 21 Corkery Papers).
63. Francis Mac Manus in *The Standard* 9–10–1942.
64. "Nationalism with the Adjective Off" lecture at UCD 8–3–1946, TS Box 4 Corkery papers.
65. "Mr Eliot on Regional Cultures" *Irish Press* 7 April 1949.
66. Ronald Hayman *Leavis* (London, 1976); Denys Thompson (ed.) *The Leavises: A Memorial Volume* (London, 1984); William Walsh *The Leavises* (London, 1980); Q.D. Leavis *Fiction and the Reading Public* (London, 1932). Eamonn Hughes "Leavis and Ireland: An Adequate Criticism?" *Text and Context* Autumn 1988 is a misguided attempt to present Leavis as a propagandist of Empire (he was a pacifist Liberal Little Englander permanently scarred by memories of the First World War) and Corkery as a "radical populist". Francis Mulhern *The Moment of Scrutiny* (London, 1981) gives a valuable overview of the background, associations and influence of the Leavises.
67. "Ourselves and Literature – II" *The Standard* December 13 1930.

68. "What is Wrong With Our Writers?" *Irish Press* August 19th 1938 p. 8: "The Twenty Club" MS lecture Box 92 Torna papers.

69. "Culture and Language Struggles" MS Box 81 Torna Papers.

70. Interview with Bill and Mary Corkery.

71. "Nationalism with the Adjective Off" *op.cit.*

72. *What's This About The Gaelic League? op.cit.* p. 23; (Sean O Faolain) "The Synthetic Gael" *Bell* November 1942. Notes and plans for *The Romance of Nation Building*, with several lectures meant for incorporation in the completed work, are in Box 4 Corkery Papers.

73. Corkery to O Muircheartaigh 1–3–1946, 15–7–1946 Folder 2 Box 16. Despite political differences Hogan and Corkery maintained a guarded respect for each other; Hogan saw Corkery as "a gifted man but one who shrank from life" (information from the late Professor James Barry).

74. Saul *Corkery op.cit.*; Corkery to O Muircheartaigh, 12–4–49, 24–4–49, 17–5–49, 12–11–49, 26–2–50, 14–3–50, 21–9–50; interviews with Dan O'Donovan 9–5–89, Diarmuid O Murchu 21–5–89, Maighread Ni Mhurchu 26–5–89.

75. Interview with Dan O'Donovan *op. cit.*

76. Saul *Corkery op.cit.*; interviews with Diarmuid O Murchu 21–5–89; Maighread Ni Mhurchu 26–5–89, Clara Ni hAnnrachain 10–12–89. This was Corkery's only experience of the Oireachtas, although some writers have confused him with the Macroom flour merchant Dan Corkery, Commandant Mid-Cork IRA Brigade in War of Independence and Mid-Cork TD 1920–48.

77. Saul *Corkery op.cit.*

78. Benedict Kiely *Modern Irish Fiction* (Dublin, 1950).

79. Francis MacManus "Three First Meetings" *Capuchin Annual* 1959 p. 53–9.

80. MacLaverty letters in Corkery Papers Box 21.

81. *Ibid;* Sophia Hillan King *The Silken Twine: A Study of the Works of Michael MacLaverty* (Dublin, 1992); Sophia Hillan King (ed.) *In Quiet Places: The Uncollected Stories, Letters and Collected Prose of Michael MacLaverty* (Dublin, 1989).

82. Corkery to O Muircheartaigh 15–7–1946 Folder 2 Box 16.

83. O Muircheartaigh letters to Corkery, Box 14 Corkery Papers; Corkery letters to O Muircheartaigh Box 16.

84. MS attached to Corkery to O Muircheartaigh 24–3–1958 Folder 5 Box 16.

85. Anon. "Tomas O Muircheartaigh" in Diarmuid Breathnach & Maire Ni Mhurchu *Beathaisneis a hAon* (Dublin, 1988) p. 92.

86. O Riordain Diary Vol. 29 p. 32 31–12–1964 UCD Library Special Collections.

87. Hilary Pyle *Irish Art 1900–50 op.cit.* p. 81.

88. Interviews with Diarmuid O Murchu 21–5–89, Clara Ni hAnnrachain 10–12–89.
89. Interview with Maire Mac an tSaoi *An Droichead/The Bridge* Summer 1989 p. 14; "Ca Bhfuil ar dtriall-Filiocht" MS dated 18–3–1947 Box 1 Corkery Papers.
90. Interview with Clara Ni hAnnrachain *op.cit.*
91. O Riordain Diary 17 Deireadh Fomhar 1960 quoted in Sean O Coileain *Sean O Riordain – Beatha agus Saothar* (Dublin, 1982) p. 259; O Riordain diary Vol. 21 5–4–1960 P. 69; "Do Dhonall O Corcora" *An Siol* 1948.
92. "An Braon Firinneach" *Feasta* February 1949 p. 13–4; "Cre na Cille" *Feasta* May 1950 p. 14–15.
93. O Riordain Diary Vol. 24 15–2–1962 p. 20–1.
94. Martin O Cadhain *The Irish Language Movement – A Movement Astray* pamphlet Communist Party of Ireland n.d. (translation of a lecture given 1969 or 1970).
95. "Dan Cruinn Beo-Inquisitio 1584" *Feasta* February 1953 p. 16–17.
96. O Riordain Diary Vol. 16 12–4–57 p. 55.
97. *Ibid.* Vol. 21 5–4–1960.
98. *Ibid.* Vol. 24 12–2–1962 9.45p.m.
99. Matthews *Voices op.cit.* p. 340.
100. "Fubun Fuibh" *Feasta* December 1952 p. 13–14.
101. "An Stat Agus An Duine" *Feasta* October 1949 p. 16–19; An tAthair Eric Mac Finn "An Stat agus an Duine" *ibid.* November 1949 p. 6–7; "Aire Teangan: Riachtanach no gan a bheith?" *ibid.* January 1950 p. 7–8.
102. O Riordain Diary Vol. 21 5–4–1960 p. 71.
103. *Ibid.* vol. 16 12–4–57 p. 61–2.
104. Interview with Diarmuid O Murchu 21–5–89; O Riordain diary Vol. 19 16–2–1958 P. 2.
105. Interview with James N. Healy 18–1–1990.
106. Interview with Diarmuid O Murchu 21–5–1989.
107. "The Tradition of Nationality" *Irish Press* 3 April 1956; "A Story of Two Indians" *Irish Press* 27 September 1953.
108. Interview with Clara Ni hAnnrachain 10–12–1989.
109. Interview with Bill and Mary Corkery 17–8–1988.
110. Flor O'Donoghue Tomas MacCurtain (Tralee, 1958); Moirin Chevasse *Terence MacSwiney* (Cork, 1962); Liam O Suilleabhain *Where Mountainy Men Have Sown* (Cork, 1965); Kathleen Keyes McDonnell *There Is A Bridge At Bandon* (Cork, 1972); Corkery to O'Donoghue, Flor O'Donoghue Papers NLI.
111. Denis Gwynn "Now and Then" *Cork Examiner* January 5, 1965 p. 6.
112. Interview with Diarmuid O Murchu 21–5–1989.
113. Interview with Mairead Ni Mhurchu 26–5–1989; "Modern Sculpture" MS lecture Box 1 Corkery Papers.

114. Interview with Dan O'Donovan 9–5–1989.
115. Saul *Corkery op.cit.*
116. Fergal Tobin *The Best of Decades: Ireland in the Sixties* (Dublin, 1986). Corkery's sister was annoyed when a reporter mistook a photograph of Terence MacSwiney for her brother (Interview with Bill and Mary Corkery 17–8–1988).

SOURCES

Manuscript

University College Cork
Corkery Papers (now being catalogued, 1992).
Torna Papers. Boxes 81 and 92 contain Corkery material; apparently these were originally in the Corkery Papers and have now been reincorporated in them.
Administrative Records. Access for period of Corkery's professorship restricted; I only saw file and Governing Body minutes on his appointment.

Cork Municipal Museum
L313 – Corkery material given to the Museum by his sister. Contains letters from MacSwiney, Pearse, de Valera. A small collection.
G1057 – MS introduction to projected book of MacSwiney plays "The South Mon and Myself" short MS lecture donated by Seamus Ware. Letters from Frank O'Connor to Hendrick – some references to Corkery.

Cork Archives Institute
Liam de Roiste Papers.

University College Dublin Archives
MacSwiney Papers
W.P. Ryan Papers – some material on *Irish Tribune*.
Fr. Timothy Corcoran Papers – contain Corkery acceptance of membership of proposed National Academy of Ireland

UCD Special Collections
Sean O Riordain Diaries
Constantine P. Curran Papers – contain small but interesting collection of Corkery letters from 1920s & 1930s.

National Library of Ireland
Thomas MacDonagh Papers (MS 20, 642) – one Corkery letter with MacDonagh notes for reply.

Matthew O'Mahony Papers (MS 24, 900) – one Corkery letter on performances of *Yellow Bittern*.

Flor O'Donoghue Papers – one letter from Corkery on biography of MacCurtain, copies of some de Roiste diaries.

RTE Sound Archives – recordings of Corkery and of O Faolain.

Published Books by Daniel Corkery

A Munster Twilight (Dublin, 1916). Short stories.

The Threshold of Quiet (Dublin, 1917) Novel.

(with Seamus O hAodha) *An Clochair* (The Convent) (Dublin, 1919) school play.

Three Plays (*King and Hermit, Clan Falvey, The Yellow Bittern*) (Dublin, 1920).

The Hounds of Banba (Dublin, 1920). Short Stories.

The Labour Leader (Dublin, 1920) Three-act play.

Ui Bhreasail (Dublin, 1921) Poems and Lyrics.

(under pen-name "An Reiltin Siubhlach") *Rebel Songs* (Cork, 1922). Verse.

The Hidden Ireland (Dublin, 1924) Cultural history.

The Stormy Hills (Dublin, 1929) Short stories. (The Mercier Press edition published after Corkery's death should be avoided. It omits several stories, apparently through sheer carelessness).

Synge and Anglo-Irish Literature (Cork, 1931). Literary criticism.

Earth out of Earth (Dublin, 1939). Short stories.

Resurrection (Dublin, 1942). Play.

What's This About the Gaelic League? (Dublin, 1942). Pamphlet.

The Philosophy of the Gaelic League (Dublin, 1943). Pamphlet.

The Wager (New York, 1950). Selection from previous short story collections.

An Doras Dunta (Dublin, 1953). Two-act play in Irish. (The Closed Door).

The Fortunes of the Irish Language (Dublin, 1954). Cultural history.

G.B. Saul (ed.) *Fohnam the Sculptor* (Proscenium Press, New Jersey, 1974). Play.

Nightfall and Other Stories (Dublin, 1987). Selection from short story collections.

R. Hogan & R. Burnham (eds.) *Lost Plays of the Irish Renaissance III – Cork Dramatic Society* (Proscenium Press, New Jersey 1984). Contains two plays by Corkery, *The Embers* and *The Onus of Ownership*.

Articles in Periodicals

My list of known Corkery articles has been deposited in UCC Archives; it is almost certainly incomplete.

Biographies (published)

G.B. Saul *Daniel Corkery* (Bucknell, 1974). Short and unsympathetic, though admires the short stories and some plays. More interested in literary criticism than historical context.

Seamus de Roiste *Daniel Corkery* (Cork, 1974) Pamphlet accompanying exhibition of Corkery material.

Unpublished Theses

Arthur H. Fedel *The Miracle and the Quaking Sod* (MA English Department UCD 1951). On the works of Corkery; contains interview and letter extracts.

Ione Malloy *Corkery, O'Connor and O Faolain: A Literary Relationship in the Emerging Irish Free State* (University of Texas Ph.D. 1979) Some useful information and comments. Available on microfilm.

Patrick Maume *"Life That Is Exile": Daniel Corkery and the Search for Irish Ireland 1878–1964.* Contains some useful information and quotations omitted from this book; but excessively long and diffuse, with some ill-considered and undeveloped ideas.

Vivian Mercier *Realism in Anglo-Irish Fiction 1916–40* (Ph.D. Department of English TCD 1944). Literary criticism. Chapter IV (on Corkery) has extracts from a Corkery letter to the author. I have also had access to Brian S. Murphy *Politics and Ideology: Mary MacSwiney and Irish Republicanism, 1872–1942*, Ph.D., N.U.I., Forthcoming. *Mary MacSwiney*.

Published Material

Primary Sources – I: Books

Chevasse, Moirin — *Terence MacSwiney* (Cork, 1962).

de Blaghd, Earnan — *Gael A Mhuscailt* (Dublin, 1973).

de Roiste, Seamus — *Daniel Corkery* (Cork, 1974).

Doyle, Paul A. — *Sean O Faolain* (New York, 1968).

Hogan, Robert & M. O'Neill (eds.) — *Joseph Holloway's Abbey Theatre* (3 vols. Southern Illinois V.P. 1967, Proscenium Press 1969, 1970).

ibid. & James Kilroy — *A History Of Modern Irish Drama III: The Years of Synge 1905–1909* (Dublin, 1978).

ibid. & Richard Burnham & Daniel P. Poteet — *ibid. IV: The Rise of the Realists 1910–1915* (Dublin, 1979).

ibid. & Richard Burnham — *ibid V: The Art of the Amateur 1916–20* (Portlaoise, 1984).

ibid. & Richard Burnham (eds.)	*Lost Plays of the Irish Renaissance III: The Cork Dramatic Society* (New Jersey, 1984).
King, Sophia Hillan (ed.)	*In Quiet Places: The Uncollected Stories, Letters and Prose of Michael Mac Laverty* (Dublin, 1989).
McDonnell, Kathleen Keyes	*There is a Bridge at Bandon* (Cork, 1982).
McElligott, T.J.	*This Teaching Life* (Gigginstown, 1986).
Matthews, James	*Voices: A Life of Frank O'Connor* (Dublin, 1985).
O Buachalla, Seamus (ed.)	*Letters of Padraic Pearse* (Dublin, 1980).
O Coileain, Sean	*Sean O Riordain – Beatha agus Saor* (Dublin, 1982).
O'Connor, Frank	*An Only Child* (London, 1961).
Idem.	*My Father's Son* (London, 1968).
O'Donoghue, Flor	*Tomas MacCurtain* (Tralee, 1958).
O Dulaing, Donncha (ed.)	*Voices of Ireland* (Dublin, 1984).
O Faolain, Sean	*Vive Moi!* (London, 1965).
O'Hegarty, P.S.	*Terence MacSwiney – A Memoir* (Dublin, 1922).
O'Neill, Michael J.	*Lennox Robinson* (New York, 1964).
Ruiseal, Liam	*Liam Ruiseal Remembers* (Cork, 1978).
Saul, G.B.	*Daniel Corkery* (Bucknell, 1973).
Twohig, Patrick J.	*The Dark Secret of Beal na mBlath* (Cork, 1991).

II – Articles

Anon. "Obituary – D.L. Kelleher" *Cork University Record* Easter 1958.

Breathnach, Riobaird "Daniel Corkery – Creative Writer and Critic" *UCC Record* 1965.

Dawson, William "Arthur Clery" *Studies* March 1933.

Farrell, Michael "Drama in Cork" *Bell* December 1941.

"D.G." "Con O'Leary" *Cork University Review* Easter 1959.

Gwynn, Denis "Now and Then" *Cork Examiner* January 5 1965.

Hogan, Barry "Heroic Days in the Dun Theatre" *Cork Examiner* September 8 1956.

idem. "A Gallant Effort Begins to Wilt" *ibid.* September 15 1956.

idem. "Splinter Groups: Offshoots of the Parent Body" *ibid.* September 22 1956.

Leland, Mary "Interview with Seamus Murphy, Spring 1975 *Cork Review* 1980.

MacEoin, Finn "Irish Emancipation" *Leader* September 8 1923.

MacManus, Francis "Three First Meetings" *Capuchin Annual* 1959.

(Moran, D.P.) "Confessions of a Converted West Briton" *Leader* September 1, 1900.

Moran, Nuala "Memories of D.P. Moran" *Leader* September 1950.

Murphy, John A. "The Friday Night Court" *Cork Review* 1980.

Murphy, Diarmuid "Donal" *Capuchin Annual* 1967.

Murphy, Seamus "Daniel Corkery – An Appreciation" *Irish Times* January 2 1965.

O Buachalla, Breandan "Daniel Corkery agus an Hidden Ireland" *Scriobh* 4 (1978).

Anon. (O'Hegarty, P.S.) "D.P. Moran" *Dublin Magazine* April–June 1936.

O Tuama, Sean "Donall O Corcora" *Scriobh* 4 (1978).

idem. "Daniel Corkery, Cultural Philosopher, Literary Critic: a memoir" in Birgit Bramsback and Martin Croghan (eds.) *Irish and Anglo–Irish Literature: Studies in Literature and Culture* (Uppsala, 1988).

Ruiseal, Liam "Daniel Corkery and the Cork Dramatic Society" *Cork Examiner* January 6 1965.

Swanton, J.A. "Memories of the Leeside Players" *Cork Weekly Examiner and Holly Bough* 1963.

Secondary Sources

I – Books

Bannon, Michael J. (ed.)	*The Emergence of Irish Planning 1880–1920* (Dublin, 1985).
Boyd, E.A.	*Ireland's Literary Renaissance.*
Breathnach, Diarmuid & Maire Ni Mhurchu	*Beathaisneis a hAon* (Dublin, 1986)
British and Irish Communist Organisation	*"Hidden Ulster" Explored* (Belfast, 1973).
Brown, Terence	*Ireland: A Social and Cultural History 1922–85* (rev. ed. Dublin, 1986).
Clery, Arthur	*Dublin Essays* (Dublin, 1920).
Coakley, Davis & Mary	*Wit and Wine* (Dublin, 1975).
Coldrey, Barry	*Faith and Fatherland* (Dublin, 1988)
Cullen, L.M.	*The Hidden Ireland: Reassessment of a Concept* (Gigginstown, 1988).
Dudley Edwards, Ruth	*Patrick Pearse: The Triumph of Failure* (London, 1977).
Dwyer, T. Ryle	*Michael Collins – The Man Who Won The War* (Cork, 1990).
Dunne, Sean (ed.)	*Cork Review* Sean O Faolain issue 1991.
Ellmann, Richard	*James Joyce* (rev. ed. Oxford U.P. 1988).
Finneran, Richard J. (ed.)	*Anglo-Irish Literature; A Review of*

	Research (New York, 1976).
Garvin, Tom	*Nationalist Revolutionaries in Ireland 1858–1928* (Oxford 1987).
Gaughan, Fr. J.A.	*Alfred O'Rahilly*: vol. I *Academic* (Dublin, 1986); vol. II *Public Figure* (Dublin, 1989).
Greene, David & Edward Stephenson	*John M. Synge 1871–1909* (London 1959, rev. ed. 1990).
Harmon, Maurice	*Sean O Faolain – A Critical Introduction* (rev. ed. Dublin 1984).
Hill, Myrtle & Sarah Barber (eds.)	*Aspects of Irish Studies* (Belfast 1990).
Hone J.M.	*Life of W.B. Yeats* (Pelican edn. London 1971).
Hopkinson, Michael	*Green Against Green: The Irish Civil War* (Dublin, 1989).
Kiely, Benedict	*Modern Irish Fiction* (Dublin, 1950)
King, Sophia Hillan	*The Silken Twine: A Study of the work of Michael MacLaverty* (Belfast, 1992).
Lankford, Siobhan	*The Hope and the Sadness* (Cork, 1980)
Larkin, Emmet	*Jim Larkin; Irish Labour Leader* (London, 1965; new ed. 1989).
Lee J.J.	*Ireland 1912–1985; Politics and Society* (Cambridge U.P. 1989).
MacManus, Francis	*The Years of the Great Test: Ireland 1922–39* (Cork, 1967).
MacSwiney, Terence	*The Revolutionist* (Dublin, 1914)
"Malone, Andrew E"	*The Irish Drama* (Dublin, 1928).
Martin, F.X. (ed.)	*Leaders and Men of the Easter Rising* (London, 1967).
Miller, D.A.	*Church, State and Nation in Ireland 1898–1921* (Dublin, 1973).
Moran, D.P.	*The Philosophy of Irish Ireland* (Dublin, 1905).
Norstedt, Johann	*Thomas MacDonagh* (Charlottesville, North Carolina 1980).
O'Brien, Conor Cruise	*Maria Cross* (London, 1950).
O'Brien, Gerard (ed.) Maureen Wall	*Catholic Ireland in the Eighteenth Century* (Dublin 1989).
O Cadhain, Mairtin	*The Language Movement – A Movement Astray* (Dublin, n.d.)
O'Connor, Frank	*The Big Fellow* (London, 1937; rev.ed. Dublin, 1965).
idem.	*Dutch Interior* (London, 1940).
idem.	*The Lonely Voice* (London, 1962).

O'Connor, Garry	*Sean O'Casey – A Life* (London, 1988).
O Faolain, Sean	*King of the Beggars* (London, 1938).
idem.	*An Irish Journey* (London, 1941).
idem.	*The Great O'Neill* (London, 1942).
idem.	*The Irish* (London, 1947; rev.ed. Dublin, 1980).
O Murchada, Diarmuid	*Liam de Roiste* (Dublin, 1976).
O'Riordan, Michelle	*The Gaelic Mind and the Collapse of the Gaelic World* (Cork, 1990).
O'Sullivan, Daniel J.	*The Literary Periodical and the Anglo-Irish Revival* (Ph.D. UCD 1969).
O Tuama, Sean (ed.)	*The Gaelic League Idea* (Cork, 1972).
Parks, E.W. & A.W.	*Thomas MacDonagh* (University of Georgia Press 1967).
Pearse, P.H.	*Collected Works; Plays, Stories, Poems* (Dublin, 1922).
Porter, Raymond J.	*P.H. Pearse* (New York, 1973).
Pyle, Hilary	*Irish Art 1900–50: An Exhibition at the Crawford Gallery* (Cork, 1975)
Rockett, Kevin & Luke Gibbons & S. Hill (eds.)	*Cinema and Ireland* (London, 1988 edn.)
Saunders, Norah & A.A. Kelly	*Joseph Campbell; a Critical Biography* (Dublin, 1988).
The Hidden Ireland Ltd.	*The Hidden Ireland* (Dublin, 1988 & subsequent edns.).
Tobin, Fergal	*The Best of Decades: Ireland in the Sixties* (Dublin, 1986).

Articles

Gibbons, Luke "Romanticism, Realism and Irish Cinema" in Rockett et al *Cinema and Ireland* (see above).

Gough, Michael "Socio-Economic Conditions and the Genesis of Planning in Cork" in Bannon (ed.) *Emergence of Irish Planning* (See above).

Harmon, Maurice "The Chair at UCC" in *The Cork Review* Sean O Faolain issue (Cork, 1991).

Heaney, Seamus "Forked tongues, Celts and incubators" in Bell *et al.* (eds.) *Troubled Times* (Belfast, 1992).

Hughes, Eamonn "Leavis and Ireland: An Adequate Criticism?" *Text and Context* Autumn 1988.

Hutchins, Patricia "Daniel Corkery: Artist of Time and Place" *Irish Writing* 1956.

Kearney, Colbert "Donall O Corcora agus an Litriocht Angla-Eireannach" *Scriobh* 4 (1978).

Anon. (Kelleher, D.L.) "A City Ruskin" *Q.C.C.* June 10 1905.

Kelleher, D.L. "Canon Sheehan: Philosopher and Friend" *Capuchin Annual* 1952.

Kelly, John S. "The Fall of Parnell and the Rise of Anglo-Irish Literature" *Anglo-Irish Studies II* (1976).

Kennedy, Brian "Irish Landscape Painting in a Political Setting 1922–48" in Hill and Barber (eds.) *Aspects of Irish Studies* (see above).

Keogh, Dermot "Democracy gone dotty" in *The Cork Review* Sean O Faolain issue (Cork, 1991).

King, Sophia Hillan "Quiet Desperation: Variations on a Theme in the Writings of Daniel Corkery, Michael MacLaverty, & John McGahern" in Hill & Barber (eds.) *Aspects of Irish Studies* (see above).

Lahiff, Eddie "Class Struggles in the South of Ireland 1890–1922" unpublished paper.

Larkin, Emmet "A Reconsideration: Daniel Corkery and his ideas on Cultural Nationalism" *Eire-Ireland* Spring 1973.

Lucy, Sean "The Short Stories of Daniel Corkery" in P. Rafroidi (ed.) *The Irish Short Story* (Lille).

"T.G.M." "Daniel Corkery – Dramatist" *Irish Statesman* October 11 1919.

Mac an tSaoi, Maire Interview, *An Droichead* Summer 1989.

MacAodha, Breandan S. "Was This a Social Revolution?" in O Tuama (ed.) *The Gaelic League Idea* (see above).

McCaffrey, Laurence J. "Daniel Corkery and Irish Cultural Nationalism" *Eire-Ireland* Spring 1973.

McCartney, Donal "Hyde, D.P. Moran and Irish Ireland" in F.X. Martin (ed.) *Leaders and Men of 1916* (see above).

MacManus, Francis "The Literature of the Period" in MacManus (ed.) *Years of the Great Test* (see above).

Murphy, Maura "Nineteenth-Century Cork" in Harkness & O'Dowd (eds.) *The Town In Ireland* (see above).

O'Brien, Conor Cruise "The Parnellism Of Sean O Faolain" in O'Brien *Maria Cross* (see above).

O'Connor, Frank "A Triumph for the Gaelic Players" *Irish Statesman* January 14th 1928.

O Faolain, Sean "Daniel Corkery" *Dublin Magazine* April–June 1936.

O'Hegarty, P.S. "Synge and Irish Literature" *Dublin Magazine* January–March 1932.

O Tuama, Sean "Donall O Corcora agus Filiocht na Gaeilge" *Studia Hibernica* 1965.

O Tuathaigh, Gearoid "Is do chuala croi cine soleir" *Scriobh* 4 (1978)

INDEX